SUNK
IN
KULA GULF

Related Titles from Potomac Books

Shattered Sword: The Untold Story of the Battle of Midway
—Jonathan Parshall and Anthony Tully

War in the Boats: My WWII Submarine Battles
—William J. Ruhe

The Pearl Harbor Myth: Rethinking the Unthinkable
—George Victor

SUNK
IN
KULA GULF

THE FINAL VOYAGE OF THE USS *HELENA* AND THE INCREDIBLE STORY OF HER SURVIVORS IN WORLD WAR II

JOHN J. DOMAGALSKI

Potomac Books
Washington, D.C.

Copyright © 2012 John J. Domagalski

Published in the United States by Potomac Books, Inc. All rights reserved. No part of this book may be reproduced in any manner whatsoever without written permission from the publisher, except in the case of brief quotations embodied in critical articles and reviews.

Library of Congress Cataloging-in-Publication Data
Domagalski, John J., 1969–
  Sunk in Kula Gulf : the final voyage of the USS *Helena* and the incredible story of her survivors in World War II / John J. Domagalski. — 1st ed.
    p. cm.
  Includes bibliographical references and index.
  ISBN 978-1-59797-839-2 (hbk. : alk. paper)
  ISBN 978-1-59797-840-8 (electronic)
  1. Helena (Cruiser) 2. World War, 1939–1945—Campaigns—Solomon Islands. 3. World War, 1939–1945—Naval operations, American. I. Title.
  D774.H4D66 2012
  940.54'2695931—dc23
                                                                    2012023651

Printed in the United States of America on acid-free paper that meets the American National Standards Institute Z39-48 Standard.

Potomac Books
22841 Quicksilver Drive
Dulles, Virginia 20166

First Edition

10 9 8 7 6 5 4 3 2

For Two Who Served:

Harry Koziol
World War II Pacific

Edward Domagalski
Korean War

CONTENTS

	List of Maps	ix
	Acknowledgments	xiii
	Introduction	xv
1	Heading North	1
2	Voyage to the Unknown	11
3	Escape to Espiritu Santo	23
4	Down Under	35
5	Return to Kula Gulf	45
6	Turnabout	59
7	Gunfight	71
8	Fatal Damage	85
9	Abandon Ship	91
10	A Night in Kula Gulf	105
11	The Captain's Flotilla	119
12	Return	127
13	Adrift	133
14	The Island	147
15	Hideouts	159
16	Rescue Operation	175
17	Home	191
	Epilogue	201
	Notes	207
	Bibliography	223
	Index	231
	About the Author	239

MAPS

Kula Gulf Area, 1943	xi
Battle of Kula Gulf, Part 1	75
Battle of Kula Gulf, Part 2	108
Battle of Kula Gulf, Part 3	113
Route of *Helena* Survivors	141

Kula Gulf Area
1943

Adapted from U.S. Navy, *Combat Narrative IX*.

ACKNOWLEDGMENTS

A project of this magnitude cannot be completed without the help of many individuals, and the number of people is often too lengthy to publish. Topping the list of those who deserve special acknowledgment are the veterans who gave freely of their time, sharing their recollections about the Pacific War days aboard USS *Helena*. In a few instances in which a veteran had passed away, his family graciously provided me with pictures and written recollections that the sailor wrote years ago. As with any naval history project, the excellent staffs at the National Archives and the Naval History and Heritage Command provided great assistance in locating documents and photos. The fine staff at Potomac Books provided superb guidance throughout the publishing process with Elizabeth Demers championing the project from the start and Kathryn Owens offering great support during the latter stages of the project. Lastly, I want to thank my wife, Sandy. Without her enduring support this book could not have been written.

INTRODUCTION

The light cruiser USS *Helena* was one of hundreds of American naval vessels that participated in the hard-fought victory over Japan on the Pacific side of World War II. A Pearl Harbor survivor, she ventured to the South Pacific and participated in some of the vicious naval battles fought in the embattled Solomon Islands. The pages that follow document the final months of the ship's life as seen through the eyes of the men who were aboard.

The sinking of the *Helena* during the Battle of Kula Gulf in July 1943 began an epic struggle of survival for her crew. Nearly two hundred men perished. Hundreds of sailors were rescued the night of the sinking, and a second group made it to a nearby island and was saved the next day. A third group, however, was missed entirely. They endured several arduous days at sea before landing on a Japanese-held island well behind front lines. With the help of a coastwatcher, a missionary priest, and friendly natives, the *Helena*'s survivors disappeared into the interior jungle of the island. While they lived a meager existence, American naval leaders almost a thousand miles away grappled with how to save them.

Like thousands of other World War II stories, the episode slowly faded from memory and became lost in history. *Sunk in Kula Gulf* resurrects a story that is nearly seven decades old. The stories of individual sailors are woven together with overall events—reconstructed using official navy documents, personal stories, and interviews—to form a continuous narrative that documents the last days of a great American warship and her sailors. The book serves as a tribute to a great generation of American sailors who sacrificed so much to help ensure that our way of life perseveres.

1
Heading North

The early afternoon of January 21, 1943, found USS *Neosho* on the move. The oiler was operating as the service tanker for the U.S. Navy's base at Espiritu Santo deep in the South Pacific. Her role was to provide precious fuel to American warships battling the Japanese farther north in the Solomon Islands. The ship was methodically maneuvering through Segond Channel—a narrow waterway that served as an anchorage area for an assortment of allied warships—and soon began to close in on one particular vessel.

Just after 2 p.m. the *Neosho* slowly pulled up to the starboard side of the *Helena*. Crewmen on both ships began the laborious process of connecting hoses and opening valves so that the oil—the lifeblood of any warship—could fill the light cruiser's depleted tanks. When the process was completed about an hour and a half later, the tanker slowly cleared the side of the cruiser and moved out. The *Helena*'s replenishment that day was not limited to fuel oil. The ship also took on ammunition, hauling aboard a total of 1,033 shells for the ship's 6-inch main battery guns.

The warship had been at Espiritu Santo for almost two weeks since returning from her last stint of combat—an early January mission to bombard a Japanese airfield in the Central Solomons.[1] For the crew, the loading of fuel and supplies could only mean that the ship would soon be headed out to sea. The harbor stay was about to end.

It had been little more than a year since the *Helena* had been at the epicenter of action the day the Pacific War started. She was hit by a torpedo on her starboard side almost directly amidships during the surprise Japanese attack on Pearl Harbor. Quick damage control kept the ship afloat, but her crew suffered many casualties. After a temporary fix-up at Pearl Harbor, she was dispatched to the Mare Island Navy Yard near San Francisco for permanent repairs.

A relatively new ship at the time of the Pearl Harbor attack, the *Helena* was launched at the New York Navy Yard on August 27, 1938. When the commissioning ceremony took place more than a year later on September 18, 1939, the war in Europe had already started.[2] The *Helena* was a sleek and modern warship with an overall length of 608 feet and a beam (width) of 62 feet. She had a standard displacement of 9,700 tons.[3] After shakedown and training, the new vessel was assigned to the Pacific Fleet.

■ ■ ■ ■

During the stay at Mare Island, the *Helena* received more armament and new electronics while her damaged hull was repaired. Anti-aircraft defenses were bolstered with the addition of 20mm and 40mm guns; surface search (SG) radar, air search (SC) radar, and fire control (FD) radar sets were installed; and her crew quickly swelled to a wartime complement of 1,200 men. By the time she was heading back to the Pacific, the *Helena* was a heavily armed fighting vessel.

The American invasion of Guadalcanal, on the southern fringe of the Solomon Islands, had just begun when the repaired light cruiser arrived in the South Pacific on August 11, 1942, ready to support the war effort. Only two days earlier the U.S. Navy had been dealt a stinging loss during the Battle of Savo Island. Four Allied heavy cruisers had been sunk in a night battle near the embattled island. Heavy fighting lay ahead, both on land and at sea, around Guadalcanal.

In September the *Helena* was escorting USS *Wasp* when the new aircraft carrier was torpedoed and sunk by a Japanese submarine. Just weeks later, the *Helena* helped to sink the Japanese heavy cruiser *Furutaka* and the destroyer *Fubuki* in the Battle of Cape Esperance off Guadalcanal.

On November 13 the warship participated in the climactic naval battle of the Guadalcanal campaign. She was part of a task force comprising five cruisers and eight destroyers that clashed with a larger group of Japanese ships. The Americans were heavily outgunned as the enemy force contained two battleships, one light cruiser, and fourteen destroyers. The opposing ships encountered each other in the waters off Guadalcanal during the early morning hours. A vicious night battle followed that was fought at close quarters and lasted about an hour. The American force suffered horrific losses, including seven ships, hundreds of sailors, and two admirals. However, the superior Japanese fleet turned back, and the *Helena* escaped with only minor damage in what was later known as the Naval Battle of Guadalcanal.[4] During a weekend of heavy fighting at sea and in the air, the Americans were able to land a large contingent of fresh troops while a Japanese attempt to reinforce their island garrison was largely thwarted.

■ ■ ■ ■

The early morning hours of January 22 saw the *Helena* full of activity. Sailors on duty in the engineering compartments deep below deck were getting the ship ready for departure from Espiritu Santo. Fires were lit under boilers. Steam pressure was cut into the main lines. At 5:46 a.m. a seaplane was hoisted out for inner air patrol. Thirteen minutes later the *Helena* was under way, maneuvering to clear Segond Channel and heading for the open sea. By 7:00 a.m. she was directly behind the light cruiser USS *Nashville* moving northeast at a speed of 15 knots. The two cruisers were accompanied by four destroyers. The force moved into cruising formation with the destroyers spreading out to provide an anti-submarine screen. The ships increased speed to 21 knots before turning due north.[5] The course pointed toward the area west of Guadalcanal.

In command of the *Helena* was forty-nine-year-old Capt. Charles Cecil. He had assumed control of the ship on November 23, 1942, replacing popular Capt. Gilbert Hoover.[6] Cecil brought a wealth of experience to the *Helena*, having served on a wide variety of ships since graduating from the Naval Academy in 1916. More recently, he was awarded the Navy Cross for heroism while leading a destroyer squadron in the Battle of Santa Cruz, northeast of Guadalcanal, in late October 1942.

Captain Cecil had under his command a veteran crew that hailed from points all across the United States. Some had been aboard the ship since her commissioning and had survived the Pearl Harbor attack. Others transferred aboard while the vessel was being repaired in California. Each sailor had a unique story of where he was from and how he came to the *Helena*.

As Espiritu Santo slowly faded beyond the horizon, the *Helena*'s crew went about their routine duties. The bridge was crowded with officers and enlisted men, as was normally the case when the vessel put to sea. Among them was one of the ship's two buglers, Gayle Gilbert. "I was on the bridge all the time," he said. "There was always a bugler on the bridge in case of emergency." Spending his watches inside the enclosed navigation bridge allowed Gilbert a firsthand view of all the activity. "That's where the quartermaster steered the ship, that's where officers stood their watches, and captain and the exec and the navigator and all those guys were there," he noted. "I tried to stay out of the way because it was quite a busy place."[7]

Gilbert had no intentions of becoming a bugler when he enlisted in the navy. He remembered the day when a few navy sailors were on leave in his hometown of Larned, Kansas. They stood out in the small farming community. "This is before the war started," he recalled. "Two or three guys come back and I seen 'em in that uniform and that threw me." Gilbert was a long way from the ocean and never gave much thought about joining the navy. "The only thing I ever seen wave in the wind was the wheat," he added.

What convinced him to consider the navy was his love of music. "I played trombone all through high school," he said. "I got to see the navy concert band in Hayes, Kansas. And that's what started me off." He was twenty-one years old when he jumped in a car with some friends and traveled cross-country to Los Angeles to join the navy.

Gilbert enlisted for six years on October 2, 1941. One day later he was sent to San Diego to begin boot camp. After completing basic training he wanted to join the navy band but was told there were no openings. He instead was offered the opportunity to go to specialty school to become a bugler. "I just wanted to be around music," he said. "So I was a bugler."

Granted a nine-day leave before bugler school started, Gilbert used the time to go home, boarding a Greyhound bus in California. He was only partway home when he heard the news of the attack on Pearl Harbor. "I thought, well, I just well better turn around and go back." Officials in the small town where the bus had stopped helped him to contact the base in San Diego, but he was told to keep going on his leave. When Gilbert eventually completed bugler's school, he received orders to report to the *Helena*. He boarded the ship at Mare Island on May 9, 1942.

Now a seaman second class, Gilbert marveled at the vast array of guns on the cruiser. The ship soon pulled out for sea trials. "That's the first time I'd seen the big beautiful Pacific," he said. "I never got seasick. Never got seasick for the six years I was in the service." By early 1943, Gilbert was well accustomed to his ship.

Time at sea was nothing new for Machinist's Mate 1st Class Walter Wendt, who spent his on-duty time below deck in the after engine room. "The routine at sea was to stand a watch there, which was four hours on and eight hours off," he recalled. The work often took place in extreme heat—the joint effect of the heavy machinery and tropical conditions.

Growing up near Rhinelander, Wisconsin, Wendt was a long way from home. Aboard the *Helena* from the beginning, he joined the navy in search of adventure after graduating from high school in 1939. "It was something to do," he recalled of his decision to enlist. "There wasn't much work here. I wanted to travel and see the world."[8] After enlisting in Green Bay, Wendt traveled south to the Great Lakes Naval Training Center near Chicago for three months of training. "It was pretty tough," he remembered. "They'd give us a good boot to the butt. Boot training or anything like that is to impress you that you're just part of a unit and not running it." Wendt graduated from the training center with the rank of apprentice seaman.

After a short leave Wendt and the rest of his company were put to work. "We were cleaning up old barracks that were used in World War I. They were dirtier than the dickens," he recalled of the training center buildings that had apparently been abandoned at the end of the war. "We were scrubbing 'em up and just getting 'em cleaned up good enough to put new recruits in." The arduous duty was apparently reserved for each outgoing group of recent graduates. Fortunately Wendt was soon given a ship assignment. "I was kind of relieved when they said they needed a bunch of guys to go on the *Helena* in the Brooklyn Navy Yard," he said. "There [were] about a hundred of us that went out there."

After traveling east by train, the group arrived at the receiving station in Brooklyn, where trucks took them over to the navy yard. Wendt boarded the *Helena* one day after she was commissioned. He was thus considered a plank holder of the vessel—an honor only bestowed on a ship's initial crew. "It was quite a ship," he said. "It was brand new. It was a big surprise."

Wendt soon learned what it was like to be seasick when the *Helena* sailed out into the Atlantic. "Part of it was going out and having too much beer the night before, but part of it was that the North Atlantic in the winter time is the roughest ocean in the world," he said. "It has big black waves that were straight up and straight down." After a mandatory stint of mess hall duty, Wendt was assigned to the engineering spaces of the ship. He spent his days working on the engines and machinery that made the *Helena* move.

When not at his battle station, Pharmacist's Mate 2nd Class Jim Layton worked in *Helena*'s medical compartments. "We had a real nice arrangement aboard ship," Layton remembered. "Every few months . . . you would rotate to a different [medical] department. That kept your hands so to speak in the whole pie instead of just in one piece." The medical men split up during battle conditions. "The medical staff were scattered all over the ship," he said. "If they were all together and they took a hit in a certain spot, then they would lose the whole medical department."

As part of the rotation, Layton spent his share of time working in the sick bay. The area was a complete and modern medical facility. "The first thing that happened in the medical office in the mornings was sick call," he said. "That was [when] anyone aboard ship who had something wrong with them, or even thought they had something wrong with them, could make sick call. They would come down and get in line and wait their turn." As a pharmacist's mate, Layton functioned as a physician's assistant. Duties for the position ranged from doing minor surgery to administering medicine.[9]

Layton joined the navy to stay out of the army. "I didn't want to be a soldier," he recalled. Growing up in Roxton, Texas, a small farming community northeast of Dallas, he struggled through the tough years of the Depression living with an aunt and uncle after his mother died young. "There [were] no jobs," he said. "People who lived on the farms still ate pretty well because they raised their own food. The average going wage in this area at that time was a dollar a day for labor work."[10] Layton was working in a local drug store when he decided to enlist right after high school. When he volunteered just a few months before Pearl Harbor, he suspected that the United States was heading toward war. "I think most everyone did," he added.

After completing basic training in San Diego, Layton decided to enter the medical field with the goal of becoming a pharmacist's mate. "I guess because I worked in a drug store," he said of the reason behind his decision, which meant attending a specialty school that involved a variety of training. "I was in what was called hospital corps school. You had to learn all the bones in the body, the circulatory system and pharmacy, lab, X-ray," he continued. The program also contained a heavy dose of first-aid training. "Before you graduated from hospital corps school you had to observe an autopsy." He was fulfilling the requirement when the Japanese attacked Pearl Harbor. The school lasted about six weeks. "You took an exam when you finished and you were on your way."

Upon graduation Layton became a hospital apprentice second class. Instead of going to sea, he was assigned land duty in the navy hospital at Mare Island, California. The facility was part of the large naval yard complex where the *Helena* was undergoing repairs. Although far from the front lines, Layton quickly learned about the realities of war. Shortly after his arrival, the hospital started receiving large numbers of casualties from Pearl Harbor. Layton initially helped transport the wounded to Mare Island from the receiving station at nearby Treasure Island in an antiquated paddle-wheeled boat. It was not long before his work shifted to inside the hospital. "First I did ward duty," he said. "You were kind of functioning like a nurse in the hospital." His basic duties included dispensing medication and checking on patients. Being low in seniority, he also regularly handled bedpans.

Layton remained at the hospital for about six months before his orders suddenly arrived for sea duty aboard the *Helena*. Since it had already departed Mare Island for the Pacific, Layton had to hitch rides on several transports before he eventually caught up with the ship at Espiritu Santo.

As a junior officer aboard the *Helena*, Lt. j.g. Mason Miller remembered a typical day as being hectic. "It was pretty much trying to keep up with everything that was going on," he said. When not under battle conditions, a day normally included standing watch.

Miller was a long way from his hometown of Roanoke, Virginia. He first thought of joining the navy during his days at Roanoke College. "I was in the class of '39 in Roanoke. However, I needed a couple of quality credits [to graduate]," he recalled. Unknown to Miller, his uncle had already found him a job. Right after the school year ended, his uncle told him, "Get ready, I want you to go meet your boss." He then took Miller to meet the head of the accounting department at Norfolk and Western Railroad. "So I went to work over there as a messenger," Miller continued. "The following year I took a leave of absence and went back to Roanoke and got my degree. I actually graduated in 1940."[11]

It was while working for the railroad in 1941 that Miller began to seriously think about the navy. Given the world events of the time, he did not know how much longer the United States would be at peace. "I knew that I was going to be in a prime position to go into the armed forces," he said. "I had just finished up there and a friend of mine came by and he said some of the boys at Roanoke College were joining some sort of a naval reserve program where they would go away during the summer for some training. After they graduated, they would go for some additional training and then get a commission in the navy." It sounded like an interesting proposition.

Miller went down to the recruiting station at the local post office. A recruiter answered his questions about the program and told him to fill out an application, paying careful attention to answer all of the questions correctly. "I figured if I could get a commission, I'd be better off with that rather than being in the navy as a seaman. So that's what I did." The navy notified Miller in late 1941 that he was accepted into the program. He left for Northwestern University in Chicago at the end of January 1942.

Before Miller had formally entered the navy, the United States was at war. "I was at home sitting in my living room and listening to the radio," he recalled of the moment he heard about Pearl Harbor. "I remember it [was] on Sunday afternoon. It was pretty gloomy for me because I already had my papers to leave town next month and go to Chicago. I took it all in real fast."

The long journey to Chicago took the form of a slow train ride. After a chance meeting at the train station, Miller traveled with two other young men from the area who had also been accepted into the naval reserve program. Upon their arrival the three men from Virginia were given separate room assignments. Miller was assigned to Tower Hall, just north of the downtown area. "We lived on the sixth floor and there were eight of us in the room," he recalled. "We had plenty of room. We had a nice desk to study at night. I think we had four bunks, upper and lower."

Midshipman school amounted to a crash course in becoming a naval officer. Graduates became an ensign in the U.S. Naval Reserve, but wartime meant immediate active duty. "The first three weeks were mostly general classes," Miller recalled. "We assembled in a gigantic auditorium. There were something like fourteen or fifteen hundred in the class to start." The class size, however, soon dwindled. "Every thirty days there would be a hundred people that wouldn't make it. They would be dismissed and sent home." For those that made the cut, the advanced classes focused on seamanship, navigation, and gunnery. "We were kept busy all the time," Miller added, although the cadets were afforded some free time on the weekends, enough to go out for a meal and to see some of the city.

Miller graduated as an ensign on May 14, 1942. He soon had orders to report to a recruiting station in Richmond, Virginia. Although he was now a commissioned naval officer, Miller had never actually been to sea and felt uneasy about the situation. He wondered what it would be like to have land duty for an extended period of time. "You're going to feel a little bit awkward if you've been in [the navy] that length of time and never been to sea." Less than two weeks after being issued, the orders to Richmond were unexpectedly cancelled and replaced with new orders to go aboard the *Helena*.

Taking advantage of a leave before reporting to his ship, Miller decided to go back home. He and his girlfriend Helen used the time to get married. "I'd known her for years," he said of his new bride. "It was a Sunday afternoon wedding. Three days after I graduated." The newlyweds stayed in Roanoke for about two weeks before traveling to San Francisco together.

Moving to the West Coast meant both a new ship and a new home. "We were able to find a nice lady that had a room to rent," Miller said. "We lived up there for about a month with her." The couple resided in Vallejo, very close to the *Helena*'s temporary home at Mare Island. "It was there being repaired and I didn't know that she had been damaged." Miller learned about his new ship and married life at the same time. "I'd go to the ship every day," he remembered. "I hardly ever had to spend a night aboard, unless I had a duty or something." He occasionally brought his wife aboard for dinner. When the *Helena* left for the Pacific, the newlyweds parted ways after less than six weeks together.

■ ■ ■ ■

Back in the South Pacific the *Helena*'s sailors went about their routine duties as the ship sailed north to an unknown destination. The fading of daylight of January 22, 1943, marked the end of an otherwise uneventful day.

2

Voyage to the Unknown

Sunrise on January 23 saw the *Helena* approaching Guadalcanal from the southeast. By now the sailors knew that it was not going to be a routine patrol—the task force was on a dangerous mission to bombard a Japanese airfield on Kolombangara Island in the Central Solomons. The crew would become well acquainted with the area during the next six months.

As the Japanese slowly lost the fight for Guadalcanal, they began shifting their focus north. Any route to the interior of the Japanese Empire from the Solomon Islands area would have to go past Rabaul, a large air and sea base on the island of New Britain about six hundred miles northwest of Guadalcanal. Japanese commanders needed to create a barrier stong enough to block the advancing Americans short of their fortress base. In late 1942 the Japanese began to fortify islands in the Central Solomons, the half way point to Rabaul from Guadacanal.

The Central Solomons are dominated by the large island of New Georgia. Situated to the northwest is Kolombangara, a circular island lush with tropical vegetation and dominated by a large volcano cone. New Georgia and Kolombangara are separated by a body of water known as Kula Gulf. Both islands were occupied by Imperial troops, and by early 1943 the area was a hotbed of Japanese activity. The Japanese built a new airfield at Munda Point on New Georgia, with the workers cleverly concealing its construction by rigging cables to support the tops of palm trees over the runway.[1] In early January, *Helena* had been part of a task force that conducted a night bombardment of the Munda airfield.

A coconut plantation on the southeastern corner of Kolombangara, the Vila-Stanmore area, first became of interest to American planners in late 1942 when radio intelligence analysts linked it to Japanese messages associated with air units further north.[2] It appeared that the Japanese were initially using the area as a staging point for the transfer of supplies to Munda Point. Large ships frequently made nightly runs from bases north and west to drop off troops and supplies to Vila-Stanmore. Kept well hidden during the daylight hours, the cargo was transferred to barges and various other types of small craft for the trip across Kula Gulf. With the completion of the Munda airfield, the Japanese began work on a satellite air base at Vila-Stanmore.[3] It was quickly detected by Allied aerial reconnaissance.

The commander of the South Pacific area, Adm. William Halsey, decided that action against Vila-Stanmore was warranted. He issued an operational order on January 19. The new airfield and related facilities would be subjected to a two-phased punch. The area would first be bombarded from the sea and then hit from the air. Rear Adm. Walden Ainsworth was tapped to lead the sea portion of the operation, since he ably led the force that hit Munda only a few short weeks ago.

In addition to his flagship, the light cruiser *Nashville*, Ainsworth selected the *Helena* and the destroyers *Nicholas*, *DeHaven*, *Radford*, and *O'Bannon* for the operation. The force had to be limited to two light cruisers due to a shortage of 6-inch ammunition. Operating as a task force, the ships were simply known as the bombardment group.

Going to Kula Gulf first meant a run up the Slot—the narrow body of water that runs northwest from Guadalcanal to the Central Solomons. Positioned between two parallel columns of islands, the deep water passageway is easily navigable by larger ships. Considered Japanese waters, the route offered few places to hide for ships caught by the opposing side's airplanes. Kula Gulf, on the other hand, was only accessible by large ships from the north and is merely twelve miles wide at its opening. The waterway then narrows as it progresses south toward Vila-Stanmore.

Admiral Ainsworth was under no illusion as to how dangerous the mission would be for his bombardment group. "Kula Gulf was somewhat more difficult [to] access, and afforded less sea room than outside Munda," he later wrote. "Study of the chart showed Kula Gulf would not afford much maneuvering room and that it would be a mean place to be boxed in. The fact that this was a second venture in the same direction made us quite dubious about catching the [Japanese] asleep."[4] The undertaking required careful planning, skill, and perhaps even some good luck.

The admiral's operation plan called for the bombardment force to travel southeast after entering Kula Gulf, favoring the New Georgia side of the waterway. The destroyer *O'Bannon* would proceed into the gulf ahead of the other ships to sweep the area for any signs of trouble before maintaining station off the coast of Kolombangara. She would act as a sentry to block any Japanese ships from entering the gulf from the north. The five remaining ships were to continue into the gulf before making a sharp turn to the right at a point almost due east of Vila-Stanmore. Dividing into two parallel firing lines, the ships were to open fire on the target area, with one destroyer, the *Nicholas*, providing a screen and not participating in the firing. To improve gunfire accuracy, the ships were to be aided by two Black Cats. Hidden in the dark sky above, the night equipped Catalina flying boats contained spotters that would be in direct radio contact with the ships below. After delivering a thorough blasting to the target, the five ships would rejoin the *O'Bannon* and speed out of the gulf.

■ ■ ■ ■

Ainsworth's hope of staying undetected ended at 10:30 on the morning of January 23. While still south of Guadalcanal the force was spotted by a Japanese reconnaissance plane. By noon, the task force was less than fifty miles due south of the island.

Land-based fighter planes from Guadalcanal provided a protective umbrella over the bombardment group for much of the day. However, one or more Japanese scouts still attempted to shadow the ships. Thus began a cat and mouse game that lingered on during the remainder of the day. Crewmen on the ships below periodically had strange radar contacts. The

Helena made one at 11:25 a.m. when an unidentified aircraft appeared on her scope at a distance of twenty-one miles. Sailors also caught fleeting glimpses of the snoopers on at least one occasion.

Throughout the day fighters vectored out in an attempt to find the shadowers, but were never able to make any firm contacts. "We could see the fighters go out and hear them talking to one another, but the [Japanese] trailers would always come back on the screen after short intervals," Ainsworth recorded. Intelligence reports later revealed that Japanese planes radioed at least five contact reports during the day.[5]

The last of the covering fighters turned back toward Guadalcanal just before 7 p.m. Only minutes later, a lone Japanese plane was spotted hovering to the west. Lookouts aboard the *Helena* were among those to make visual contact. The scout likely submitted the last contact report of the daylight hours. Positioned almost due west of Guadalcanal, the bombardment group was now on its own.

For most of the afternoon hours, the force had been heading in a northwesterly direction. The track pointed almost directly to the south side of New Georgia. It is very possible that the Japanese concluded the ships were on the way to give Munda another pounding and the bombing of that airfield by American planes throughout the day may have helped to support the conclusion. On at least one airbase to the north, Japanese twin engine bombers readied for a possible night torpedo attack.[6] The bombardment group, however, was not to be found.

As twilight faded into darkness, clouds overtook the area. The sky soon became completely overcast. The bombardment force turned north to begin the run into the Slot. Ainsworth believed that he had finally given his Japanese followers the slip. "It was very dark and our course change to the northward could not have been detected," he later wrote. An occasional rainsquall popped up as the ships steamed north at 26 knots and simply disappeared into the black night.

The last hours of January 23 passed away uneventfully as the bombardment group moved up the Slot. The force was running roughly parallel to the northern coast of New Georgia, but well out to sea. A radar-equipped Black Cat, positioned directly ahead of the ships, was on the lookout for any signs of trouble.

As with the other ships, the crew of the *Helena* went to condition of readiness two during the late evening hours. The arrangement meant that half of the crew manned their battle stations, while the second half was off duty. The groups alternated on four-hour shifts. The warship was ready for battle.

■ ■ ■ ■

Inside turret five, Lt. j.g. Bin Cochran was ready for action. Short of the Pearl Harbor attack, he had been aboard the ship for every stint of combat. Cochran had come to the *Helena* via the United States Naval Academy.

From Holly Springs, Mississippi, Cochran won an appointment from his local congressman and entered the academy in 1939. "I just saw the movie *Navy Blue and Gold* and that was the way I wanted to go," he recalled. The first year of the program was heavily tilted toward physical activities, while later years focused on the specifics of being a naval officer. "There was always an argument about which was the hardest year there and it was between the first year and the second year," he said. "You just had to stay with it."[7]

Life at the academy changed after the Pacific War started. "The main thing that I remember is we immediately [became] security guards. They gave us a forty-five [pistol] and put us around at the gates and doors and things." With the United States now at war, class work was accelerated with the standard four-year program condensed into three years. The extra work meant little time off for the midshipmen. "There [were] no holidays," he continued. "We stayed there the first Christmas after [Pearl Harbor]." Cochran made it through his remaining academy days without any major problems. "I tolerated it all right," he said of the time. "I just took things as they came." Almost a year earlier than anticipated, he graduated on June 19, 1942, and was commissioned as an ensign. He received orders for the *Helena* and was granted a thirty day leave.

It was not exactly easy for Cochran to get to the West Coast after his leave. "You had to get priorities for flight tickets," he said. He was not able to board his scheduled military flight at the Memphis airport. "Somebody with a better priority had booted me off." He loitered around the airport, waiting for more planes to arrive. "I met every bomber that landed at the airport there, and it was one right after the other. None of them were going to the West Coast." He eventually ended up on a commercial airliner. "In the mean time, some nice lady there, she arranged me a way to get there. I had to fly out of Chicago." He arrived at Mare Island in the middle of July.

Cochran's only previous shipboard experience was short stay aboard the old battleship *Arkansas* during his academy days. Boarding the *Helena* gave him the chance to be on a new modern warship. "It was ready to go," he said of his new ship. "I wasn't here very long, and we were hitting the course due west."

■ ■ ■ ■

Jim Layton did not get to see much of the topside action while at his battle station. "My general quarter's station was midship repair party." The group met on the second deck amidships, a position that was right under the stacks. It was one of several repair parties stationed around the ship, each consisting of as many as twenty-five men and assigned to cover a specific portion of the vessel. "A repair party takes care of anything that needs to be done during general quarters within that area of the ship," he said.[8] A chief petty officer was in charge of the group.

As pharmacist's mate second class, Layton's duty was to provide medical support. "If there was anyone that needed any medical attention in that area of the ship [it] was my responsibility. I had two stretcher bearers assigned to me," he said, noting that he was the only actual medic in the group. "They were just stretcher bearers." He also had a first aid kit at his disposal that was well stocked with tape, gauze, antiseptics, and morphine.

Although he did not have a headset, Layton took orders from central station, where the ship's damage control officer was located. "They would give me instructions before I left the repair party," he added. "If someone needed attention, they directed me where to go and how to get there. They told me what watertight integrity I could open." Depending on the situation, Layton could be all over the middle part of the ship.

■ ■ ■ ■

The *Helena* was a ship with plenty of firepower. Her main armament consisted of fifteen 6-inch guns arranged in five triple-barreled turrets. Each turret was designated a number, with one being the most forward and numbers four and five in the rear part of the ship. The main battery guns would be taking center stage during the upcoming bombardment mission. Eight 5-inch guns, arranged in four double-barreled turrets, comprised the secondary battery. The weapons were considered dual purpose in that they could be fired at air or surface targets.

Although it was a bombardment mission, Captain Cecil knew that his ship had to be ready for a variety of actions. The barrage itself required the main battery guns to use high capacity (explosive) ammunition. A surface fight called for common ammunition, the standard shells with armor piercing ability. The men in the turrets had to have quick access to both types of ammunition as the situation warranted. "In the main battery, 6-inch common was kept in the hoist until the leading destroyer had completed its sweep of the inner areas of the gulf," Cecil later wrote of the situation. "Shift was made to [high capacity] bombardment projectiles about ten minutes before firing."[9] Although it meant extra work for the ammunition handlers, the arrangement kept the *Helena* well prepared for any possible situation that might arise during the dangerous voyage.

Throughout the operation, Cecil would rely heavily on his combat information center, which was a relatively new concept. Operations in the Solomon Islands had clearly established the need for a type of clearing house—a place where information from lookouts, radio reports, radar plots, and more could be analyzed and interpreted away from the busy bridge. The solution was to designate a room in the superstructure, equip it with the radar scope, and call it a combat information center.[10] Often manned by the executive officer during combat conditions, the area collected and analyzed important information that could then be disseminated to the bridge, gunnery department, and other locations.

■ ■ ■ ■

Just after midnight the bombardment force neared the northern tip of New Georgia. At about this time three unidentified planes, all showing lights, approached the force. Aboard the *Nashville*, Ainsworth wondered if the planes were the Black Cats. "They had small white wing tip lights and a large white light in the tail portion of the fuselage," he noticed. A lookout reported that the aircraft looked like Catalina seaplanes and Ainsworth cursed them for carelessly flying without turning off their lights.

The mysterious planes were also seen from the *Helena*. Cecil reported the incident in the ship's war diary. He noticed that the planes challenged the ships by blinking a recognition signal from a lamp. "First tried letter U, next W, next O, and finally AA," he wrote of the signals.[11] None of the ships answered the challenge as the codes did not match anything currently being used by Allied aircraft.

The planes eventually moved on without incident after circling for about a half an hour. Back aboard the *Nashville*, Ainsworth concluded that the planes were Japanese. "This light near the tail was a new wrinkle to all of us and although they were very large planes, they looked somewhat too straight in the fuselage to be Catalinas," he noted. The admiral drew his own conclusion of the events. "They probably figured we were a friendly force on our way home, and must have thought us excessively cautious in not answering their challenge. Whether or not they reported us we shall probably never know." Ainsworth's belief was shared by his ship commanders.

Moving in a single column the ships turned southwest into the unknown waters of Kula Gulf just before 1 a.m. Following the operation plan, the *O'Bannon* pulled ahead of the other ships and scanned the area. As a precaution, the *Nicholas* moved into a position slightly ahead of the remaining four ships. Moving at half speed the *O'Bannon* cautiously crept along as if entering a blind alley. Silence shrouded her bridge as lookouts trained their eyes for anything amiss. Minutes seemed to take an eternity to pass.[12] Satisfied that the gulf was clear of any enemy ships, the destroyer turned north at 1:28 a.m. and moved to her station position at the entrance of the gulf. The remaining ships slowed to 17 knots and moved deeper into the gulf.

An important factor to the success of the operation hinged on the force getting a good navigational fix in the confined waters of Kula Gulf. "Due to land configurations, it was considered unlikely that fire control radars would be of any value in determining the ship's position or in determining the opening range and bearing," Captain Cecil later wrote. "It was therefore planned to utilize the SG radar for this purpose." The radar performed the task well with Sasamboki Island being used as the point of fixation. The small land mass is located just off the coast from the Vila-Stanmore plantation area. In spite of it being a low lying island, the SC radar sets on the cruisers accurately located it.

At exactly 1:55 a.m. the bombardment ships reached their deepest penetration into the gulf. The *Nashville* swung hard to the right and began to move on the firing line. The two Black Cats from Guadalcanal now arrived over the target area and made contact with the ships below. Careful not to warn the Japanese of the impending attack, the planes had patrolled to the north and south as the bombardment ships made their way up the Slot. A day earlier—during a heavy air attack on Munda so as to not attract any unwarranted attention—the planes had made a quick pass over the target so that the spotters could become familiar with the land area below. The third plane, which had accompanied the force up the Slot, fanned out to search the general area for any signs of approaching Japanese ships.

Five minutes after turning onto the firing line, and exactly on schedule, the *Nashville* fired a salvo from her main battery guns. The deafening noise shattered the silence of the night. A plane above reported that it landed near the center of the runway. After adjustments for spots, the cruiser began to rain shells down onto her assigned target area.

Two minutes after the flagship started shooting, the *Helena* turned onto the firing line. Her five main battery turrets were pointed off her port side. Lookouts aboard the ship made out individual palm trees on the distant land. A spotter plane checked in with the *Helena* just as she was preparing to open fire. "How do you receive me?" A radioman aboard the ship replied, "Receive you fine."[13]

The ship's guns suddenly opened fire with a thunderous roar. Her first salvo fell into the water about a hundred yards from land. "Down five," came over the radio from the overhead plane guiding the *Helena* to adjust her fire. However, the adjustment came too late as the second salvo had already hit land. An observer in the plane saw the shells fall near a cluster of buildings. "From this time on the *Helena*'s salvos covered the land area north and west of the Vila Plantation buildings for about 1,800 yards. The area east to the Vila River was also worked over," the observer later reported.[14] When the main battery switched to rapid fire, the cruiser's 5-inch secondary batteries joined the bombardment. Throughout the mission, an occasional announcement was made via the *Helena*'s internal speaker system to keep the men below decks appraised of what was happening.

High atop the *Helena*'s superstructure in director control, Lt. Cdr. James Baird stood transfixed as the 6-inch guns below him sent a parade of shells streaming out toward land. His role in the operation was to visually check the accuracy of the gunfire. A young sailor with a headset stood at his side ready to communicate any spot corrections. From his commanding position, Baird could see a panoramic view of the *Helena* each time the dim glow of the orange shells left the main battery guns. Below director control, Cecil stood among the crowd of sailors huddled on the bridge. All eyes were glued to the distant land that was being rocked by fiery explosions.

Admiral Ainsworth seemed pleased with the accurate gunfire contributed by the *Helena*. He later reported that shells from the ship caused a number of "good sized fires" ashore. Some occurred in an area believed to be an unloading facility used by the Japanese to store ammunition.

As the cruiser's shells streamed toward the target area, the *DeHaven* and *Radford* continued into the gulf before turning to create the second parallel firing line. Both ships then opened fire on the assigned target area. The same plane that was assisting the *Helena* also spotted for the destroyers. The first salvos from the small ships created a brilliant fire that only seemed to spread as the battery continued.

The Japanese mounted no effective response to the bombardment. Only the *DeHaven* and *Nashville* reported seeing some weak anti-aircraft fire coming from the beach area. None was threatening. It appeared as though the enemy was truly taken by surprise.

Six minutes into the bombardment, the Black Cat spotting for the *Nashville* reported a small ship fleeing the area. The vessel was seen to enter Blackett Straight, a narrow body of water just south of the Vila-Stanmore area. At about the same time, lookouts aboard the flagship reported seeing a torpedo wake pass near the ship. Ainsworth ordered the *Helena* to take the unidentified ship under fire. However, neither her surface search radar, nor her lookouts, could locate the target. Positioned closer to the strait, the *DeHaven* also scanned the area with radar and obtained negative results. Later, after the bombardment force had moved out of the gulf, one of the Black Cats reported seeing a cargo ship and a second unknown type of small vessel leaving the area as well. A cargo ship and destroyer were seen pulling into a harbor in the Shortlands the next morning.[15] Apparently Ainsworth's bombardment force had disrupted their quiet night.

The flagship was not the only vessel to report seeing a torpedo wake that night; lookouts aboard the *Helena* also thought they spotted one. In the course of the operations within the gulf, her SG radar scanned the immediate area around the ship on several occasions to investigate suspicious objects sighted by topside lookouts. None turned out to be enemy ships.

■ ■ ■ ■

Mason Miller's anti-aircraft gun did not see action during the bombardment. "At that time I was assigned to a 40mm gun on the port side aft," he said."[16] Surrounded by a metal shield, the gun mount was positioned precariously between a 5-inch battery and the after main turrets. Miller, who oversaw a group of about twelve sailors, had become very familiar with his gun since coming aboard the *Helena*. "It was a quadruple gun and we had quite a crew on there," he recalled. The gun lacked the range needed to hit the target area at Vila-Stanmore. "We didn't shoot anything at night," he said. "We had to stay out of the way."

The angle from which the *Helena* was firing meant extra steps had to be taken by Miller and his gunners. "When the main battery trained out to port side and the 5-inch battery, which was almost over our head trained around, we had to head to the other side of the ship to keep from getting killed by the blast from the guns," he recalled. "Usually you used cotton to plug your ears. If you didn't, you might get some pretty serious blast to your ears." It was all in the nights work for the forty-millimeter gun crew.

■ ■ ■ ■

Just before 2:15 a.m. the *Nashville* completed her time on the firing line and made a hard turn to the right. The flagship was now pointed northeast toward the entrance of the gulf. The movement signified the beginning of the end of the bombardment phase of the operation. The *O'Bannon*, stationed near Waugh Rock off the northeast coast of Kolombangara, began to move east away from the island. As the remaining ships began to move out of the gulf, the *DeHaven* and *Radford* briefly poured heavy gunfire into two small harbor areas north of Vila-Stanmore. Apparently neither destroyer knew that the *Nicholas* had just determined by radar sweep that no Japanese ships were in the harbors. As a parting farewell both Black Cat planes dropped two 500-pound bombs on the target area to close out the operation while the bombardment force slipped away.

The men inside the *Helena*'s main battery turrets quickly reshuffled their ammunition, moving the common shells into position for use in a possible surface engagement. The nature of the threat now changed. "Total firing time was eleven minutes and forty-one seconds," Cecil reported. The guns had delivered a total of 990 6-inch shells onto the target area.

The firing from the *Helena* did not go off entirely without any hitches. "Although all turrets suffered stoppage during the firing, all were able to get out their ammunition allowance during the time allowed except turret [five]," Cecil noted. All three guns of that turret suffered some type of problem. However, all of the troubles were temporary and overall the captain was pleased with the performance of his gun crews.

During the height of the bombardment, the *Helena*'s SG radar set had suddenly lost power. A quick check of the equipment determined a switch kicked out due to the vibration of the main battery guns. The set was back running after only a minute.

It was about 3 a.m. when the *O'Bannon* linked up with the other ships near the entrance of Kula Gulf. She joined the *Nicholas* in position out in front of the two cruisers. The *DeHaven* and *Radford* spread out to the rear of the formation. The four destroyers created a box formation for anti-aircraft defense around the *Nashville* and *Helena*. The ships revved up speed to 29 knots as the force began the long and dangerous journey home.

3
Escape to Espiritu Santo

Luck must have been riding with Admiral Ainsworth—his ships had successfully slipped into Kula Gulf undetected and delivered the Japanese a punishing night barrage. As quickly as the bombardment portion of the operation had ended, however, the admiral changed the focus to getting his force out of harm's way. Now fully alerted to the presence of enemy ships, the Japanese were on the hunt. The greatest threat to the escaping American ships was from the air.

With the *Helena* gearing up for anti-aircraft defense, Seaman 1st Class Gene Robinson knew he might see some action. Robinson's battle station was a 20mm gun mount on the port side. Positioned on the main deck about even with the space between the smoke stacks, the gun was pretty close to being in the exact middle of the ship.

Robinson was one of many new sailors who had boarded the *Helena* while the ship was in California for repairs. His life had changed dramatically since the war started. He was thousands of miles away from his native Ohio, and his wife back home surely must have been worried about his well-being.

Growing up in the Cleveland area, Robinson entered the navy in January 1942. "I was what they called a Pearl Harbor avenger," he said. "A lot of guys got steaming mad [about the Japanese attack] and wanted to get even."

With his older brother already drafted into the army, Robinson decided to enlist in the navy. "I think I was twenty-two," he continued. "I just barely made the eye test. I think the guy let me hunch up a little bit closer and I passed the exam."[1]

Robinson's introduction to navy life started with his arrival in Chicago. "It was cold and the training officer wouldn't let us put ear muffs on. He went around with his cap and no ear muffs," he remembered. "Most of us when we left home were not dressed for winter." The heaviest clothing Robinson possessed was a sport jacket, which had to suffice for a few days until uniforms and coats were issued.

After a period of training that was much shorter than a typical boot camp, Robinson was on a train heading west. "We knew we were going out to the West Coast," he said, "but we didn't know what our assignment was." He was amazed at the support shown by ordinary citizens along the way. "About every stop that we'd make, why there'd be people out there greeting us. The mothers and women were giving us candy and cookies and stuff like that . . . cigarettes. It was a fairly pleasant trip."

The end of the line was San Francisco. Robinson spent a short amount of time on several small islands in the area, before learning that he was assigned to a nearby ship. He boarded the *Helena* on March 4, 1943. Seeing the cruiser in dry dock was an awe-inspiring site. "Cruisers were maybe as long as a battleship, but not as big and heavy," he said. "But they were big." He was assigned quarters on a nearby barracks ship, which "was all made up with a lot of bunks, and that's where they put us for training. We would walk to the [*Helena*] and go aboard and start getting familiar with it and find out our duties."

The young sailor learned firsthand what war was all about when he came down with a case of the flu. "They took me to sick bay and I was there for a couple of days," Robinson related. "In the sick bay there were several sailors that had been injured and burned at Pearl Harbor aboard the *Helena*. I didn't talk to them too much, but they were in a lot of pain." Robinson noticed that pharmacist's mates frequently tended to the men's burns. "Everyday I'd see them go over there taking dead skin off their backs, trying to get them more comfortable." It seemed like a painful undertaking. "I hated to see that. It started me thinking: wholly catch what I am doing here?"

In addition to getting to know his new ship, Robinson had something else to accomplish—he wanted to marry his girlfriend Mae. "We'd been going around together for about two years and we were engaged," he said. After realizing that the ship would not be departing anytime soon, Robinson asked Mae to come out from Cleveland and bring the rings. Contacting a distant aunt in nearby Oakland, he arranged for a late June ceremony. "We had the wedding right there in their home," he recalled. "I had several of my sailor buddies along there with me. One of them was my best man." As an unintended result of the wedding, word spread among Robinson's circle of sailor friends that his aunt had three daughters. "Everyone wanted to go with me on liberty because I'd go to my aunt's house with all these nice looking nineteen, twenty-year old girls. So I was fairly popular."

Mae stayed in the San Francisco area until shortly after Robinson departed with the *Helena*. "After I'd been out to sea for a while I got in touch with her by letter. I told her to go back home." He was not comfortable with the idea of his new wife living in a sailor's town. She soon went back home to live with her parents near Cleveland.

■ ■ ■ ■

Having let the bombardment force sneak in undetected, the Japanese were determined not to the let the ships get away. After the assault ended, eleven float planes fanned out to search for Ainsworth's ships. Thirty twin engine bombers took off from bases at Rabaul on a search and destroy mission.[2] The Japanese airmen were prepared to use newly developed night torpedo attack tactics.

As the ships sped out of the gulf, a green flare suddenly appeared over the mountaintop on Kolombangara. Japanese planes soon began to shadow the ships, with red, white, and green flares occasionally falling from the sky, apparently marking the position and movement of the task force. "The flares burned for three or four minutes on their way down, and the float boxes burned with frequent flare-ups for about ten minutes," Admiral Ainsworth later reported.[3]

Shortly after 2:30 a.m. the ships moved into anti-aircraft formation. Radar screens immediately began to show contacts. "Sometimes in groups, and sometimes the groups would separate into smaller groups, or single aircraft," Ainsworth wrote. "The number of planes is estimated at anywhere from a half a dozen up to twenty."

Aboard the *Helena*, Captain Cecil believed that the current weather conditions were somewhat favorable for an air attack. "Surface visibility was about 8,000 yards," he recalled. "Cloud cover, though fairly dense, merely diffused the bright moonlight." A full moon had occurred only two days earlier. "Destroyers could be seen at 4,000 yards with the unaided eye."[4] Moving at high speed, the ships left a telltale wake that could be easily spotted from above. Cecil later heard from one of the Black Cat spotters that the wakes of the two cruisers could be seen five miles away.

Lookouts on the *Helena* first sighted a floating flare marker at about 2:49 a.m. Blinking white, it seemed to be about six miles away from the ship. "Thereafter additional float markers were observed indicating that a shadowing plane was efficiently marking the track of the task group," Cecil reported. At about the same time, a plane was picked up by the *Helena*'s SC radar set. It proved to be a busy night for the radar men on duty in the combat information center. "Tracking and attacking the force under prevailing weather conditions was entirely feasible, particularly with excellent float markers with blinking characteristics dropped by the shadower, marking the track of the task group," the captain added.

The weather soon began to change for the better. Upon sighting several dark squalls on the horizon from his flagship, Ainsworth changed course slightly to enter the dark masses. The ships were able to stay intermittently hidden under the cloud cover for almost an hour. However, the coverage provided by the squalls was not complete and when the enemy planes began to move closer, the admiral directed the *Helena* to open fire at her discretion. Cecil received the order just after 3:30 a.m. The cruiser's speaker system immediately barked the order for the crew to stand by for an air attack.

Just after 3:45 a.m. one of the *Helena*'s 5-inch gun batteries opened fire on a shadowing plane when it closed to within 7,000 yards off the starboard bow of the ship. The gun was operating under full radar control. "At the first flash the plane maneuvered radically and withdrew," Cecil noted. Lookouts were able to get a brief visual glimpse of the plane. It appeared to be a large flying boat. Less than fifteen minutes later, the process was repeated with the shadower again moving into range before withdrawing after a burst of gunfire. A short time later the *Helena* again changed course, following the force into another squall. Although not a heavy storm, the partial protection it afforded was better than nothing.

At 4:19 a.m. the *Helena*'s SC radar obtained a new contact. The initial report, made by the *Nashville*, had the planes about eighteen miles from the ships. Three groups were soon being tracked and radar operators kept a good eye on them as they moved steadily closer to the ships. "At no time thereafter was the air defense officer in ignorance of the exact location of the attacking groups," Cecil noted, "owing to the efficient functioning of both SC and FD radars, and the splendid coordination of information in the combat operations center."

Less than a half an hour after the initial sighting, the enemy planes closed in for an attack. Groups of planes, tentatively identified as twin engine torpedo bombers, made two advances toward the ships, and the *Helena*'s 5-inch gun batteries quickly crackled with fire. The *Nashville* and some of the destroyers joined the fusillade in what appeared to be the most serious threat encountered thus far in the mission. However, both attacks stalled. "After each attack the planes withdrew upon meeting effective radar controlled anti-aircraft fire," Cecil wrote. The *Helena* also used her 6-inch main battery guns to help defend the ship during the second attack. Using high capacity ammunition with timed fuses, the six guns of two of the forward turrets let loose with a single salvo. Radar and the bursts from the 5-inch guns were used to aim the shells toward the approaching planes. "The 6-inch bursts showed on the radar screen not far from the range of the [Japanese] planes, and undoubtedly influenced the enemy to retire immediately," Cecil added.

Although unconfirmed, one enemy plane was thought to have been downed during the two attacks. Gunfire from either the *O'Bannon* or *Radford* may have hit the mark and sailors on both ships reported seeing a plane go down in flames.

By now more rainsqualls of heavy intensity began to appear. Ainsworth did his best to use the cloud banks to his advantage. As soon as his ships left one cloud bank, he changed course to enter a new one.

The last blast of anti-aircraft fire came from the *O'Bannon* just before dawn. The task force had managed to escape from the dangerous situation. Daylight brought a flight of five P-38 fighter planes from Henderson Field to their aid. As the friendly planes took station over the ships, the second round of the bombardment plan was about to take place. Fifty-nine planes from USS *Saratoga*—an assortment of SBD Dauntless dive bombers, TBF Avengers, and Wildcat fighters—showed up to hit the Vila-Stanmore area. The airmen flew back to their carrier after giving the area a thorough drubbing.[5]

The ships pulled into Port Purvis late in the morning of January 24.[6] The anchorage was located adjacent to the island of Tulagi, directly across from Guadalcanal. Although he considered his mission a success, Admiral Ainsworth knew that the bombardment offered only a very temporary cure to the menace of the Japanese airfields. "We may destroy large quantities of gasoline and stores, and we may render these fields unusable at critical times, but the only real answer is to take the field away from them," he concluded. The admiral was correct in his assumption. As the months ahead would bear out, no matter how hard the Americans pounded the Japanese airfields from the sea or air, the bases never seemed to be out of action for any great length of time.

Aboard the *Helena*, Cecil was pleased with the way his crew performed during the operation. "The performance of all personnel, officers and men, was exemplary," he wrote. "The bombardment was carefully planned by the gunnery officer in cooperation with the ship control party and the officer in charge, combat operations center." The captain directed special praise toward the fire control area. "It is considered that the performance of the fire control party was above reproach and functioned exactly as planned, and that our assigned target areas were properly and effectively covered." With a job well accomplished, it was time for the *Helena* to head home.

■ ■ ■ ■

The stay at Tulagi was a short one, and the *Helena* returned to Espiritu Santo on January 25 from the voyage to Kula Gulf. She had departed the area only days before, but for many aboard it had felt much longer.

Although not offering the luxuries found at Pearl Harbor or on the West Coast, Espiritu Santo was home for the *Helena*'s sailors. The largest island in the New Hebrides group, the base was about 500 miles southeast of Guadalcanal. By early 1943 the island was a well established forward operating base used by sailors, soldiers, and airmen alike. The naval facilities on Espiritu Santo were congregated on the southeast part of the island. A secure harbor area was established in Segond Channel, a narrow body of water that separated the mainland from Aore Island. Naval support facilities of all types stretched for almost two miles.[7] Ships of all sizes regularly dropped anchor at various designated berthing positions throughout the waterway.

The return to Espiritu Santo marked the beginning of a period of relative calm for the sailors. The ship did not participate in any major sea actions over the next couple of months. Throughout the remaining days of February, she darted in and out of Segond Channel as she spent time at sea patrolling with Ainsworth's cruisers and destroyers. If the *Helena* was at the base for any length of time, her sailors had the opportunity to spend some time ashore.

As Espiritu Santo grew in importance as a naval base, so did the amenities ashore for sailors. A recreation center was built on a nearby island, which contained a number of sporting facilities ranging from baseball diamonds to a boxing ring. A rudimentary nine-hole golf course was even built, although grazing cows and vegetation made it somewhat hazardous to play.[8]

The recreation activities were not limited to sports. A walk through the jungle led a sailor to Paradise Beach. Positioned at the end of a bay, the horseshoe-shaped beach offered plenty of sand and was surrounded by coconut trees. A native village stood off in the distance.[9]

Not one for sports, Gayle Gilbert preferred to spend his time ashore at the beach. "We could go down to the beach and swim if [we] wanted," he recalled.[10] He often wondered about the long distance that stood between him and his family. "I'd look out at that water and say, 'Oh look, my people are way, way over that way, all this water between me and them.'"

Although maybe not quite as good as being back at home, the area offered war-weary sailors a place to relax. One *Helena* sailor summed up the situation on the island in a letter to his mother: "Our life out here may not be what we would like it to be, but we're a long way from what you might call hardship."[11]

"It wasn't a bad place," Jim Layton said. "Espiritu Santo had been made really into a recreational island. If you wanted to, you could play volleyball, horseshoes [and] softball." Baseball was another popular sport on the island, although the coral ground was known to occasionally leave sailors with painful injuries.[12] Layton simply remembered it as a place to put his feet on solid ground and occasionally enjoyed going ashore for a beverage, where he recalled a small stand being set up there for the purpose. "Before we left the ship they gave us two beer chits," Layton continued.[13]

However, one did not necessarily have to go ashore at Espiritu Santo to find excitement. Layton recalled a pilot aboard the ship from San Antonio, Texas, named "Tex" O'Neil, who was known for taking guest passengers for wild airborne rides. After treating him in the sick bay, Layton reluctantly accepted an offer for a plane ride, expecting a smooth water takeoff.

He arrived at the fantail at the appointed time only to find, much to his dismay, a plane mounted up on the catapult. "He pulled a fast one. How he arranged to have them use the catapults, I don't know," Layton said. He quickly issued O'Neil a stern warning. "I told him that if he flew me upside down that [he] had better not come to sick bay again because [he didn't] know what [was] going to happen to [him]." Although he was less than happy, the pharmacist's mate survived the sudden jolt of the catapult launch. The pilot, however, wisely heeded Layton's warning and kept the plane on an even keel.

A port stay also allowed for an occasional movie to be shown aboard ship. "They'd rig up a screen by the catapults," Robinson said. Unlike the theaters of the day that ran multiple movie projectors, the *Helena* had only one machine. "Every time a reel would end, there was nothing there until a new reel was put on," he continued. Although it may not have been as pleasant of an experience as being in a theater, the movie offered the sailors a connection to the outside world.

Stays in port often meant little time spent at battle stations. When not on duty or ashore, the crew often spent much of their time in the *Helena*'s living compartments. Gilbert slept toward the back of the ship. "I was right over one of the screws," he said. "I think I was the second or third deck below quarter deck. Way down below." At least it was better than the mess deck, where he first bunked after boarding the ship, in which temporary bunks had to be set up and taken down daily to make way for the food service. Robinson had no complaints about his sleeping arrangements. "The living quarters were fine," he recalled. "The lower deck was spit and polished. We had bright red linoleum decks. The bunks were about . . . maybe three high." When not in use the bunks folded up into the overhead of the compartment.

As a junior officer, Mason Miller was also satisfied with the small stateroom he shared with three others. "The supply officer and the junior medical officer had the bunks that were installed in the room," he recalled. "Then there were two of us that were put in the room on cots. We had plenty of room, everybody was happy."

Since he spent his time while on duty below decks, Walter Wendt was not opposed to sleeping topside. "It depended quite a bit on where you were and how hot it was on topside," he said. "In the tropics you get about three rain showers every night. You'd have to grab your blanket and head underneath until it dried up just a little bit and then you go up again." Sleeping topside could pose a problem in making it to duty on time. "If you wanted to sleep on topside, you had to find a messenger that had the preceding watch. He had to know exactly where you were." The process seemed to work for everyone involved.

The time at Espiritu Santo also meant some extra work for the crew. The tasks needed to keep a ship like the *Helena* operating never seemed to stop. Cleaning and routine inspections were regular affairs. Loading supplies and ammunition was an additional chore during port stays. Bin Cochran recalled his turn. "I had to take a boat over on a couple of days, one right after another, and bring back ammunition. That's not the best way to do it," he said. Loading 6-inch shells into the whale boat and then transferring the cargo over to the *Helena* was a slow and dangerous task. "You just had to know what the capacity of the whale boat was and not exceed it."

■ ■ ■ ■

The temporary lull in the action allowed the *Helena*'s new captain to take stock of his ship. With only a short time in command, Charles Cecil was not well known by his crew. Like many of the enlisted men aboard, Robinson never even met him. "I don't think anybody disliked him," Robinson recalled. "We just didn't know that much about him, and I think he was just another captain, that's all."

Some of the junior officers may have had a little more contact with Cecil. "He was alright," said Cochran. "There was no dislike there."[14] Cochran occasionally stood deck watches with him on the bridge. Miller simply remembered that Cecil seemed to be liked by the crew. "I never did get to know him very well," he added.[15]

■ ■ ■ ■

Some of the sailors aboard the *Helena* fought an enemy besides the Japanese: loneliness. Being a young sailor thousands of miles from home certainly must have caused an emotional strain for those who were enduring the long days at sea. The occasional stop over at Espiritu Santo offered temporary breaks from the war. The port visits did not, however, provide a cure for the feelings of loneliness and isolation that could occur while being confined on a warship at sea.

Each sailor was affected differently. Walter Wendt found that focusing on his job helped to stave off homesick feelings. "I guess I was a little homesick," he admitted. "Memories of home were behind us, so I was just trying to do a good job."[16] For Robinson, the feelings seemed to only hit while in port. Layton simply came to the realization that being away from home was just something that had to be coped with to survive. "You learned to live with it because you knew that there was nothing you could do about it" he recalled. "I never let it bother me a lot."

Mail was one of the sailor's few lifelines to home. It was not uncommon for many sailors to regularly pen a note to family or a friend. For Robinson, it was the only way to keep in touch with his new wife back home in Cleveland. "A lot of times I'd go off by myself in one of the corners of the mess halls and write. At least once a week I would write." His letters often took a while to make it home. "I numbered the letters," he said. "Sometimes she would get letter number ten, but she didn't get letter number seven or six, so she knew that something was missing. I couldn't tell you exactly how long it took to get there." Robinson looked forward to the letters that he received from his wife in return. "She'd send me letters back with big lipstick prints all over 'em."

Robinson and his shipmates soon learned that the *Helena* was going on another voyage, but not one that would take them to the front lines.

4

Down Under

The last day of February found the *Helena* getting ready to put to sea. Just before 4 p.m. the ship began the necessary maneuvers to clear Segond Channel. Less than an hour later she was in the open sea. Cruising at 17 knots the *Helena* was heading almost due south.

Rumors had been circulating for about a month that the ship would soon be going to an unknown liberty port. The same gossip came about after almost every mission, but this time it was for real.[1] The crew was overjoyed when the rumor became official. The ship was going to be taking a break from the war. She was en route to a much-needed overhaul at Sydney, Australia.

For the crew this meant liberty, off-duty time ashore and away from the cramped quarters of the ship. Sailors started to shave off their beards. The ship's band began to rehearse some new songs. Young sailors pressed veterans for details about the much-revered liberty port. Even Cecil seemed to have a smile glued to his face.[2] It was a happy ship indeed.

After a brief stop at New Caledonia and several days in the open waters of the far South Pacific, the *Helena* was nearing her destination. During the early morning hours of March 6, the destroyer USS *Henley* took station near the cruiser to provide an anti-submarine screen. In mid-afternoon lookouts on the *Helena* sighted land forty-two miles away. Within an hour the ship slowed to begin maneuvering into the channel that led to Sydney. A harbor pilot then came aboard and guided the ship to a buoy in Jackson Harbor. Sailors who were topside were able to take in the welcome sights along the route. Tugboats sounded their whistles in salutation, spectators cheered from ashore, and people in pleasure craft waved from their boats.[3] At exactly 6:01 p.m. the *Helena* dropped anchor.

The Australians were glad to see the American sailors and the men on the *Helena* were just as happy to be there. Sydney was a sailor's town. It had paved streets, buildings, eating establishments, bars, pretty girls, and trolley cars. It had been a welcome port for American sailors even before the war started.

"Liberty was better than candy," Walter Wendt exclaimed. "We would go to a bar in groups of four [or] five shipmates and get stupid. In just a few hours we tried to catch up for a year of being away from most things like pretty ladies and good beer."[4] With the country at war since 1939, there seemed to be more ladies around than men. "The Australian ladies were beautiful," Wendt added.

"We had two ship's parties," Gene Robinson recalled of the stay in Sydney. "Our ship had one of the best bands in the whole fleet." The gatherings were held ashore in a large dance hall. "It was pretty big and there were tables and a big dance floor." He remembered many sailors stopping to grab some liquor on the way. "We'd pick up a girl where ever we could find one and we'd dance and drink." It was a pleasant evening for sailors who were far from home.

Making the most of his visit to the popular liberty port, Robinson was one of many sailors who spent a night ashore. "Me and a buddy had a room in Sydney," he recalled. "We had a hotel room for whatever occasion would occur. Why we'd just had the hotel room to take advantage of it." However, he soon found himself in hot water.

The trouble began at one of the ship's parties. "I got loaded pretty good," he explained. "I went back to the hotel room, climbed in, and fell asleep." After the party ended, several shipmates came by to take him back to the ship, but Robinson waved them off. "I will be all right," he told them. "I woke up the next morning a little bit late and found out my money was gone. It was probably about twenty bucks. I rushed back to the ship as fast as I could." However, he was two hours late.

Returning sailors had to report to the officer of the deck when boarding the ship. The officer on duty at the time turned out to be from Robinson's division. He remembered that it was an awkward meeting. "He knows you're late, you know you're late." The officer told him that he had already turned in the list of overdue people.

Being reported for tardiness resulted in a trip to captain's mast—an informal court held for minor infractions. Robinson's division officer accompanied him to the hearing. On this particular day the executive officer was serving as the judge. "So our division officer says that I was a good man and that [I] was just a few minutes late," Robinson continued. "The executive officer gave me three days restrictions. That's the only time I got put on restriction. I couldn't get off the ship." The sentence temporarily put a damper on Robinson's fun ashore.

Gayle Gilbert remembered his stay in Sydney very simply. "It was a good time," he said. His first liberty ashore, however, ended badly. He went ashore with Nicholas Gazis. "He was a fireman down in the boiler rooms and for some reason or another, he and I seemed to pal up together."[5] Once ashore Gazis suggested that they get a hold of some gin. Gilbert readily agreed, but in retrospect realized that probably was not a good idea since he was not used to drinking much.

"I remember going down into the subway and that's the last thing I remember," Gilbert continued. "I'd taken a few drinks and it knocked me out." He woke up the next morning on the side of the road. "I was in my white uniform sitting by a telephone pole. My clothes were all dirty and I didn't have my hat." His companion was gone. Something else was missing, too—his money. "I only had thirty bucks, but back in those days thirty dollars was a lot of money." He soon realized that he had to get back to the ship. Suddenly someone yelled out, "Hey Gilbert, get over here," from a nearby bus. Looking up he quickly saw that it was several shipmates. When Gilbert told them that he did not have any money, they offered to pay his way. He graciously accepted their offer and jumped aboard. The group knew that they were fighting a deadline. "I got back in time. I didn't get into any trouble." Learning his lesson, he made a vow, "I won't do that again."

A later liberty proved to be much tamer. Gilbert made his way to the USO where he enjoyed a show and some Coke. "At the USO I met a girl," he said. "She was a very nice person and she invited me to go out to her house." The two traveled together on a trolley car. The girl lived with her parents. "Went out to her home and they fed me crumpets . . . tea and crumpets. I had that and had a little visit with her and came back to the ship. There was nothing going on, just a friendly person," Gilbert added.

The good times in port were not only limited to the enlisted men. Bin Cochran also enjoyed the visit. "We had a great time," he said. "We'd get about two days ashore and then one day on the ship. They were pretty good about giving us good liberties." Cochran had a chance meeting in a hotel. "I [saw] a guy I grew up with, right across the street from me in Holly Springs."[6] The old friend was in the U.S. Army Air Force. "They'd go on liberty down there. He had an apartment. So I was able to get his apartment when he left, which made our three weeks there even better. It was great." He also remembered Cecil organizing an evening party for the officers that included a performance by the ship's band.

When not ashore on liberty, Cochran and the other officers had duties aboard the ship. "There was a lot to do on the ship to kind of get it back in shape and getting things working right," he said. "In the gunnery we had to do things, like checking the turrets. They don't roll 100 percent true and you have [to make] corrections." The vast array of equipment aboard the ship had to be restored to good working order for the next combat mission.

Jim Layton said of Sydney "The food was excellent. The women were excellent," he recalled. "They loved the yanks."[7]

■ ■ ■ ■

While many of *Helena* sailors were enjoying time ashore, Marine 1st Lt. Remmel Dudley was on a flight to Australia from Admiral Halsey's headquarters in New Caledonia to join the *Helena*. "It was rather ironic, I thought, that I ended up on a ship," he later recalled.

The youngest of four siblings, Dudley had grown up in Jonesboro, Arkansas. Like many, his family tightened their belts to make it through the 1930s. His father died at the onset of the Depression when Dudley was only twelve years old. "He was an attorney," he said of his father. "He was a lawyer, had been a judge, and left the bench and went into private practice. My mother was just a housewife," Dudley added. "We didn't spend a lot of money." The family was able to struggle through the Depression with meager means.

Dudley's decision to join the military was an easy one. "You didn't have to be a Rhodes Scholar to know you were going into the service either voluntarily or involuntarily in those days," he said. "Life was very uncertain and I wanted to control my own destiny and did not want to be drafted." He had recently graduated from the University of Arkansas and was attending law school there when he started to think about joining the service. "There were recruiters coming through the university towns all over the country," he continued.[8] Dudley was progressing through his classes at an accelerated schedule and completed his degree in early February 1942. After considering all of the military branches, he decided the Marine Corps was the best fit. "They were looking for a strong back and a weak mind. In the navy, I had to have just the opposite," he explained. The twenty-four year old formally entered the service on Valentine's Day.

Shipping out to Virginia, Dudley soon completed marine officer training at Quantico, graduating as a second lieutenant. "Then they sent me to field artillery school," he continued. "[I] finished that and then went out to San Diego and was sent out in a replacement battalion. I was headed for the First Marine Division in Australia." However, Dudley and a few others were unexpectedly dropped off at New Caledonia. He ended up with an office job at Admiral Halsey's headquarters. "I was doing coding and decoding, you know, top secret stuff." It was routine work that involved sending and receiving radio messages. Dudley soon heard a rumor that the *Helena* was in need of a marine officer. "So violating my rules, 'don't be volunteering too much,' I went up to the personnel officer and told him I sure would like to be considered for that job, and sure enough I got it." The marine was heading to sea.

Dudley received a warm welcome after boarding the *Helena* in Sydney. "I remember very fondly, how gracious the officers in the wardroom were to a brand new second lieutenant just joining the ship," he said. "The young junior officers all came up and introduced themselves. They made me feel right at home." Although Dudley had plenty to learn about his new ship, he also had time for some liberty. "I tell people that's when I had a full head of hair and a nice trim waist line," he said. He also had some money. Working on an island base in the South Pacific did not afford him the opportunity for much spending. "All the Australian boys were out fighting the wars and left all those poor girls home. We met some nice young ladies." However, as the stay in Australia drew to a close, Dudley focused on learning about his new duties.

■ ■ ■ ■

The liberty lasted twenty-four days.[9] While many of the men were enjoying their time ashore, the ship had undergone some much needed maintenance. The stay included a stint in a dry dock so that her bottom could be scraped free of barnacles. Some minor damage, suffered during the Naval Battle of Guadalcanal, was also repaired.

The sailors surely must have realized that the port call would eventually come to an end. In a scene that was almost fit for a movie, one sailor arrived back to the ship just prior to departure with two attractive young ladies dressed only in night attire.[10] The trip to Sydney had been a welcome break from the war. For some of the sailors, it would be the last liberty port that they would ever see. On the morning of March 26 the cruiser slowly began making her way toward the open sea.

■ ■ ■ ■

The *Helena* arrived back at Espiritu Santo on the afternoon of March 30 to resume her duties with Admiral Ainsworth's cruisers and destroyers. While the *Helena* was gone from the war zone the U.S. Navy had stayed busy. New construction ships were arriving in the South Pacific at an ever increasing pace. Groups of cruisers and destroyers made nightly patrols up the Slot, almost to the entrance of Kula Gulf, searching the area for enemy shipping. Although no battles resulted from the increased patrols, the Japanese seemed well aware of the stepped-up activity.[11]

The Japanese airbases on Munda and Vila-Stanmore still posed a threat to the Americans. Both seemed to be able to stay operational in spite of continuous air attacks and several sea bombardments. On one early March bombardment mission to Kula Gulf, a group of American ships stumbled across two Japanese destroyers. The *Minegumo* and *Murasame* were on their way out of the gulf from a routine supply drop at Vila-Stanmore and were apparently unaware of the danger ahead. The approaching American ships pounced on the unsuspecting prey, quickly smothering both in a hail of gunfire. Neither Japanese ship made it out of Kula Gulf. After sinking both destroyers the mission continued without further incident.

The U.S. Navy was not the only one on the move in the Solomons. With Guadalcanal secured in early February, American land forces now occupied the adjacent Russell Islands. Planning then began for a larger amphibious operation to take place up the Slot sometime during the summer.

■ ■ ■ ■

For much of the next few months, the *Helena* operated in a period of relative calm, occasionally going to sea for routine patrols and training. She did, however, have a few scrapes with danger.

The cruiser was at Tulagi on the morning of April 7 with light cruisers USS *Honolulu* and *St. Louis* and six destroyers. Preparations were under way for another mission up the Slot when word suddenly came of an approaching Japanese air attack. The Guadalcanal area was full of American shipping with about forty large vessels of various types as well as many smaller ones.

Admiral Ainsworth wisely made for open water. The *Helena* had just finished refueling from a tanker when the order came to get under way in a hurry. Captain Cecil sent his men to general quarters fearing the worst. "Bogies reported at various ranges and bearings," he recorded.[12] Lookouts were clearly able to make out the enemy planes as they approached Tulagi by overflying adjacent Florida Island. The ships safely made it out of the immediate area and were not attacked. A total of 177 enemy planes swooped in to attack the ships in the harbor and surrounding area. Two tankers were damaged, including the *Kanawha*, which had just fueled the *Helena*. A destroyer and minesweeper were sunk.[13] Ainsworth's ships remained at sea northwest of Savo Island until learning mid-afternoon that their mission was cancelled. The *Helena* had escaped unharmed from a very dangerous situation.

The cruiser again participated in a voyage to shell Vila-Stanmore on the night of May 12–13. It would be the *Helena*'s first stint of combat since early in the year. The mission was part of a three-pronged operation that included the simultaneous bombardment of Munda and Vila-Stanmore and laying of mines in Blackett Strait at the southern end of Kula Gulf. The attack on Vila-Stanmore went off as planned, with the *Helena* hurling exactly one thousand 6-inch shells onto Japanese positions. The combined operation was considered a success. However, unknown to the Americans at the time, the Japanese discovered the minefield and cleared it out only a day later.

■ ■ ■ ■

Even when the *Helena* did not see combat for a stretch of time, the crew kept busy with duties and training. The lull in the action gave Robinson a chance to target practice with his 20mm gun mount. The routine often involved one of the *Helena*'s planes towing a target sleeve at a safe distance behind it. Robinson recalled that trying to hit a moving target was not as easy as it looked. "You had a big gigantic round gun sight and a point on the barrel up front," Robinson said. "It's not that easy to hit something that's flying pretty fast. Coming towards you it'd be easier to hit, but flying past you, boy you would have to lead that target a hundred yards or whatever in order to hit it."[14] Every third round was a tracer to aid in the aiming process, but it did not help much on a bright sunny day. For the gun crews, however, it was the closest thing to a combat simulator available.

The work never seemed to stop for Wendt. He kept busy below deck in the after engine room. It took a lot of men to ensure that the machinery needed to keep the *Helena* running stayed in good order. "There were four main engines, but each engine room would only take care of two of them," Went explained. Each steam turbine was connected to a large reduction gear. "Those reduction gears were connected to the main shaft. So the steam turbines would be turning much faster than the screw was turning."[15] Wendt spent a good amount of time overseeing pumps. "Usually I was on the lower level, either on the lube oil pumps or there were a bunch of pumps that would take the water out of the main condensers," he said of his duties. The men in the engine room drank plenty of strong black coffee as they kept busy with their work.

■ ■ ■ ■

By late spring Sydney was a distant, but pleasant, memory for the crew. The general lull in action of the past few months would soon come to an end. The next major American amphibious operation was about to begin.

5

Return to Kula Gulf

After months of planning and preparations that lasted through the spring of 1943, the navy was ready for its next large amphibious operation in the Solomons. It was a move up the Slot to the island of New Georgia. The ultimate goal: to capture the Japanese airfield at Munda. Guadalcanal veteran Rear Adm. Richmond K. Turner was chosen to lead the amphibious portion of the offensive, soon dubbed Operation Toenails. The landing was planned for the last day of June 1943.

As Turner's amphibious force moved north, a powerful assortment of American warships were in position to provide support. The bulk of Admiral Halsey's fighting ships, designated as Task Force Thirty-Six, were arranged in several groups to the south patrolling the waters of the Coral and Solomon Seas. The warships were ready to quickly intervene should any Japanese naval units try to interfere with the landings. Targeting multiple points on New Georgia, the invasion took place as scheduled without incident.

■ ■ ■ ■

While the amphibious portion of Operation Toenails proceeded as planned, the *Helena* patrolled the northern fringe of the Coral Sea. She was with familiar company: Adm. Walden Ainsworth in his flagship *Honolulu*, the light cruiser *St. Louis*, and a destroyer screen. On the morning of July 1 the force was just over three hundred miles south and slightly west of New Georgia.[1] The destroyer USS *Strong* joined the formation right after sunrise. Along with the *O'Bannon*, *Nicholas*, and *Chevalier*, the new addition formed the anti-submarine screen around the cruisers. The four destroyers were under the command of Capt. Francis X. McInerney, who was using the *Nicholas* as his flagship.

Ainsworth and his captains were waiting for the word to move north. But, with no serious seaborne threat to the New Georgia operation mounted by the Japanese, the call never came. The ships spent much of the day cruising at moderate speeds with an occasional zigzag.

During the late morning hours of July 3, the ships dropped anchor for a brief stay at Tulagi. No sooner had the anchors fallen than the general quarters alarms began to sound in response to a report of approaching enemy planes. Within fifteen minutes, however, it was the determined to be a false alarm.

By this stage of the war, running to his battle station was nothing new for Gayle Gilbert. Although he spent much of his on duty time as the bugler on the bridge, his general quarter's battle station was battle two. "We drilled and drilled and drilled and it was just a natural thing to go to that battle station," he recalled. "Everyone knew their place, and boy I'm telling you they'd really run for it. It was unreal."

Occasionally referred to as secondary con, battle two was located immediately behind the after smoke stack. It was a small perch with a 5-inch gun turret on either side and a director on top. The small, fully enclosed armored room served as an emergency bridge. "If anything happened to the bridge, the secondary con would take over," Gilbert explained. "They had a little enunciator there and we could steer the ship with that."[2] It was the normal battle station for the executive officer. "We had the lieutenant for the secondary navigation and we had a chief, I think it was a chief gunner with us," he explained. "We had quartermasters, and of course I was there too." Gilbert's role at secondary con was the same as when he was on the bridge.

Dimly lit by a small blue light, the room was largely barren except for a big table positioned in the center. "Just something to lay out the maps," Gilbert noted. The air in the small room quickly became clouded when people lit up cigarettes. "Everyone was smoking in this little room and you could cut the smoke with your knife." The end of a night often found the deck piled with ashes. A sweeper would come by to clear it out the next morning. Although Gilbert thought about starting to smoke, he decided against it. He did not like the taste of cigarettes.

■ ■ ■ ■

Pleased with the initial progress of the New Georgia operation, and perhaps encouraged by the lack of strong Japanese opposition, Halsey on July 2 directed Turner to start the drive toward Munda.[3] A previously devised plan for a second landing on the opposite site of New Georgia was put into effect. A force of army and Marine troops stationed at Guadalcanal stood ready to be transported into Kula Gulf to land on New Georgia at Rice Anchorage. In one bold strike the operation would cut off both the main Japanese supply line and the escape route. If the landing was successful, the Munda garrison would be trapped.

While the decision to land troops on the Kula Gulf side of New Georgia was being made by Admiral Halsey, Ainsworth's ships were still operating in close proximity to Guadalcanal. The task group was called upon to participate in the operation. At Turner's request, Ainsworth dispatched the destroyer *Strong* to Koli Point, Guadalcanal to pick up a copy of the basic plan for the Rice Anchorage operation. A transport group consisting of seven destroyer transports, two minesweepers, and escorting destroyers was set to conduct the actual landing. Ainsworth's force was to cover the transport group's journey north and then shell Japanese land positions in advance of the actual landing.

Unlike previous trips up the Slot, the mission was to hit both sides of Kula Gulf. The Vila-Stanmore area on Kolombangara was the first target. The force would then move across the gulf to hit Bairoko Harbor on New Georgia. In addition to the bombardments, Ainsworth's force was charged with destroying any Japanese surface forces encountered during the operation. "With Rear Admiral Turner's operational order as a basis, our own operation order was prepared," Ainsworth later wrote. The ships pulled into Tulagi Harbor as the admiral and his staff worked out the seemingly endless list of operational details. The planners studied aerial photos dated

May 1, as well as a more up-to-date grid map that came with Turner's orders. Ainsworth met with his ship captains at Tulagi to discuss the operation.

The admiral knew the risks were higher than during his previous trips into the gulf. "It was perfectly evident that the presence of twenty ships on various courses in the constricted waters of Kula Gulf in the presence of an alerted enemy presented problems in coordination not experienced on previous bombardments," he recorded.[4] The purpose of the mission was not necessarily the wholesale destruction of the Japanese installations but to hit the key targets needed to help protect the amphibious operation. He was not expecting the Japanese to be taken by surprise. "The preliminary estimate showed very little probability of surprise for this operation, so our heaviest fire was placed on the battery emplacements," Ainsworth wrote. "We also hoped to knock out all artillery which might prove embarrassing for our landing force later." During the planning process Ainsworth strongly urged Turner to let him add the Enogai Inlet to the target list, but the request was denied because aerial reconnaissance did not show any gun emplacements.[5]

By now the voyage to Kula Gulf was routine for Captain Cecil and the other cruiser commanders. Cecil carefully reviewed the operational orders to gain a complete understanding of the situation. Ainsworth specifically noted, "That increased enemy strength in the surface forces in the Buin-Shortlands area may be utilized against us in the New Georgia area at any time, particularly at night."[6] The admiral warned of the threat from both the surface and from submarines. He told his cruiser commanders of the need to be ready to get crippled ships out of the area, preferably to Tulagi. If damaged ships were unable to make it out of Kula Gulf then the orders offered an alternative. "All commanding officers were enjoined to study the Rice Anchorage and its approaches carefully with a view to beaching damaged ships there should the occasion so demand." The captains of the task group were now armed with the best possible pre-operation intelligence.

The assault troops stepped aboard the destroyer transports at Guadalcanal on the afternoon of July 4.[7] At the same time Ainsworth's ships (including the *Helena*) were making final preparations to get under way from Tulagi Harbor. Below the *Helena*'s decks fires were lit off on various boilers. Steam pressure was built up and cut into the main line. At 3:47 p.m. the *Honolulu* started the procession out of the harbor area. The *Helena* followed the *St. Louis* in getting under way a short time later. Using the normal cruising formation, the three warships moved into a single column with the flagship in the lead while the four destroyers were positioned around them as the anti-submarine screen. It appeared to be nothing more than another routine bombardment mission.

The destroyer transports were under orders to proceed independently to the entrance of Kula Gulf with the warship group providing only distant cover. Once arriving at Visuvisu Point the transport force came under Ainsworth's tactical command. The confined waters of Kula Gulf were very crowded on this particular night.

As the bombardment and transport groups traveled northwest from the Guadalcanal area, Imperial Japanese Navy ships were also preparing to make an entrance into the gulf. Japanese commanders decided that Munda needed to be reinforced quickly. Accordingly, four thousand troops were ordered to make ready for the voyage to the front lines. The first contingents of 1,300 men were loaded aboard three destroyers—the *Niizuki*, *Yunagi*, and *Nagatsuki*—which pulled out of Buin on the south side of Bougainville during mid-afternoon on July 4.[8] The nocturnal Japanese supply runs, first used during the battle for Guadalcanal, were dubbed the Tokyo Express by American sailors.

The voyage for the American ships to the entrance of Kula Gulf was uneventful. "The approach was conducted without incident and I believe both bombardment and landing force detachments succeeded in arriving off Visuvisu Point without being snooped or detected by the enemy," Ainsworth reported. The ships shifted into a single line before entering the gulf. The cruisers were in the middle of the formation with two destroyers in the front and rear. Just after midnight the bombardment force slowly crept toward Kula Gulf. It was a typical South Pacific night: overcast with intermitted rainsqualls.

The lead destroyers *Nicholas* and *Strong* pulled ahead of the formation to cautiously scan the gulf with radar and sonar. Acting as sentries, neither was to fire during the first round of the bombardment. The two destroyers, however, would participate in the second phase of the operation, "unless enemy vessels or shore batteries attacked our ships, or enemy searchlights were turned on the formation," Captain McInerney later reported.[9] The operation plan gave either ship the authority to fire without orders on any craft that threatened the force. The remaining vessels soon moved in the gulf running parallel with the Kolombangara coastline. All ships were under orders to maintain complete radio silence after passing Savo Island near Guadalcanal until five minutes before the opening of fire. At that juncture the bombardment ships established communications with the Black Cat planes circling above.

Just minutes before the cruisers were set to open fire, radar on the *Nicholas* picked up a contact moving at a high rate of speed in a westerly direction. "The contact was evaluated as an airplane and soon disappeared from the screen," McInerney later wrote. Shortly after the cruisers opened fire, the *Strong*'s radar picked up a contact. However, operators on the *Nicholas* were unable make out any contact at that time and the *Strong* soon reported that it had faded away.

The *Honolulu* opened fire four minutes ahead of schedule at 12:26 a.m. as she approached the Vila-Stanmore target area. The *Helena* did not have long to wait. "Commence firing was ordered one and one half minutes after the *Honolulu* commenced firing," Captain Cecil reported. "Two ranging salvos were fired and check fire ordered to await receipt of Black Cat air spot. No spot was received when due therefore fire was resumed." Seconds later the spotting report came to move the fire up three hundred yards. "This was assumed to apply to the initial salvo and was so applied," Cecil continued.[10] With roar after tremendous roar, the *Helena* pounded away at the shore targets.

When the *St. Louis* opened fire, all three of the big ships were in rapid-fire mode, with the 6-inch main battery guns firing at six-second intervals. Each cruiser was allocated up to one thousand rounds of high-explosive ammunition for the operation, and all were equipped with flashless gunpowder to help conceal their positions. Pulling up the rear of the formation, the destroyers *O'Bannon* and *Chevalier* joined the bombardment, sending round after round of 5-inch shells into Japanese positions. "Communication with our spotting planes was excellent, and according to reports, the high sustained bombardment fire on this leg was extremely accurate," Ainsworth later wrote.[11] The operation seemed to be going according to plan.

■ ■ ■ ■

Although gun crews and fire-control men aboard the *Helena* were kept pretty busy during a night bombardment, not all crew members played such an active role during that type of mission. Due to being in enemy waters, the ship was kept at general quarters during a bombardment. By July, Mason Miller had transferred off of the 40mm gun mount to a new battle station. "I had been put down below ship in the radio room," he said. "Down in radio three." Miller's new battle station was one of three radio facilities on the ship. Located one deck below and slightly aft of officers' country, the room contained a complete assortment of radio equipment. "Radio three served as a backup," he explained. "[It] would be there in case radio one and two were shot out."[12] Miller was the officer in charge of the station. His small group of sailors included two who were radio operators. One man was assigned to operate a set of headphones and could listen in on the various radio communications. A couple other sailors were also stationed with Miller, including a supply officer who maintained the payroll for the ship.

The night's mission was Miller's first at the new battle station. Being in a fully enclosed room was quite different for the young officer who was used to being topside at a gun mount. "I had a pretty good view of what took place topside in the two battles that I was in up there. There wasn't much that I could do about it," he said of the new situation. "You were totally out of any action because all you could do is hear somebody tell you what was going on; you couldn't see it yourself. Topside you could." Although not overly happy about the change in battle station, he took it in stride.

While the main batteries of the *Helena* fired away, Gilbert remained sequestered inside battle two. "It wasn't big at all, maybe ten by ten," he related. "It might even have been smaller than that because the front of it was rounded off." The space was sealed up tight. "We [were] all dogged down and the whole works. Watertight doors on either side, although we were way up so we didn't have to worry about the water."[13] The four or five porthole type windows in the room were not more than twelve inches in diameter, and the arrangement typically did not afford Gilbert much opportunity to see the action outside. "All we'd see was the flashes and the banging of the guns," he recalled. "That's about all. We [were] locked in there and just sweated it out." However, since it was not an actual night battle, the men stationed at battle two took an occasional peek out during the bombardment. "We'd open the hatch and you'd see the shells leaving the ship," he said. "They were red. They were hot," he said of the fireballs streaking away from the ship into the dark night. "And they [were] just kind of hanging real fast and they'd drop in real fast. All of a sudden they'd drop." It was a spectacular view.

■ ■ ■ ■

After fourteen minutes of rapid gunfire at Vila-Stanmore, the column of American ships turned due east to move across the gulf. They were now pointed almost directly toward the next target area, Rice Anchorage, and the second phase of the bombardment began as all ships opened fire. This time the gunfire was directed using a previously prepared diagram, without help from spotters above. The drubbing of Japanese positions lasted about six minutes.[14] It was during this portion of the operation that Cecil noted that a small amount of ineffective gunfire from shore batteries was seen landing near some of the cruisers. "Several minor caliber (believed to be 3-inch) splashes were observed ahead of the ship, straddling the projected track of the ship about one hundred yards ahead," he reported. None of the cruisers were hit.

Like previous missions, Cecil felt that the operations aboard the *Helena* went smoothly. "All firing by both batteries was conducted in full automatic using an initial range and bearing as furnished by [the combat information center] from the SG radar," he noted. "It appeared that these were very accurate. The functioning of the fire control parties and C.I.C. was extremely smooth and most satisfactory." The *Helena* hurled 915 6-inch shells toward the enemy, plus 235 rounds of 5-inch.

■ ■ ■ ■

Gene Robinson stood ready at his 20mm gun mount. He served as a loader on the gun. "The ammunition is loaded in a kind of a drum," he explained. "You put the drum on top of the gun and slam it down and it cocks in place."[15] Robinson knew the routine well. His job was to maintain a continuous stream of ammunition to the gun tub. Although he was ready for action, his gun stayed idle during the evening's encounter.

Watching the *Helena* fire a broadside of her main battery guns was an awe-inspiring site for Robinson. "That's something that you don't forget," he said. "The ship jumps and if [there is] anything loose around it rattles and falls and breaks." It was not uncommon to hear a crashing of a dish or two if a sailor was within an earshot of an open hatch. The 5-inch gun mounts were much closer to his battle station than the main batteries. "The noise of a 6-inch is not as bad as the noise of a 5-inch going off," he recalled. The smaller guns had a sharp bark that pierced a sailor's ears. None of the men at Robinson's gun were equipped with earplugs to muffle the sound, but Robinson and his gun mates were wearing protective clothing. "It was supposed to be flash proof," he said. "They'd tell you that [you] should not have any bare skin showing during battle because you can be burnt very easy." The clothing resembled something along the lines of an overcoat. "I really don't know what it was [made of]," he added. "You could move around all right. It was flexible." Robinson fortunately did not need the protection offered by the clothing during this particular trip to the gulf.

■ ■ ■ ■

As the bombardment portion of the operation neared an end, the transport group slowly moved into Kula Gulf. The ships were under orders to stay within one mile of the New Georgia coast at all times until the bombardment force passed. Neither the bombardment group nor the transport group had any inkling that a third group of ships were also in the gulf that night.

It would be Ainsworth's first brush with the Tokyo Express. After passing south of Choiseul Island, the destroyers *Niizuki*, *Yunagi*, and *Nagatsuki* entered Kula Gulf to begin the run down to Vila-Stanmore. The lead ship, *Niizuki*, was the only Japanese vessel fitted with a radar set. Ainsworth's force was already deep in the gulf pouring fire onto the target areas. The Japanese quickly spotted the American ships at a distance of just over six miles. The bombardment force was tentatively identified as four light cruisers and four destroyers.

With the last phase of the shelling over, the ships were ready to begin the run out of the gulf. At about 12:39 a.m. they began to turn north. As the bombardment ships left the gulf, the transport force moved into position off Rice Anchorage.

Apparently not liking the odds of any potential battle, Japanese Capt. Kanaoka Kunizo decided to run. The plan to deliver the troops to Vila-Stanmore was abandoned. Using *Niizuki*'s radar to help with the aim, the three destroyers fired a total of fourteen torpedoes at the American warships. The attack was a long shot, since the distance to the target ships was thought to be eleven miles.[16] The destroyers then made a quick exit from the gulf to start the run back to Buin. But, as the ships sped away, Japanese lookouts reported seeing torpedoes hit a light cruiser and one destroyer.

The Japanese torpedoes actually only found one American hull. Just after the firing on Bairoko Harbor was completed and the formation started the turn north, the *Strong* was reported by a lookout to be in her assigned position directly behind the *Nicholas*. Everything appeared to be normal. Ainsworth then radioed to his forward destroyers, "Any trouble ahead?" McInerney was quick to reply, "Everything clear ahead."[17]

Just minutes later the gunnery officer on the *Strong*, Lt. James Curran, spotted a torpedo track approaching the port side. Before anything could be done, the torpedo slammed into the midsection of the destroyer. At 12:45 a.m. a radar scan aboard the *Nicholas* showed that the *Strong* was no longer in the column. "It was assumed that the *Strong* had suffered some casualty, possibly a steering casualty," McInerney reported. Ainsworth quickly knew that something was amiss when his flagship's radar also showed the incomplete column.

McInerney quickly tried to reach the *Strong* by radio. "Are you all right? Come in please." There was no response. He then notified the admiral of the situation before asking the *Chevalier* to also try to contact the *Strong*. She too was unsuccessful.

The torpedo that hit the *Strong* caused serious damage. "A violent explosion was heard and felt throughout the ship," Curran later wrote of the moment.[18] The explosion occurred in the ship's critical engineering spaces. The force of the blast was so severe that it ripped the hull open to the sea on both sides. "The ship took a list of about fifteen degrees to starboard immediately after the explosion," Curran wrote. "The list increased slowly as the ship settled in the water." The *Strong* was quickly dying.

The crippled destroyer swerved out of formation immediately after being hit. For the most part she was unseen by the three cruisers that sped past, although a lookout aboard the *Honolulu* was able to catch a fleeting glimpse of the destroyer. The flagship's log noted, "Sighted *Strong* sharp on starboard bow, damaged and smoking, dead in the water and on opposite heading."[19] Shortly after McInerney failed to raise the *Strong* via the airwaves, the two rear destroyers found the stricken ship dead in the water about two miles west of Rice Anchorage.[20] The *Chevalier* pulled alongside to communicate by blinker and then radioed Ainsworth, "*Strong* needs aid." The admiral asked for more information. He received it a few minutes later when the *Chevalier* reported, "*Strong* is sinking."

It soon became apparent that that *Strong* was not going to stay afloat for much longer. Both the *O'Bannon* and *Chevalier* were ordered to start the rescue operation. The latter ship pulled up to the port side of the *Strong* while the *O'Bannon* stayed in the immediate area to assist when needed. The *Chevalier* came a bit too close to the damaged destroyer. Her bow crashed into the side of the *Strong*, ripping open a ten-foot hole in the hull of the rescue ship. However, all of the damage seemed to be above the waterline, so the incident did not delay the rescue.

Once the condition of the *Strong* was determined, Ainsworth slowed the speed of his remaining ships down to 15 knots. He needed to know more details as to what happened to the destroyer to know if the remaining ships were in imminent danger. He radioed the *Chevalier*, "As soon as you can, find out and let me know how she got hurt." A short time later he asked, "Was it torpedo or gunfire? Must know whether it was gunfire or torpedo." The *Chevalier* responded that the damage was done by a torpedo.

The admiral now knew that the rest of his ships could be in great danger. He immediately ordered speed increased to 28 knots and told the *Chevalier* and *O'Bannon* to rendezvous outside of the gulf when the rescue was completed. However, he also wanted to make sure that all the sailors from the *Strong* would be picked up. "Take your time," he advised the two destroyers. "Get everybody, and rejoin outside." Having no radar contacts, Ainsworth concluded that the *Strong* had fallen victim to a submarine. As the remaining ships of the bombardment force moved toward the entrance of the gulf, he radioed McInerney to keep a close watch. The destroyer captain in turn told the *Chevalier* and *O'Bannon* to "keep your sound gear going, sub may be within 5,000 yards of you." No Japanese submarine was found.

Quickly passing the damaged destroyer, few aboard the *Helena* knew what had happened to the *Strong*. It would have been nothing new to most of the cruiser's sailors. They had previously seen ships sink near Guadalcanal.

After the initial mishap with her bow, sailors aboard the *Chevalier* sent manila ropes and cargo nets over to the *Strong*. The starboard side of the *Strong*'s deck was already awash as the destroyer started to go under.

No sooner had the rescue operation begun than Japanese shore batteries, silent during the bombardment, opened fire. The Japanese gunners apparently felt the damaged destroyer was an easy target. The fire was coming from four batteries at the Enogai Inlet—the place that Ainsworth wanted to hit but was denied. The sudden appearance of flares overhead only made matters worse. The *O'Bannon* quickly commenced counter battery fire, but at least two shells hit the *Strong* during her final minutes of life.

At 1:22 a.m. the *Strong* rolled over and sank, with her depth charges exploding as she went down. The force of the explosions violently shook the *Chevalier*, knocking out her radar and compass.[21] The destroyer rescued 239 men, but a number of survivors left just as the ship went down and were not seen by either the *Chevalier* or *O'Bannon*. Forty-six other sailors were lost with the ship.

With all of the *Strong* survivors that could be found safely aboard, the *Chevalier* and *O'Bannon* pulled out of Kula Gulf. On the way out the *Chevalier* radioed to commanding officer of the destroyers that were escorting the transports about the possibility of additional survivors being in the water. "Would appreciate it if you would pick up any people you find." At 2:15 a.m. the two rescue ships rejoined the rest of the bombardment force. Ainsworth then pointed his ships for home.

As the bombardment force retired, the amphibious portion of the operation began in earnest. Just after 1:30 a.m. the first wave of small boats headed for shore. The same shore guns that had fired on the *Strong* opened up on the transports. Several destroyers returned fire. Although the two sides intermittently dueled throughout the night, no casualties were suffered on the American side. During the landing, one of the escorting destroyers spotted a raft. Moving closer it was found to be a group of survivors from the *Strong*. Many of the rescued sailors, including the destroyer's commanding officer Cdr. Joseph H. Wellings, had suffered concussions when the sinking ship's depth charges went off. By 6:00 a.m. the transport group was heading out of the gulf.

In spite of the loss of the *Strong*, the operation in Kula Gulf on the night of July 4–5 was considered a success. "The bombardment was carried out exactly in accordance with plan," Ainsworth reported. He heaped praise on the commanding officers of the *Chevalier* and *O'Bannon* for their heroic effort to rescue the *Strong* survivors in the face of shore gunfire.

As the force sped down the Slot toward Tulagi, its leaders pondered what really happened to the lost destroyer. McInerney initially thought that an enemy submarine was to blame. After learning that several ships of the transport group reported experiencing fleeting radar contacts in the far northwest corner of the gulf, he concluded that the torpedo came from above the waves. "It is believed that these contacts were two destroyers which left the gulf at a high speed. Either or both of these ships could have fired torpedoes from long range," he later wrote. The captain wondered why none of the bombardment ships were able to spot the enemy vessels on radar. Ainsworth disagreed with his subordinate's opinion. The admiral wrote in his after action report that the *Strong* was most likely sunk by a torpedo fired from a submarine.

6

Turnabout

It had been a long night of hard work for the men of the *Helena*'s gunnery department. Cdr. Rodman Smith headed up the department, and John Chew and Warren Boles, both lieutenant commanders, served as his assistants. Remmel Dudley did not have much contact with Smith. "I wouldn't have any reason to," he said. "The one that we would work with was Warren Boles. He was the one who was kind of in charge, so to speak, of what we were doing."[1] Bin Cochran remembered that Boles was a strong advocate of rapid fire with the main battery guns. "He was the one who was just sold on this continuous fire," he recalled. "Get on a target and just rock it with continuous fire up and down. He thought it was just the thing." Cochran, however, harbored doubts as to the true worth of the rapid fire. "We thought that we were a lot more effective than we really were. He would try to adjust the range so that it would be over a little and under a little . . . all these bullets coming in you figured you just had to be making a lot of hits, but we weren't making as many as we thought."[2]

Since transferring to the gunnery department, Cochran had become quite knowledgeable on the 6-inch guns. He was now the officer in charge of turret five. Located at the back of the ship, just forward of the aviation area, it was the aftermost turret. "I had a little learning to do when I got back there," he said. "I had a very good turret captain." Chief Turret Capt. Otis Point worked directly under Cochran and taught him the ropes. As the senior enlisted man in the turret, Point took charge of the guns and crew.[3] Cochran wore a headset that usually gave him all that he needed to know in terms of gunnery-related information. "It was a circuit that went to all the other turrets and to the control up on the flag bridge and of course to the computer room and the spotter . . . all of them were on the same circuit." Communication to the crew inside the turret was accomplished using a one-way loudspeaker. It was rudimentary, but it worked.

Cochran remembered the hard labor endured by his gun crews during the night bombardments. "Sometimes we'd fire continuous fire and sometimes we'd fire salvo fire," he said. "It was mainly just getting out the ammunition the way they called for it." Although they didn't last long, the missions often required grueling work of great intensity.

■ ■ ■ ■

Dudley was also in charge of a main battery gun. "I was assigned to the number three turret," he said. "Our class of cruisers had five turrets, unlike the traditional ones with four turrets, and the Marine detachments of our class of ship manned number three turret. So that's where I was, that was my battle station." Having gone through artillery school, overseeing a gun was not exactly foreign to the marine. The last of the three forward turrets, Dudley's gun was positioned just forward of the superstructure. It was, however, facing the rear of the ship and thus could only be used for firing broadsides.

Chief Turret Capt. John Sharp was the only navy man in the number three turret. "He taught me a lot," Dudley remembers. "I was his boss, but I was smart enough not to push him too much. He was very, very competent and he was a good sailor." A level of mutual respect existed between the two men. "He respected me as an officer. I mean not me personally, but the rank, and he was very helpful to me." The marine and the sailor worked well together.

The turrets that Cochran and Dudley commanded each mounted three 6-inch guns. "Down below decks [we] had the ammunition room," Dudley said in describing the operation of the turret. "The bullets, the projectile, came up a hoist, a hydraulic hoist from down below. The men down there would load the hoist, send it up to us." The shells would come up to a small platform in front of each gun. Each armor-piercing shell, the type typically used against other ships, weighed 130 pounds. A separate gunpowder-filled casing weighed about twenty-eight pounds.[4] "The men inside the turret would take it and load the weapons," Dudley continued. "Each gun had its own hoist. They could all operate simultaneously."[5]

In the end it was teamwork that made each turret work efficiently. "You take forty men, you split them up to those various positions, you can use them up very fast," Dudley recalled. "I'm also including the ammunition handlers and the projectile handlers." The latter sailors were usually stationed on the shell deck directly below each turret. After the night bombardment mission neither Cochran nor Dudley suspected their turrets would again be seeing action in short order.

■ ■ ■ ■

At sunrise on the morning of July 5, the task group was well south of New Georgia Island steaming at 24 knots. The *Helena* had experienced problems in two of her main battery turrets during the bombardment. As she sailed away from the front lines, crewmen were able get to work on both. "The projectile hoist to the left gun of turret five failed at about the sixth salvo and did not function during the remainder of the bombardment," wrote Captain Cecil. "The hoist was repaired during the following day and functioned perfectly during the subsequent firing."

The second gun issue was more serious and required a good deal of time to resolve. Powder cases became jammed in the gun barrels of turret two on three different occasions during the bombardment. In the first two instances, the cases were removed without incident. Cecil picked up the story. "The third, in the left gun, at about the sixth salvo, jammed and when the case was extracted the cork plug stuck in the bore of the gun making it impossible to load another case into the gun." In the process of trying to remove the stuck canister some gunpowder spilled inside of the turret creating a dangerous situation. "Most of this was quickly cleared from the bore and the breech was closed with the projectile, but no powder case in the gun. Two fire hoses were applied to the gun, one on the outside and the other into the bore through the muzzle." The gun crew had been cleared out of the turret as soon as the *Helena* departed Kula Gulf, leaving several buckets to collect leaking water. A group of three men occasionally entered the turret to empty out the buckets. "This was continued for five and one half hours at which time a specially prepared short powder case was inserted and the gun unloaded through the muzzle," Cecil concluded. It seemed like a lot of work, but the gun was restored to working order.

It had been a long night in Kula Gulf, and the sailors on all of the ships must have looked forward to the possibility of dropping anchor at Tulagi. Seaman 1st Class Edwin Rick remembered the strain that a night bombardment mission put on the crew. "You don't get a whole lot of sleep, and the next day you have to stand watches," he later recalled. It made for exhausted sailors.[6]

The task group headed toward a refueling rendezvous southwest of San Cristobal Island. The refueling schedule would likely take up a good part of the day. A brief stopover at Tulagi was also slated. If the ships ventured back down to Espiritu Santo, then maybe the near future held some recreation time ashore for the *Helena*'s crew.

The destroyer *Jenkins* joined the formation at 7:00 a.m., taking station near the *Helena* in the anti-submarine screen.[7] About a half an hour later the ships passed the Russell Islands; the land mass was visible directly off the starboard beam of the formation. An earlier condition red report warning that an enemy air attack on the area was imminent had been lifted.

At 8:30 a.m. the ships sighted Savo Island twelve miles away. Twenty-five minutes later the flagship pulled even with Cape Esperance near the northwest corner of Guadalcanal. It was in these very waters less than a year previously that the *Helena* had first traded gunfire with Japanese ships on an October night. The formation slowed a bit to allow the *Helena* to pull in two of her seaplanes that had been up on patrol. At about the same time, the *Chevalier* and *Jenkins* turned away to proceed independently to Tulagi. The rest of the force was to arrive in port later in the afternoon after rendezvousing with the tanker to top off with fuel.

As the ships entered the narrow waters near Guadalcanal, the remaining two destroyers moved ahead of the three cruisers. The *Nicholas* took the lead in sweeping the channel as late morning faded into early afternoon.

With the afternoon came the heat. It seemed to grow in intensity as the South Pacific sun rose higher in the sky. Moving through the Southern Solomons, topside crewmen caught an occasional glimpse of the lush green hills that covered the nearby islands.

It was about this time that Admiral Ainsworth received an urgent dispatch from Admiral Halsey. A force of Japanese destroyers was spotted pulling out of Buin. It could only mean one thing: the Tokyo Express would be making a night run into Kula Gulf. Ainsworth's orders were to stop it. "In obedience to these orders, this force reversed course, proceeded via Indispensable Strait and close to the southern extremity of Santa Isabel Island at 29 knots in order to reach the vicinity of Kula Gulf in time to intercept," Ainsworth recorded.[8] The admiral notified his ships of the new orders at about 3 p.m.[9]

Aboard the *Helena*, Cecil wondered if the force would make it back up to the gulf in time to catch the Japanese.[10] After a quick study of the charts, he concluded that his ship had enough fuel and the force would probably meet with the enemy at about midnight. He sent an officer from the radio room to notify all the department heads of the new orders.

Aborting the refueling rendezvous, the force soon reverted back to cruising formation and was heading toward open waters. The light cruisers formed a single column, with the *Honolulu* in the lead. The *Helena* assumed her usual middle position in the line. The destroyer *O'Bannon* moved into a screening position off the flagship's port bow, while the *Nicholas* took the starboard side. The fuel supply aboard the two destroyers was low, but the tanks held enough for the quick run back up the Slot.

With the task group down two destroyers, the *Jenkins* and *Radford* were assigned to take the place of the sunken *Strong* and damaged *Chevalier*. Cdr. William K. Romoser had *Radford* refueling from the tanker *Erskine Phelps* near Tulagi when he received a message from Admiral Turner's command to get under way immediately. However, his ship was extremely low on 5-inch shells. The destroyer had conducted counter battery fire the previous night in Kula Gulf while escorting the transport group. Romoser quickly notified the Tulagi port director that he would be delayed. As soon as the fueling was completed, the destroyer made for Tulagi. The nearby *Jenkins* followed her into port, and the two destroyers moored alongside each other. "The *Jenkins* transferred 300 rounds of her ammunition to *Radford* in the short period of about twenty-two minutes," Romoser later recalled.[11] He picked up two hundred more rounds from the *Chevalier*. At the same time crewmen offloaded about nine hundred empty shell casings. By the time the yard boat pulled up to the *Radford* with a load of ammunition, it was too late to accept it. Romoser thanked the port director for getting the ammunition boat to him so quickly, but then headed out for sea.

■ ■ ■ ■

The sudden increase in speed was the first indication to the *Helena*'s enlisted men that something was amiss. Then, the ship made an abrupt turn. The task group was doing an about face and the force was heading back to the Slot.

The *Helena* had definitely been a lucky ship in her nearly one year of combat duty in the South Pacific. She made it through sea battles, air attacks, bombardment missions, and submarine attacks with not much more than minor scratches. One junior officer remembered that the mood aboard the ship seemed to have shifted during the summer months.[12] More ominous feelings began to circulate around the vessel with a sense that the lucky streak was going to end. The sudden move toward the battle zone rekindled the uneasiness and raised it to a fever pitch.

Scuttlebutt soon spread around the ship that the force was going back up to Kula Gulf to intercept the Tokyo Express. The veterans aboard who had lived through the Guadalcanal campaign knew exactly what it meant: another vicious night battle.

Seaman 1st Class Robert Howe started to get nervous shortly after hearing that the ship was going back north. "I was already nervous, and we were not even out of [the] Guadalcanal area," he later wrote. "My nerves were shot. I wondered if I could go through another battle. I had heard of sailors having nervous breakdowns and that scared me more than anything." He soon came to the simple realization that, "There wasn't anything I could do except go along for the ride."[13]

Resting in his cabin at the time was Lieutenant j.g. William McKeckney. "I looked out the bunkroom door and saw the *Honolulu* turning one eight and with signal hoisted for speed 29 knots," he later said. "That seemed to indicate that we were going back on another business trip."[14] There was no easy way to prepare for a battle. McKeckney summed up the feelings of many aboard the light cruiser. "We were naturally rather scared or a little bit apprehensive of what was to take place," he said. "Most of us had been through a number of engagements and, no matter how many experiences we had, we were still very much afraid that the next one would be the last one for all of us." In order to be able to function during the approaching battle, the sailors simply had to put fears aside and let their training take over.

On her way toward the Slot the *Helena* passed Guadalcanal just as the sun was setting. What was left of the red sun danced about the island's mountain peaks as the land mass slowly faded out of sight. Many sailors aboard the light cruiser must have wondered if they would see the familiar coastline again.[15] No one knew what the night would bring.

■ ■ ■ ■

Halsey's intelligence was right on target. With the previous night's run to Kolombangara aborted, the Japanese now undertook a much larger operation to get the much needed troops into the supply pipeline line for Munda. Rear Adm. Teruo Akiyama was directed to lead the voyage. He assembled a group of ten destroyers—soon designated as the Reinforcement Group—and then organized the ships into three smaller units. The First Transport Unit consisted of the *Mochizuki*, *Mikazuki*, and *Hamakaze*. The Second Transport Unit included the *Amagiri*, *Hatsuyuki*, *Nagatsuki*, and *Satsuki*. The seven warships were loaded with twenty-four hundred troops and 180 tons of supplies.[16] Designated as the Support Unit, the third group of ships comprised *Niizuki*, *Suzukaze*, and *Tanikazi*. These destroyers carried no cargo, but were supposed to safeguard the two transport groups.

Akiyama's orders were to travel down the east side of Kolombangara to deliver the men and materiel to Vila-Stanmore during the early morning hours and then exit the gulf via the same route. The admiral used the *Niizuki* as his flagship. The destroyer was the only ship in his force fitted with radar. The surface search set had proved invaluable in setting up the long-range torpedo attack that sank the *Strong* the night before. The Japanese ships pulled out of the Shortland Islands at 5 p.m. under the observant eye of a coastwatcher and headed for Kula Gulf. Disappearing into a patch of bad weather, Akiyama's ships would neither be sighted by American search planes, nor found by the ever-present bombers that seemed to regularly roam the Slot.

■ ■ ■ ■

Just after 7:30 p.m. the *Radford* and *Jenkins* joined up with the rest of Ainsworth's force. The two destroyers took up screening stations on either side of the back of the cruiser column. It would be relatively easy for the four smaller ships to quickly shift into the single-column formation used in battle situations.

When formulating the tactics for the pending night battle, Ainsworth looked to a plan that was already on file. Dated March 16, 1943, Operation Plan 4-43 gave procedures for day or night encounters with enemy surface ships and aircraft.[17] It contained provisions for two possible scenarios for a night surface battle that mainly depended on the range of the enemy ships. Both plans were largely based on a heavy round of opening fire to score early hits on the enemy, and the use of radical maneuvering to put the ships in a favorable firing position. Like many senior American officers of the day, the admiral favored guns over torpedoes.

The first option, Plan A, relied heavily on the use of fire control radar. To be used in medium-range situations, Plan A called for the main batteries of the cruisers to open fire under full radar control when the enemy ships were eight thousand to ten thousand yards away. The use of radar and tracer shells would help to ensure that many early hits could be scored, perhaps even with the opening salvos. Plan B was for longer-range situations. It relied on starshells to provide the illumination needed to aid in the opening minutes of a battle. Fire control radar would also be employed. Both plans called for the use of flashless gunpowder to help conceal the position of the firing ships. Ainsworth decided to use Plan A in the coming engagement.

The admiral did not know the exact composition of the Japanese force he would be encountering. He did, however, assume that at least some of the enemy ships would have radar, although it would likely not be as accurate as the SG sets that his ships possessed. He also expected all of the opposing ships to be equipped with torpedoes. Like most American commanders at this stage of the war, Ainsworth was largely ignorant of the true range and power of Japanese torpedoes.

The Japanese torpedoes used in World War II came about as a result of more than a decade of diligent work. Shortly after World War I, Japanese leaders envisioned the possible need to fight a future naval battle with the United States. They spent the next two decades developing and perfecting weapons and tactics to defeat the numerically superior American Pacific Fleet. Among these was a powerful long-range torpedo, known to the Japanese as the Type 93 torpedo, which could propel a powerful warhead about forty thousand meters.[18] The almost unbelievable distance translates to just short of twenty-five miles. It was the best such weapon in the world. Throughout the 1930s, the Japanese emphasized night fighting tactics that centered on the use of torpedoes over gunfire. They had effectively used these in the naval battles around Guadalcanal and would soon employ them again in Kula Gulf.

■ ■ ■ ■

By the late hours of the evening, the watertight doors on the *Helena* were dogged down. The ship plodded along in darkened condition, a phosphorus wake glowing off the stern. At 11 p.m. the crew ate a snack of apples and oranges accompanied by freshly brewed cups of coffee. It would carry the men through the upcoming battle.

During the first hour of July 6, Ainsworth's ships approached Visuvisu Point on New Georgia, the now-familiar marker near the entrance of Kula Gulf. The ships slowed to 25 knots to conserve fuel. A heavy cloud layer formed a ceiling of about five thousand feet. With no moon visible it was a very dark black night.[19] "The average visibility at its best did not exceed two miles, reduced to less than one mile at times," Ainsworth recorded.

Although the gulf was familiar territory for the admiral and many of his ships' captains, it was the first time the group would be entering for the express purpose of picking a surface fight. Beyond the initial dispatches,

Ainsworth had no additional information about the Japanese force he would encounter. "No contacts had been received from our Black Cat scout planes and one of them had reported that he was returning to base because of the weather," he noted.

As the American ships approached the entrance to the gulf, the Japanese supply operation was already well under way. After closely hugging the coast of Choiseul Island, Akiyama moved south toward Kolombangara. Close to midnight the First Transport Unit broke away from the rest of the force at a point about twenty miles north of Kolombangara to begin the run down to Vila-Stanmore. At 1:06 a.m. the *Niizuki*'s radar spotted the American ships heading northwest at a distance of just over thirteen miles. Already in Kula Gulf, the Japanese ships were to the southwest of the approaching American task group. Knowing the importance of his mission to deliver the troops, Akiyama directed the Second Transport Unit to break away at 1:43 a.m.[20] He then turned his Support Unit to the north to keep a close watch on the American force.

Just before 1 a.m. the *Honolulu*'s radar picked up several contacts at a distance of about fifteen miles. The targets, though, were soon identified as land.[21] Halsey's orders were for Ainsworth's ships to head for home at 2 a.m. if definitive contact with the Japanese had not been established.[22] At 1:36 a.m. the flagship again had a radar contact a little closer than the last. This time it was the Japanese ships off the northeast Kolombangara coast.[23] "The enemy formation was very blurred but easily distinguishable," Ainsworth reported. The admiral certainly must have believed that he held the advantage of surprise. He had no way of knowing that the Japanese already spotted his force about a half an hour earlier.

Lookouts on the Japanese Support Unit ships were soon able to make out three American light cruisers and two destroyers. Akiyama now knew that he faced a formidable foe. Close to 2 a.m. he recalled his transport groups. The unloading of the troops would have to wait. The Second Transport Unit, which had just started on the path down to Vila-Stanmore, quickly reversed course.[24]

Each side had its own set of advantages and disadvantages. Ainsworth had larger ships, heavier guns, and more advanced radar, but he faced an enemy that was trained in night fighting. Akiyama possessed more ships and more long-range torpedoes. The Japanese admiral was, however, burdened by passengers and supplies loaded into all but three of his destroyers.[25] The setup for the Battle of Kula Gulf was now complete. The American task force and the Tokyo Express were on a collision course.

7

Gunfight

Admiral Ainsworth was ready to duel with the Tokyo Express. Without waiting for the details from the first firm report of contact with the enemy ships, he radioed instructions to his force. "Form for attack. Prepare to attack in battle plan Able."[1] Captain Cecil already had his ship ready for action. "The *Helena* had set condition of readiness one, material condition able, and ammunition condition of readiness one in all batteries at [midnight]," he reported. "The fire control radars were being used to supplement the search radars by periodic sweeps through 360 degrees of arch."[2]

The American ships immediately shifted into a single-column attack formation upon receipt of Ainsworth's order. The destroyers *Nicholas* and *O'Bannon* pulled ahead of the three cruisers to lead the column. "One minute later the formation turned simultaneously sixty degrees to the left in order to close the enemy," Ainsworth recorded. Only a few minutes later the ships made another turn to the right. In spite of the maneuvers, the task group maintained a speed of 25 knots.

While the admiral was maneuvering to get his ships into the best possible firing position, the information on the flagship's radarscope was becoming clearer. "At this time the first enemy group of four or five ships in column on a northerly course could be made out very clearly on the SG radar screen," Ainsworth wrote. At about the same time a second group of enemy ships began to appear on radar screens throughout the task force. These ships appeared to be larger and heavier than the first cluster. As Ainsworth pondered the best course of action, his captains were also trying to decipher the situation.

The enemy first appeared on the *Helena*'s radarscope shortly after the shift to battle formation. "I have a surface radar contact bearing 214 degrees true, nine miles," Cecil reported over the radio. A minute later he added that there appeared to be four separate enemy ships. "The main and 5-inch batteries were trained on targets and tracking commenced," he recorded. "All guns were loaded." The *Helena* was ready.

Aboard the *Nicholas*, Captain McInerney also studied the radarscope. "At this time the radar screen indicated that there were two distinct groups of ships, the first group consisting of about four or five pips which appeared to be smaller pips than those of the second group of about three ships," he reported. "The ships were headed out of Kula Gulf on course approximately 315 degrees."[3] The captain continued to keep a close eye on the enemy vessels.

The first contact seen by most American ships was most likely the Japanese Support Unit, which was positioned the farthest north at the time. The second was surely the four destroyers of the Second Transport Unit that had just been recalled from the journey south.[4] The Americans were apparently still unaware that the First Transport Unit was even further south.

The fire control radar team aboard the *Helena* was wasting no time sizing up the enemy. "The batteries were originally tracking on the nearest group when orders were received to prepare to open fire on the larger ships of the more distant group," Cecil noted. "This was attempted, but the fire control radars could not distinguish these targets owing to the proximity of the shore line and this situation was so reported."

In turret five, Bin Cochran had his men ready for action. A small area in the very back of the turret served both as a control station and as a point of entry. "[The entrance hatch] went straight out the back and then there was a little ladder that came down to the deck," he said. "In the high turrets that ladder fell a good little distance."[5] Cochran and Otis Point were positioned in the control area. They were separated from the guns by a waist-high partition containing an array of circuit switches and control lights. The lights indicated when each gun was loaded and ready to fire. A small opening on the left side of the partition allowed crewmen passage to the gun area from the access hatch. On the floor was a small chute to remove the empty powder casings that were ejected after each shot. "If your guns were not elevated too much [the casings] would go right into a tray and out on the deck outside," he said. "There were people out there that had to make sure that [the casings] stayed out of the way." In most situations the empty casings would simply be tossed over the side of the ship.

Looking straight ahead over the partition Cochran faced the breeches of the three guns. "You could look beyond that and see how each gun was operating," he said. "From there on back, some turrets have a range finder, which is the last thing behind you." Cochran's turret did not have one. "There was just space from there on back." Stationed inside of each turret were a pointer and trainer who were needed to move and elevate the guns when under manual control. The two simply stood out of the way if the guns were in automatic mode. In addition, a small cluster of men surrounded each gun. "You had a shell man, you had a paddle man and you had the gun captain," Cochran recalled. "Three men on each gun." In some cases the gun captain was a petty officer. "He could have been a first class seaman. They had to use a little judgment there," Cochran noted. The gun crews were bracing for a busy night as the battle loomed closer.

■ ■ ■ ■

Ainsworth initially thought that his ships could strike both Japanese groups simultaneously, and was getting ready to instruct his ships accordingly. However, it soon became clear that the two enemy clusters were about eight thousand yards apart. "It now appeared that it would be much better to hit them separately, even if to do so might give the second group a chance to run back into Blackett Strait," he reported.[6] Wanting to punch the first enemy cluster hard, the admiral directed the cruisers and two lead destroyers to focus their fire on the first group of ships. "My intentions are to get these, reach ahead, and make a turn and get the others on the reverse course."

Crewmen aboard the *Helena* made the appropriate adjustments. "The batteries were again shifted to the leading group, a good solution quickly obtained, and both batteries ready to open fire except that of the main battery only turrets I and II could bear on the target," Cecil reported. The Japanese ships were off the *Helena*'s port bow at a range of just over seven thousand yards.

As the ships were getting ready to fire, McInerney asked for clarification as to whether his destroyers were to fire guns or torpedoes. "Gunfire first," the admiral responded. All three cruisers soon reported that the fire control setup was complete. The order then went out for all ships to open fire. "The range by this time had closed to about 7,000 yards, but there had been nothing to indicate that the enemy had either seen us or made radar contact on our formation," Ainsworth wrote, still believing that he had the element of surprise on his side.

As the American ships prepared to open fire, Admiral Akiyama was readying an attack of his own. Adhering to Japanese doctrine for night battles, he would rely on torpedoes first. Gunfire before torpedoes only served to give away the positions of his ships. There was no shortage of the favorite Japanese weapon; the seven destroyers of the Support and Second Transport Units had a combined fifty torpedo tubes plus reloads.[7]

The battle started at about 1:57 a.m. when both sides opened fire at almost the exact same time.[8] American guns roared as a torrent of shells lashed out toward the Support Unit. In an opening barrage that lasted just over five minutes, the three cruisers fired almost fifteen hundred 6-inch rounds. Not to be left out, the *Nicholas* and *O'Bannon* contributed heavy doses of 5-inch fire. Ainsworth was certain that his ships were hitting enemy targets early and often. "Both cruisers and destroyers had demonstrated in several radar controlled target practices that they do not miss at ranges less than 7,000 yards, and the Task Force Commander has no hesitancy in expressing the firm opinion that this first group of enemy vessels were practically obliterated by the end of five minutes," Ainsworth later wrote. "All remaining pips on the screen appeared dead in the water." From his vantage point on the *Nicholas*, McInerney could see that the target his two destroyers were firing at had exploded into flames. "This ship finally blew up and disappeared from sight and from the radar screen," he said. It appeared to him to have been a large ship, and he later speculated that it was a transport.

Going into battle the quantity of flashless gunpowder was in short supply on some ships. The *Helena* had very little, having used up most of her

Battle of Kula Gulf
Part 1

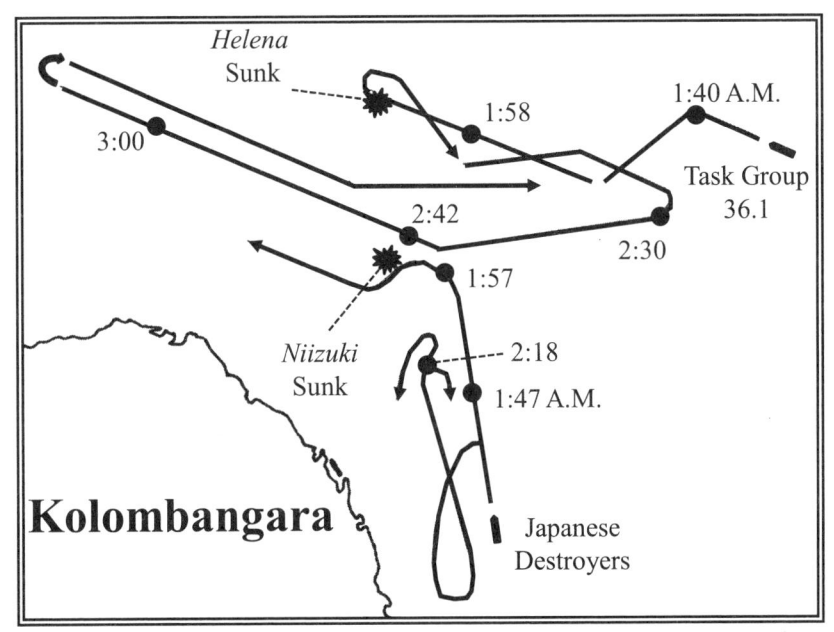

Map showing ship movements with labels: Helena Sunk, 3:00, 2:42, 1:58, 1:57, Niizuki Sunk, 2:18, 1:47 A.M., 1:40 A.M., Task Group 36.1, 2:30, Kolombangara, Japanese Destroyers

Adapted from U.S. Navy, *Combat Narrative X*, with supplemental information from Morison, *History of United States Naval Operations*.

supply during the previous night's bombardment.[9] "About fifty rounds per turret and per mount of flashless powder had been saved from the previous night's firing and was initially used by both batteries until expended, after which smokeless was used," Cecil reported. Without flashless powder, the *Helena*'s main battery guns fired with a recognizable sheet of flame. A quick flash of light momentarily removed the blackness of the night each time the cruiser's big guns roared. The flashes may have created an easy marking point for Japanese torpedo men looking to pinpoint the aim on their deadly fish.

As the battle developed Cecil positioned himself on the open air fighting bridge. Rodman Smith was in close proximity. The open air command area was just below the forward main battery directors and slightly jutted out from the rest of the superstructure. The location gave him a panoramic view of the events. As the rapid fire continued, smoke from the forward turrets drifted across the area, partially obscuring the bright muzzle flashes.

Almost directly below the captain in the enclosed pilot house, Cdr. Charles Carpenter stood with Chief Quartermaster Leroy Sweeney and others. As the *Helena*'s navigator, Carpenter oversaw the operation of the pilothouse during combat situations. The captain's orders pertaining to speed and course were relayed to the pilothouse via a voice tube.

■ ■ ■ ■

When Ainsworth gave the initial order to fire, the *Helena* was more than ready to comply. She had her sights set on the first two ships of the Japanese Support Unit. The enemy targets were heading on a mostly northerly course at the time. "The target formation was a line of bearing which as measured from the nearest ship was about twenty or thirty degrees to the right of our target bearing," Cecil wrote of the moment. "For this reason the main battery opened fire on the nearest target. The 5-inch battery, however, opened fire on the second from the nearest or what appeared to be the middle target."[10]

Both sets of batteries fired under full radar control. After about a minute and a half of rapid fire, it was momentarily paused so that observers could visually check the results. After firing on the lead target for almost three minutes, both fire control and SG radars reported that it had disappeared. The presumed destruction of the Japanese ship was a spectacular sight for those sailors who could see the action topside. Flashes of light marked the location of explosions as the vessel's superstructure seemed to be ripped to pieces. The target was most likely the Japanese flagship *Niizuki*, which had taken the brunt of American gunfire in opening minutes of the battle.

The *Helena*'s 6-inch guns then shifted to the second target. After only about two minutes word arrived from the combat information center that it too had disappeared from the radarscope. The target may have been the *Suzukaze*. She sustained damage and turned away, but did not sink.

The gun crews inside each of the *Helena*'s 6-inch turrets were working at a feverish pace to keep up with the rapid rate of fire. "These [turrets] were the latest things in fast firing fairly big guns," Cochran said. "They could really put out a lot of ammunition." The turret crews kept a steady stream of ammunition flowing to the guns.

By this time the Japanese destroyers had already fired some of their torpedoes and were responding with guns. "A considerable number of splashes from enemy gunfire was observed, most of which were 1,000 to 2,000 yards short," Cecil recalled. "At least one salvo, however, was observed to land about 200 yards on the port bow." The *Helena* was not hit by any shells.

At about the same time that the splashes were seen, the combat information center reported that a single Japanese ship seemed to have broken away from the rest of the group and was moving toward the American formation. The 5-inch gun batteries took the vessel under fire at an estimated range of five thousand yards. Although observers aboard the *Helena* reported seeing a series of hits on the target, it is unclear which Japanese ship was under attack. The ship that seemed to have been moving toward the *Helena* may have been either the *Suzukaze* or *Tanikaze*, both of which had turned to the northwest after the *Niizuki* was hit hard by gunfire. In the confusion and fog of a night battle, however, there may have been no target at all.

The *Helena*'s 6-inch guns kept hurling shells toward the enemy at a furious pace. "The battery then shifted to the next nearest target," Cecil noted. He believed that his guns greatly contributed to the demise of multiple Japanese ships. "At the time that the main battery was firing on its second target, two enemy ships were observed to be burning from end to end with a dark red solid flame," he later reported. "Three targets on which the *Helena* was firing were definitely observed to have been sunk." Cecil was once again pleased with his gunnery department. "Our gunfire was rapid and effective," he recalled. "It is considered that the rate of fire of both batteries was the highest ever attained and maintained by the *Helena*. Both batteries seemed to be firing as fast at the end as they did at the beginning of fire."

■ ■ ■ ■

Yet, contrary to what many of the American commanders believed, the Japanese Support Unit had not been obliterated. Most of the American ships had actually fired on only one target, the lead destroyer *Niizuki*. In the opening minutes of the barrage, the Japanese flagship came under withering fire. Her steering control lost, the ship veered out of formation. Just minutes into the battle the destroyer was a flaming wreck. She soon sank, taking many sailors to a watery grave. Akiyama went down with his ship.

Shortly after the American ships opened fire, the other two destroyers of the Support Unit responded. The *Suzukaze* and *Tanikaze* each fired spreads of eight torpedoes before turning sharply to avoid the burning *Niizuki*. Ainsworth noted the turn and reported it to his ships over the radio circuit. "Enemy seems to be reversing course." The two destroyers then headed northwest under the cover of smoke to reload torpedo tubes. Both of the ships made it through the hail of gunfire, but not without suffering some damage. A searchlight and torpedo mount on the *Suzukaze* were hit and the hull was damaged. The *Tanikaze* was hit with a dud shell that caused minor damage. Neither destroyer was out of the fight.

At 2:03 a.m. Ainsworth ordered his ships to make a sharp turn to the right to reverse course. It was time to go after the second group of enemy ships. Neither he, nor any of his captains knew that sixteen deadly Japanese torpedoes were speeding toward them at that very moment. Just as the ships started the turn, three torpedoes slammed into the port side of the *Helena*. The damage was serious. In an instant the ship was out of the fight, but the battle continued around her.

While the formation was turning, Ainsworth queried his four destroyers if any were able to fire torpedoes. Only the *Jenkins* replied affirmative. She had launched three torpedoes. The two rear destroyers did not heavily participate in the first round of fighting. Just after the initial order to open fire was given, the *Radford* had moved into position behind the *Jenkins*. Commander Romoser was soon eying a potential target, but when the *Jenkins* fouled his aim, he was unable to fire. As the battle continued, Romoser watched one Japanese ship move closer to the three cruisers. "This target was apparently under the fire of the cruisers and is believed to have been sunk, for it abruptly disappeared from the radar scope," Romoser later reported.[11] He was most likely watching the demise of *Niizuki*.

The other ships of the task group did not immediately notice that the *Helena* was missing. "Since the *Helena* lost all speed and became dead in the water just as the other cruisers made their simultaneous turn in reversing the action, the fact that the *Helena* had been torpedoed and had fallen out of formation was not noticed until sometime later," Ainsworth wrote. The smoke of the battlefield and sounds of gunfire may have helped to conceal *Helena*'s fate.

The American ships now turned their attention to the second group of targets. The destroyers of the Japanese Second Transport Unit were moving north at a high rate of speed after having reversed course on Akiyama's order. The ships were heading directly toward the broadside of the American formation and soon came under heavy fire.

Ainsworth's adroit maneuvers had put his ships into a commanding position against the second group of Japanese ships. Moving on an easterly course, the American ships were now about to cross the T of the approaching enemy force. This classic naval maneuver occurs when one group of ships passes perpendicular to another. It allows the first group, representing the top of the letter T, to direct full broadside fire against the second, who can only reply with forward guns. "Targets in the second group, now coming up fast on northerly courses were first taken under the fire by the *Honolulu* at 2:17 [a.m.]. This target was taken under fire at just 11,000 yards, the first salvo hitting squarely, starting fires and explosions," Ainsworth wrote. Lookouts aboard the flagship now incorrectly identified the lead Japanese ship as a light cruiser. "Keep firing on any target as you get them," the admiral told his cruiser commanders over the radio. "You may illuminate if you so desire." The battle was moving at a frantic pace and showed no signs of slowing.

Ainsworth also ordered his destroyers to fire torpedoes at any available target. The *O'Bannon* sent a spread of five toward two targets thought to be 9,000 yards away. No hits were scored. Just minutes later, McInerney saw the opportunity to fire more. "I directed the *O'Bannon* and *Nicholas* to prepare to fire five torpedoes," he noted of the moment. The only target that the *O'Bannon* could get a clear fix on was far into Kula Gulf. She fired off five torpedoes in anticipation that one or more enemy ships would be coming out of the gulf. The *Nicholas* did not fire any. "The Commanding Officer of the *Nicholas* informed me that he had no target and I directed him not to fire torpedoes," McInerney noted.

The *Radford* let loose with a spread of four torpedoes on a target that was eight thousand yards away. She then opened fire with her 5-inch guns under full radar control. "Small fire was observed on forecastle of this target," Romoser reported. "Hits were observed by director personnel and radar spotting was possible. Large explosion observed on [a ship] which had been used as target for guns and torpedoes." He speculated that at least one of his torpedoes may have found the mark. At about this time there was a large explosion off the stern of the *Radford*. It was thought to be a Japanese torpedo exploding at the end of its run. The American destroyer was not damaged.

When the *Radford* checked fire, she had sent almost two hundred shells toward the enemy. Lookouts suddenly screamed that another ship was close at hand. "Came left upon sighting what appeared to be a 2,100 ton destroyer close aboard on starboard bow," Romoser recorded. He did not know if it was a friend or foe. "Ship plainly visible, but radar could not establish its presence." The sighting prevented the *Radford* from making one of the assigned turns and as a result, the ship fell well behind the rest of the formation. "This was later established to be a phantom ship, and was most probably our own shadow silhouetted against low hanging clouds by cruiser gunfire astern," Romoser later concluded.

The destroyer *Amagiri* led the Japanese Second Transportation Unit north. She fired a spread of torpedoes toward the American ships, but none found targets. However, she was hit by four shells, which demolished her forward radio room and damaged electrical systems.[12] The *Amagiri* veered off to the right. Next in column was the *Hatsuyuki*. Navigating through the gunfire, she was struck by three dud shells, which damaged steering gear and left three crewmen dead.[13] The destroyer was able to return fire with her 5-inch guns. Moving left out of the column toward the coast of Kolombangara, she switched to manual steering control. Coming up the rear of the column, both the *Nagatsuki* and *Satsuki* apparently deduced what was happening ahead and made quick turns to the south. The *Nagatsuki* was hit by one 6-inch shell and the *Satsuki* was not damaged.

From the American standpoint it looked as though the heavy gunfire had made quick work of the second group of Japanese ships. "All the targets in this second group seemed to have been taken under fire by more than one ship, particularly as they turned away or were stopped dead in their tracks," Ainsworth noted. The radar plot on the *Honolulu* seemed to indicate that the immediate area was clear of targets. Only two enemy ships were plotted at the time. One was moving slowly in the vicinity of Waugh Rock near the coast of Kolombangara. It was assumed to be badly damaged. The second ship was moving south into the gulf. Just before 2:30

The light cruiser *Helena* rests at anchor near Boston in June 1940. The light cruiser was less than a year old at the time of the photo. *Courtesy of the National Archives*

A close-up of the *Helena*'s starboard side shows an assortment of anti-aircraft guns. The photo was taken in mid-1942 while the light cruiser was undergoing repairs in California from damage suffered during the Pearl Harbor attack. *Courtesy of the Naval History and Heritage Command*

Admiral Ainsworth's three light cruisers operate at sea on June 20, 1943. Left to right are the *Honolulu*, the *St. Louis*, and the *Helena*. *Courtesy of the National Archives*

Shells from the *Honolulu*'s 6-inch guns streak out into the night during the Battle of Kula Gulf. The main battery guns of a light cruiser could send a continuous stream of fire toward the enemy. *Courtesy of the National Archives*

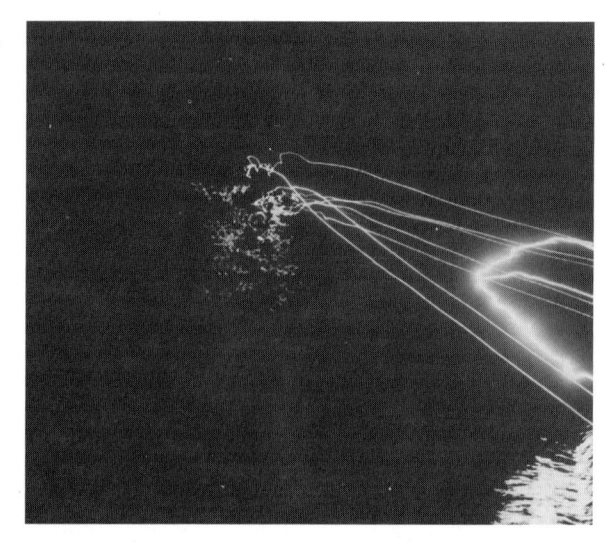

In what is likely the last photo of the doomed ship, the *Helena* unleashes a salvo from her main battery guns during the Battle of Kula Gulf. The photo was taken from the nearby *Honolulu*. *Courtesy of the National Archives*

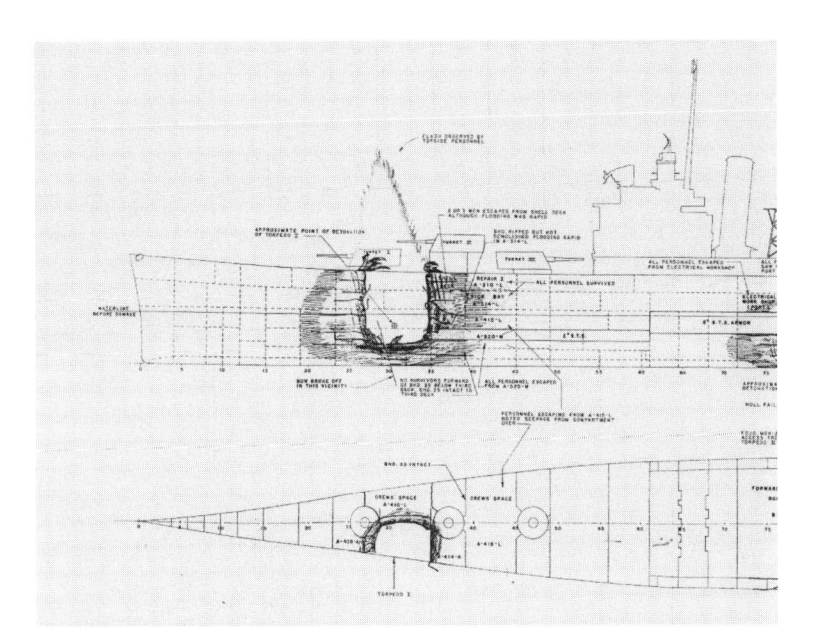

A U.S. Navy diagram shows the estimated damage caused by a torpedo that hit the forward section of the *Helena* during the Battle of Kula Gulf. The severed bow remained afloat and became a haven for survivors the morning after the sinking. *Courtesy of the National Archives*

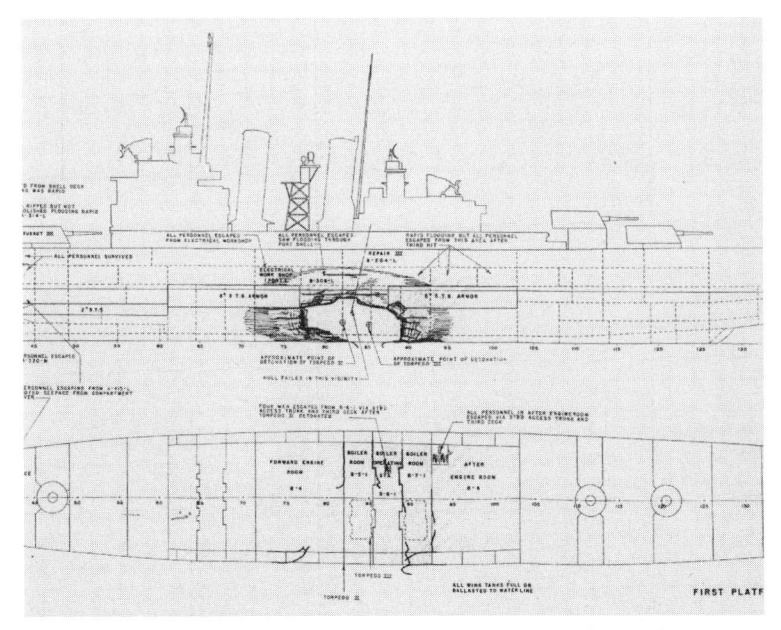

Hitting almost directly amidships, the second and third torpedoes struck the *Helena* deep below the waterline, causing fatal damage by breaking the keel of the warship. *Courtesy of the National Archives*

The wreck of the Japanese destroyer *Nagatsuki* still rests along Kolombangara in May 1944. The vessel ran aground while trying to flee American forces during the Battle of Kula Gulf. *Courtesy of the Naval History and Heritage Command*

Oil-soaked *Helena* survivors congregate aboard the *Nicholas* after being pulled from Kula Gulf the night of the sinking. *Courtesy of the National Archives*

A close-up of the *Nicholas* shows *Helena* survivors packed aboard the destroyer the morning after the sinking. The picture was taken after the ship safely reached Tulagi. *Courtesy of the National Archives*

Her decks overloaded with survivors, the *Radford* enters Tulagi Harbor the morning after the *Helena*'s sinking. The rescue destroyers had to depart Kula Gulf at daylight due to the threat of enemy air attacks. *Courtesy of the National Archives*

Stretcher cases were the first to be transferred from the *Nicholas* to the *Honolulu* at Tulagi. A steady stream of *Helena* survivors moved between the two ships after the wounded were safely across. *Courtesy of the National Archives*

Helena sailors watch a movie in the mess hall aboard the *Honolulu*. The light cruiser transported a large number of survivors from Tulagi south to Espiritu Santo. *Courtesy of the National Archives*

Admiral Ainsworth (*second from right*) shakes hands with *Helena* survivors aboard the *Honolulu* several days after the sinking. *Courtesy of the National Archives*

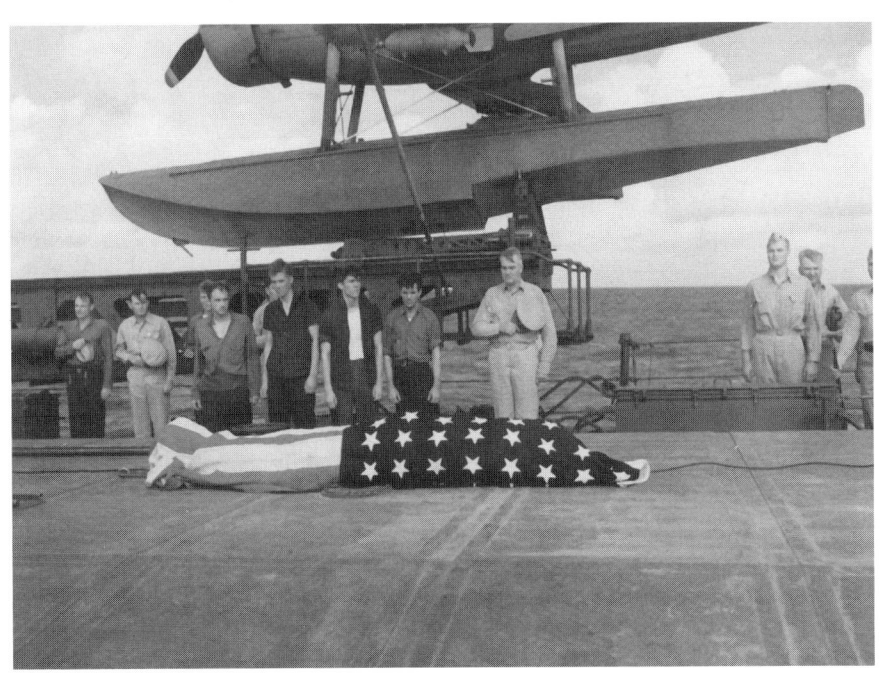

Admiral Ainsworth (*hat over chest*) pays his last respects at the funeral of Irvin Edwards aboard the *Honolulu* on July 7, 1943. The *Helena* enlisted man died aboard the *Nicholas* after being rescued from Kula Gulf. *Courtesy of the National Archives*

A boatload of *Helena* survivors heads for shore from the *Honolulu* at Espiritu Santo. Most of the homeless sailors were quickly transferred to a survivors' camp at New Caledonia. *Courtesy of the National Archives*

The destroyer transport *Dent* near Seattle on March 10, 1943, about four months before helping to rescue stranded *Helena* sailors from Vella Lavella. The outdated World War I–era destroyer found new life after being converted to a fast transport early in World War II. *Courtesy of the National Archives*

Survivors rescued from Vella Lavella wait in line for supplies at an unidentified South Pacific base. The photo may have been taken at the survivors' camp on New Caledonia. *Courtesy of the National Archives*

Crowded aboard a merchant vessel for a voyage across the Pacific, *Helena* survivors cheer their arrival at a West Coast port on August 17, 1943. Most of the men were granted a thirty-day leave before having to report to their next assignment. *Courtesy of the National Archives*

Smiles rule the moment as *Helena* men wait out their final minutes at sea while arriving at a West Coast port. It was the first trip home for most of the men since the *Helena* left for the South Pacific in 1942. *Courtesy of the National Archives*

Four *Helena* survivors stop for a dockside picture after arriving on the West Coast on August 17, 1943. Pictured left to right are: Charles Cook Jr., Gene Greene, Andy Banchero, and Bill Bunker. *Courtesy of the National Archives*

After the sinking of the light cruiser *Helena*, Capt. Charles Cecil led a small flotilla of boats and rafts to a nearby island. The group was rescued the next day. *Courtesy of the National Archives*

Lt. Cdr. John Chew was the senior officer among the *Helena* men trapped on Vella Lavella. The undated photo was most likely taken after World War II. *Courtesy of the Naval History and Heritage Command*

A graduate of the United States Naval Academy, Lt. j.g. Bin Cochran served aboard the *Helena* as a turret captain at the time of the sinking. He was among the survivors stranded on Vella Lavella. *Courtesy of Bin Cochran*

Lt. j.g. Mason Miller's battle station moved below deck just before the *Helena*'s final battle. He viewed previous actions topside from a gun mount. *Courtesy of Mason Miller*

Widely regarded as a hero for tending to the wounded on Vella Lavella, Jim Layton (*right*) is shown receiving a medal. He was stationed on land for the remainder of the war. *Courtesy of Jim Layton*

Gene Robinson (*second from left*) relaxes with friends on his first night back in the United States after the sinking of the *Helena*. The photo was taken in San Diego on September 4, 1943. *Courtesy of Gene Robinson*

Gene Robinson was among the large influx of men to join the navy in the days following the Japanese attack on Pearl Harbor. The Ohio sailor was soon assigned to the light cruiser *Helena*. *Courtesy of Gene Robinson*

A wallet and wristwatch were Gene Robinson's only personal items to survive the *Helena*'s sinking. The watch stopped when he hit the water, freezing in time the moment he left the sinking ship. *Courtesy of Gene Robinson*

Gayle Gilbert enlisted in the navy just before the start of the Pacific War. Growing up in Kansas, he was far from any ocean. *Courtesy of Gayle Gilbert*

After surviving the sinking of the *Helena*, Wisconsin native Walter Wendt was assigned to the new cruiser *Houston*. He survived the near sinking of that vessel in late 1944. *Courtesy of Walter Wendt*

Frank Cellozzi was among the *Helena* sailors stranded on a Japanese-held island after the sinking. During the ordeal he wondered if he would ever return home to Ohio. *Courtesy of Francis Cellozzi*

Paul Kavon poses for a picture during navy boot camp near Chicago. The young sailor was later among the *Helena* survivors trapped on the Japanese-held island of Vella Lavella. *Courtesy of Howard Kavon*

a.m. Ainsworth signaled his ships to make another turn. After traveling east across the column of Japanese ships, the task group was again reversing course to initially head west and then northwest. At this juncture the commanding officer of the *O'Bannon* radioed Ainsworth with a question, "Are all of our people accounted for?"[14] The admiral replied, "As far as I know yes; cannot raise *Helena*."

Once again the American perception of the action was not quite accurate. By now all four of the destroyers of the Second Transport Unit were proceeding south toward Vila-Stanmore. En route, the *Nagatsuki* ran aground near Bambari Harbor on Kolombangara. The *Satsuki* stopped to offer assistance. Unable to pull her sister ship free, she continued south.[15]

■ ■ ■ ■

The tell-tale signs that something was not right with the *Helena* began to appear shortly after 2 a.m. when Ainsworth started the turn to reverse course. Shortly after the maneuver he radioed the *St. Louis* and *Helena*, "Open up as soon as you have target." Only the *St. Louis* replied with an affirmative. The American ships completed two additional turns in the next ten minutes. The *Helena* did not acknowledge either of the maneuvers via T.B.S. radio. "It was now increasingly evident that the *Helena* was no longer in formation and the signal for the next maneuver, a turn one five at 2:25 [a.m.], was sent out on all radio circuits and by bridge searchlight both ahead and astern," Ainsworth wrote. "*Helena* failed to reply to any of these signals."

After firing on the second group of Japanese ships and subsequently completing another reversal of course at about 2:30 a.m., the task group was heading northwest and running somewhat parallel with the northern coast of Kolombangara.

With some of the ships out of position, lookouts on the American vessels gazed skeptically about, unsure if there were enemy vessels mixed in among friends. During one exchange, Ainsworth radioed the *Radford* to warn of a possible enemy ship. "There seems to be a target well astern of you. Can you get anything on the screen?" Romoser replied, "I am trying to pick it up. I am about 8,000 yards astern of you." The admiral then realized that the *Radford* was his mark. "Target dead astern of us is the *Radford*," he quickly told all ships. In a confusing night battle, friendly fire could be just as dangerous as that from an enemy.

The American ships were looking for any sign of the Japanese. At one point the *St. Louis* began to fire a series of star shells to aid in the search for targets.[16] Other than what was thought to be a damaged ship beached near Waugh Rock, only phantoms were sighted. Ainsworth reported the beached ship to area headquarters in the hopes that planes could finish her off in the morning. There was in fact, no ship in that area as *Nagatsuki* had gone aground well to the south. The phantom target may have been one of the destroyers of the Second Transport Unit on her way south, or may it have been nothing.

At about 3 a.m. the task group was directly north of Kolombangara. The force was approaching the entrance to Vella Gulf, the body of water on the west side of Kolombangara. Ainsworth wanted to see if there were any remaining Japanese ships either ahead or behind his formation. He directed the *Nicholas* to nudge her way ahead and make a radar sweep of Vella Gulf. At the same time, he wanted the *Radford* to complete a scan of Kula Gulf. "Both ships reported negative results on these sweeps," Ainsworth noted. With no apparent targets in sight, the task group turned to take on a southeast heading to begin the voyage back toward Kula Gulf.

It was not long after they reversed course that several ships reported seeing a thick smoke hanging over the horizon. The destroyer *Jenkins* was among the first to report the possible sighting of a distant smoking ship. The destroyer's commanding officer asked over the radio, "Are any of our cruisers smoking heavily?" Ainsworth replied that it could be the missing *Helena*. He directed the *Radford* to make another radar sweep, but the results were negative. Only a few minutes later the *St. Louis* reported sighting black smoke off her port bow, the general direction of where the American ships had been during the opening round of the battle. Based on the disjointed information at hand, Ainsworth asked the *Radford* to make yet another radar sweep. "Report if you can see enemy anywhere ahead," he radioed. Minutes later he made the same request of the *St. Louis*.

At 3:13 a.m. a small dot appeared on the *Radford*'s radarscope.[17] "I have a surface contact," radioed Romoser. "Range 5,000." The unknown contact was only a small dot on the radarscope, but it was definitely something.

Ainsworth ordered him to investigate and open fire if it proved to be an enemy vessel. Moving cautiously closer, lookouts on the destroyer began to make out a faint shape. "The contact which I reported is the bow of a ship sticking out of the water," Romoser radioed. The admiral directed him to move still closer and illuminate it. At the same time he wanted the other ships to turn on their lights. "Illuminate all ships except cruisers now in formation. Trying to find *Helena*." After several more anxious minutes ticked away, Romoser had more information to report. "Think we see a two digit number on ship." A short time passed before he reported back the dreadful news. "I regret to report the number is fifty." The fate of the *Helena* was no longer a mystery.

8
Fatal Damage

The *Helena* had been firing on the third target for about two minutes when a Japanese torpedo slammed into the vessel at 2:03 a.m. Hitting without warning, the torpedo struck the port side about 150 feet from the bow of the ship directly below the back half of turret one. All indications are that it was a shallow hit, perhaps just five feet below the waterline.[1] Men stationed topside reported seeing a brief flash immediately followed by a large column of water that rose high into the air behind turret one before crashing down on the forward deck area and superstructure. The ship seemed to lurch but kept moving forward. The hit caused some vibrations throughout the ship, perhaps felt more by crewmen in the upper areas than by those below the waterline.

There was far more to the torpedo hit than was seen from topside. A violent explosion took place above and below the waterline. Whether the blast was solely from the torpedo's warhead or fueled by 6-inch shells and powder cases stored below the turrets is unclear. The blast ripped a gaping hole even with the forward edge of the barbette below turret two. The damage extended deep below the waterline, but not quite as far as the keel. The explosion was, however, enough to rip the bow of the ship completely off. Turret one was completely destroyed by the explosion, while the shell deck and handling room directly below were also demolished. Under turret two, the force of the explosion breached a bulkhead causing rapid flooding. Two or three men escaped from the immediate area, but no one survived from the compartments underneath. No fires broke out as a result of the hit.

Although the damage was well contained to the forward part of the ship, the sailors in the compartment immediately aft of the impact must have certainly felt the effects of the blast. Repair station one was located one deck below topside. Positioned between turrets two and three, the area was less than fifty feet from the hit and suffered shock damage. Ventilation blowers broke free from mountings, with at least one hitting the overhead of the compartment. Damage control tools and anything else that was not securely fastened down was tossed about.[2]

Edwin Rick was a member of the repair party. "I had the phone on connected with central station at repair one," he recalled of the early stage of the battle. He was listening intently as the damage control officer reported the progress of the battle over the circuit. "I had been writing down the number of ships sunk," he later said. "We had sunk three from their report."

At five minute intervals, Rick had been reporting back to central station that repair one's area was secure. He had just given a report when the first torpedo hit a few compartments forward. The men in repair one took the hit pretty hard. "It threw me up in the air and turned me around, and when I landed I was sitting down. And the first thing I knew, water hit me in the back." The stream of water pushed Rick a distance of five or six feet into a nearby repair locker. After regaining his senses, he quickly reported the hit to central station. "Well, that's the last report they got from anyone. We had to evacuate repair one and go aft to the wardroom, which was right underneath the bridge."[3] Men of the repair party reported their compartment partially filled with smoke and gas that likely came in through the vent ducts. However, the group was able to stay intact with few injuries.

One deck below the repair station was the sick bay. The force of the explosion ruptured the forward bulkhead, sending a rush of water into the compartment. Although many sailors were momentarily stunned, everyone in sick bay managed to leave the area through an escape shuttle. It was, however, a narrow escape with the water reaching to within two feet of the overhead just as the last sailors made it out. All personnel were also safely evacuated from underneath the sick bay, where the compartments were reported to be dry, with all of the bulkheads intact.

The missing bow was not immediately noticed due to the high rate of fire by the main battery guns. "Gun flashes were blinding and, through this volume of fire, no person in a position to observe the forward part of the ship was able to do so, and the fact that turret one had been lost and no fire was coming from that turret escaped our notice," Captain Cecil later wrote.[4] The torpedo, though, did not damage the critical machinery that was necessary to keep the *Helena* moving and operating. "The main propelling plant was undamaged," Cecil reported. "Steam pressure remained up and the engines continued to generate power for 25 knots though the turns started to drop off due to the added resistance to headway."[5]

The first torpedo was definitely not a fatal blow to the *Helena*. Other American cruisers had suffered critical bow damage in the waters off Guadalcanal and survived to fight another day. The after main battery turrets, which by now were in action, continued to fire after the hit.[6] The cruiser was not yet out of the fight.

Two minutes had passed since the first torpedo struck. The *Helena* seemed to have just recovered from the initial shock, when two more torpedoes crashed into the ship. Separated by barely a minute, the torpedoes struck the port side of the ship directly under the after stack and almost dead amidships. The hits sent up a tower of water.

The second and third torpedoes delivered a devastating blow to the *Helena* in the form of a large explosion. At the epicenter of the blast were the critical engineering spaces: the boiler, engine, and generator rooms that created the power needed to keep the ship alive. The force of the blast ripped open a large section of the hull below the waterline, instantly flooding the forward engine room and the boiler rooms directly behind. The forward bulkhead of the after engine room was breeched, but did not collapse. A torrent of water rushed into the compartment. The damage extended all the way down to the keel.

In one fatal blow both sets of engine rooms were knocked out of commission. "Damage from the third torpedo hit was imposed on that caused by the second hit and overlapped it," Cecil later said. "Hit number two was in the Achilles Heel of this class of cruiser."[7] The captain knew that his ship was in serious trouble. "It struck in the one position where it is possible, in a single stroke, to render inoperative all of the main propelling machinery."[8] With all propulsion power lost, the *Helena* slowly drifted to a stop. Communication circuits went dead in short order. Normal lighting disappeared, only to be replaced by the dim glow of emergency battle lanterns. More than one hundred of these lanterns were scattered around the ship, mostly positioned along exit routes. Ruptured fuel tanks, which were more than half full, belched oil into the water around the stricken ship.

All over the *Helena*, men who had been thrown down by the force of the explosions slowly began to pick themselves up from the deck. Many groped around in the dim glow, trying to come to their senses. The battle lanterns provided enough light to reveal a layer of dust hanging in the air after being stirred up from unknown spaces by the violent shaking.

Reports of damage and distress quickly began to reach Cecil's position on the bridge. "The plotting room reported that no power was available, that the plotting room could be of no further use for gunfire, and requested permission to evacuate," he recalled. The order was given. "Within about a minute permission was also given to evacuate central station." It was at this juncture that the communication circuits went dead. "Execute" was the last word reported to have been heard over the *Helena*'s communication circuit before it went silent.[9] It was most likely a reference to the turn that Admiral Ainsworth had ordered just before the torpedoes made contact. Scattered about the ship in various compartments, many sailors were on their own to interpret what was happening.

The *Helena* was now in a desperate fight for survival. One thing seemed pretty clear to many on board: the ship was probably going to sink. "About two minutes after the third torpedo hit orders were given by word of mouth to man abandon ship stations," Cecil wrote. "At this time the ship was dead in the water, the bow including all of turret [one] had been blown completely off and was not in sight. It is not considered possible that the ship could have been saved by any additional action on the part of ship's personnel or by other ships," he concluded.

With no functioning communication system, the abandon ship order had to be spread verbally. Many sailors simply concluded that the ship was not going to stay afloat for long and immediately went into the water.

Others worked to get ropes over the side and cut free life rafts. "Practically all rafts were successfully launched and it is believed that practically all surviving personnel succeeded in abandoning ship," Cecil remembered.

The bridge was a scene of intense activity during the *Helena*'s final minutes. Chief Signalman Charles Flood stood near Cecil and relentlessly flashed a distress message on a blinker lamp. Apparently no American ships picked it up. Radioman James Sandridge rushed to the bridge from the captain's cabin with an armful of confidential materials.[10] At Cecil's direction, he tossed everything over the side. The bridge area was soon evacuated as all personnel made their way down to the main deck. Bill Barnet and Ozzie Koerner, both junior grade lieutenants, were the last to leave the bridge. Both decided to get out after seeing Cecil depart. Just a short time earlier, the two had helped free another officer who was hit by a falling radio antenna.[11] The struggle to try to save the *Helena* was over almost as soon as it had begun.

■ ■ ■ ■

Either of the two midship torpedo hits taken alone could very possibly have been fatal blows to the *Helena*. Since both struck almost the same place, the chances of saving the warship were slim. The fact that the power plants were knocked off line did not necessarily mean that the ship would sink. However, the structural damage to the hull below the waterline was so severe that the *Helena* was doomed.

The second and third torpedoes also hit much deeper than the first. It is thought that the two struck as much as fifteen feet below the waterline.[12] Much of the damage occurred below the five-inch-thick armor plating that straddled the ocean's surface. The middle section of the ship began to sag immediately after the torpedoes hit. The *Helena*'s keel—a long center beam located at the very bottom of a vessel's hull and often referred to as a ship's backbone—was broken by the force of the explosion. Severing the keel began to put great strain on the girder system, an interconnected network of beams and bulkheads that held *Helena*'s hull together. With a broken keel and failing girders, internal pressure built rapidly and the *Helena*'s midsection began collapse, leaving the ship to bend and ultimately break in two.

The noises of collapsing girders could soon be heard as the ship's midsection began to sag even further. It was the sounds of the ship in her death throes. Before long, the center of the light cruiser was sinking into the sea. The front and back sections of the ship began to rise out of the water. The middle part of the ship where the keel had been broken acted as a hinge for the rest of the hull. The *Helena* was slowly sinking in a jackknife fashion. The after part of the ship eventually stood straight up in a near vertical position. The front portion tilted at an angle of at least forty-five degrees. Both sections then slowly went down. Twenty-two minutes after the first torpedo hit, the last of the *Helena*'s hull disappeared beneath the waves. It was 2:25 a.m.[13]

9

Abandon Ship

While the effort to save the *Helena* had ended, the struggle for the crewmen to stay alive had just begun. Sailors unable to find a way off the ship in her final minutes would perish.

Unlike the previous night's bombardment mission, Gayle Gilbert had stayed inside of battle two. He was in full battle gear, including dungarees and a long sleeve shirt. "We had helmets on and we had life jackets, but we didn't have a flash proof thing for our legs or our hands," he said. "That was strictly for the gun crews." Not wearing a headset, he had to rely on periodic announcements over the loudspeakers to keep abreast of what was happening. Once the firing started, Gilbert and the rest of the men at his battle station had to contend with the noise. "It was loud," he said. "We didn't have ear plugs; we had nothing."[1]

When the first torpedo hit, the men in battle two felt the aftershock. "It knocked me right down on my fanny," Gilbert recalled. "That was a rough one." He does not remember if others in his immediate area fell down because it was dark. The aftershock effects were substantially greater with the second and third hits. "That knocked us over again." He was able to regain his footing without injury.

With communications out, the executive officer decided to leave battle two and go to the bridge to find out what was happening. He instructed the men to stay put as he began his journey along the port side. Gilbert never saw Cdr. Elmer Buerkle again and speculated that he may have encountered trouble on the damaged port side. Although he did not return to battle two, Buerkle did make it off the ship.

All the men in battle two could do now was wait. "We just kind of sat there and listened and heard and watched," Gilbert said. "I heard a lot of yelling." One of the men decided that he had had enough. "I'm not staying here," exclaimed the unknown sailor. "I'm getting off this thing. It's going to sink." The idea was quickly accepted by the others.

The group soon decided that it was time to get out. Gilbert left battle two on the starboard side. "It seemed to me that you had to crawl over something to get down there to the quarter deck," he recalled. "It might have been a ladder." The water was rising quickly on the side of the ship. Gilbert was wearing a kapok life jacket, which gave him some level of comfort. "You felt good then because you felt you had some protection," he said. He did not have a flashlight or whistle attached to the vest as many others did. "By the time I got down to the quarter deck, all I had to do was step into water. It was going down that fast. I walked right off," he said. "I don't remember leaving my helmet on, I know I took it off and I just jumped in the water with my kapok life jacket." In the process of getting off the ship, Gilbert cut his leg. Once in the water his main concern was to get away. Worried about the suction created by the sinking ship, he began to swim away from the *Helena*.

Turret three kept firing at a frantic pace in spite of the first torpedo hitting not much more than fifty feet away. The explosion did not knock Remmel Dudley off his feet and no men in his turret were injured. "We felt it, but I could not have told you, if you'd asked me at the time, what part of the ship it had hit," he said. "I didn't know, because we were inside the turret and [had] no windows of course." The main battery communication circuit initially stayed in operation.

Dudley knew that the ship was in great peril immediately after the second and third torpedoes struck. "That knocked out all communications, knocked out the lights, and electricity. Everything was out," he said. The operation of the turret quickly came to a halt. "We knew that we would be abandoning ship," Dudley said. "There's no point in staying inside there.

You couldn't shoot."[2] He decided to order all of his men to get out. The sailors in turret three started to leave through the entrance hatch. "The hatch is I'm guessing, three-, maybe three-and-a-half-feet tall and maybe thirty-inches wide," Dudley recalled. "So it's small. You have to stick your feet out first and then kind of pull yourself out." Getting the large group out of the turret could not be done quickly. The men below in the handling rooms had to come up a ladder to be able to get out through the turret. "It's a long way up from the ammunition room and the projectile room," Dudley said. "It seemed like it took forever and I'm sure they were going as fast as they could." He waited for all of his men to leave before exiting. "I was the last one out of the turret."

Shortly after leaving turret three Dudley came across his commanding officer, Maj. Bernard Kelly. He had come down to make sure that everyone had made it out. The two Marine officers soon parted ways. Dudley was wearing a life belt, as the large and bulky kapok vest was too constricting for the cramped spaces inside the turret. It was nothing more than a small belt that fit around one's waist and was self-inflating. "It's about six inches wide," he recalled. "It's just a belt literally." Seeing a cargo net that some deck hands had put over the side, Dudley decided to use it. "I inflated my life belt and I went over on the port side." He was venturing into the unknown, but was happy to be off the sinking ship.

Inside turret five, Bin Cochran was far away from all of the torpedo hits. That did not stop him from feeling the aftershocks. "We knew something had happened," he recalled. The first hit seemed to be mild. The next two hits violently shook the turret, which seemed to rise up about ten feet before falling back down. "We continued to fire right up until the third one hit," Cochran recalled.[3] The final hits cut all power and communication, rendering the turret useless.

The sailors inside the turret immediately started to run for the door, but Cochran quickly stopped the exodus. He needed to find out more about the situation. He directed one sailor to put on a life jacket, find out what was happening on the outside, and report back. It seemed like a long time, but the sailor eventually returned with the abandon ship order. One by one the men then left the turret, grabbing a life jacket from Cochran or Otis Point before sliding out the hatch.

When Cochran himself made it out he immediately knew that things were bad. Looking aft he saw the stern rising out of the water. Cochran caught a brief glimpse of a man jumping off the ship only to have a raft immediately thrown on top of him. For a moment he wondered if the sailor survived. He began to assist others in getting some of the life rafts over the side. In the mist of the fury of activity, he vaguely noticed the other ships of the task force reverse course. The main battery guns on all of the vessels seemed to be firing at a rapid pace. He thought the ships passed within two thousand yards of the stricken *Helena*. Then, he continued to usher men over the side.

After waiting for most of the men in his immediate area to leave the ship, Cochran decided it was time to go. Not knowing if he would need them later, he decided to keep on his shoes. He did not inflate his life belt as he felt it would slow down his swimming if he needed to get away from the sinking ship in a hurry. Prepared for a steep drop down into the water, Cochran tried to slowly lower himself over the side as best he could. He soon found, however, that the water was only a few feet below the deck. Once in the water he quickly began to swim away.

All that Gene Robinson could really do from his gun station was to watch the battle as it developed around him. As in the previous night's bombardment mission, the 20 mm gun played no role in the action. He was in a good position to see 6-inch shells departing the *Helena*. "You could see the shells flying through the air," he said. The bullets were red hot. "You can't see it when it immediately leaves, but after a few seconds why you could see it in the sky going towards a target. You couldn't see what they were hitting, but you could see that they did explode." As a veteran of the sea battles off Guadalcanal, Robinson knew that the fire was a two-way street. "Then you would see shells coming towards us, but not exactly at us," he said. "They were coming towards some of the other ships." The thin splinter shield around the 20mm could only offer little protection if a shell landed nearby.

Since they were unable to participate, Robinson and his crew tried to keep up with the events. "We heard the talker [speaking] about how close a target was and then we started firing," he recalled. "Our ship was lit up quite a bit because we ran out of flashless powder." But the routine of the battle was quickly broken. "All of a sudden the ship jumped and the torpedo hit the bow." Although some distance from the hit, Robinson had no trouble hearing the explosion. "The whole ship [shook], shuddered, and stopped, but then it started taking off again," he recalled of the moment, "I don't think it knocked us down."

The men at the anti-aircraft gun did not have long to wait the before the next torpedoes hit dangerously close to home. "It was just below our battle station," Robinson said of the next hit. Both of the subsequent torpedoes struck almost directly below his gun mount. The underwater explosions sent up a wave of water that hit Robinson and his gun mates head on. The men were blown through the narrow passageway between the stacks, under a searchlight platform toward the starboard side. "It didn't hurt us, but just blew us through there to the other side of the ship," he said. Not a man was left at the gun station. Unhurt, but dazed and wet, Robinson slowly got back on his feet and tried to ascertain what was happening. His helmet and life jacket may have helped him escape injury.

It took less than five minutes for Robinson to abandon ship. He could plainly see the situation was dire. "The ship was sinking from the middle," he observed. "The bow went up and the stern went up." Losing track of the other men from his gun, Robinson was soon alone. He had to make some quick decisions before leaving the ship. "I think somebody told us don't take the shoes off because if you have to walk up the beach, there's a lot of sharp coral along the beach and if you're in your bare feet, your feet will be bleeding pretty bad." He decided to keep his shoes on. "You do silly things," he said of the next decision. "I had my wrist watch on and I took it off and put it in my pocket so it wouldn't get wet." He then stepped two feet off the starboard side into the dark water below.

"I seldom saw any of the battles," Jim Layton said. As part of the midship repair party he was not in any position to see the topside action. "That was one thing about being below deck," he observed. "You never really knew what was going on. They would occasionally give us some information over the PA system."

Layton had no doubt that the ship had been damaged when the first torpedo hit. "Well, it was a jolt," he said. "Anything that will knock the bow off the ship is quite a [shock]."[4] The group had been sitting on the deck just before the next torpedoes struck. "I recall that one of the chiefs at the repair party said 'we better get ready men, we got work to do.'" No sooner did Layton start to get up when the next torpedoes crashed into the *Helena* almost directly underneath him. The blow shook the compartment with a thunderous force causing him to hit the ceiling twice. Unhurt, he came to his senses in time to quickly realize that water was entering the compartment from below. "I never knew whether there was anyone injured there or not because the compartment started to flood," he recalled. "You just knew it was time to go." Everyone immediately ran for an enclosed ladder that led up topside to the main deck. "When I got up [topside] I reached for the life line and it wasn't there." The small line ran the perimeter of the ship and was often the last hope to prevent someone from going overboard.

The repair party had become completely separated. "It was kind of every man for [himself] at that point," Layton recalled. "I was pretty positive that [the ship] was going down. Everyone was abandoning ship." He was lucky enough to be wearing both a life belt and a life vest. "I never inflated the belt. The kapok did a great job." Finding himself amidships near the two stacks, Layton made a quick decision. He decided to jump for it. "I figured that I had quite a ways to hit the water," he said. "It wasn't." It turned out to only be a three-foot drop. He was in the ocean after just a short fall.

Sequestered down in radio three, all Mason Miller could do was to wait and listen. There was little doubt in his mind that the ship was in trouble after the first torpedo hit. "We felt it all right, no question about that," he recalled. "We knew we were in deep trouble as soon as that happened."[5] Miller had no idea as to the location or extent of the damage. The subsequent blasts only confirmed his initial belief.

From the deck above suddenly came the clamoring sound of running feet. Miller had a hunch that people were getting ready to leave the ship and decided that it was worthy of investigation. A ladder led up to a heavy door at the top of the compartment. "It was about four inches thick and I had to lift that thing up with my shoulders. I climbed up the ladder and put my shoulder against that door and lifted up." It was a difficult but brief struggle to get the heavy door open. "There's a mechanism that catches that door when you open all the way," he described. "You just push it back and it's caught." Miller then encountered the running people that he had heard from his radio room. He thought that they were coming from the forward battle dressing area in the wardroom. "Sure enough the people said we were abandoning ship," he remembered. He then had the rest of his men come up the ladder and out of the compartment.

No sooner did Miller make it out of the radio room, then a friend of his arrived on the scene. Lt. j.g. Edward De Jon had come from another compartment. "He and another buddy came by and checked to see that we got out." After seeing that Miller was in good shape, the two went separate ways.

"When we got topside we could tell that things were getting pretty bad," Miller said. "Everybody [was] trying his best to get over the side." He spotted a line going into the water and decided to use it. "I tried to get down as best I could without jumping. That could have been dangerous for somebody already in the water and also, it was a pretty good jump from the main deck down to the waterline." He made it into the water without incident.

■ ■ ■ ■

Being down in the after engine room while the battle was raging topside was nothing new for Walter Wendt. "It was very noisy," he recalled. There were plenty of noises and vibrations in the engine room due to the various pieces of machinery that were running. Adding to that were the reverberations every time the 6-inch guns fired. "There was a lot of burnt cork and powder," he said of the after-effects of the shaking.[6]

The air in the engineering spaces was usually oppressively hot. "It would get hotter and hotter," Wendt remembered of the battle conditions. "It would get so hot then you couldn't stand it. So they had air going in the engine spaces during a battle." A rudimentary ventilation system supplied a steady stream of outside air. Blowers pulled air through metal ductwork from intakes that were positioned on the main deck. "It would have been too hot to stay there without some ventilation," he concluded.

The men in the after engineering spaces were well equipped for the battle. Wendt recalled that while helmets were always worn in the engine room during battle conditions, life belts were not. "It was with you, sometimes around your neck," he remembered of the inflatable belts. "It would be on your person." It was simply too cumbersome for the men to wear a fully inflated belt in the cramped engineering spaces.

Even with the normal noises and rattling, Wendt knew that something had happened when the first torpedo struck the bow of the ship. "You knew you were hit," he said. "There are so many watertight compartments that if you were a little ways away from where the torpedo hit, you would know you were hit. The ship would be shaking very bad." At the moment he had no immediate knowledge of where the torpedo struck or the extent of the damage. That would not last for very long. The second torpedo pierced the adjacent compartments just forward of the after engine room. The blast slammed Wendt and his coworkers about with tremendous force. "It would throw you right up against the overhead," he said. The fall back down to the floor plates left Wendt in a scrambled heap. The violent process was repeated just minutes later when the third torpedo hit. He likely had the steel helmet to thank for saving his life.

Wendt knew almost instantly after the third torpedo hit that the *Helena* was not going to survive. "Nobody tells you to abandon ship," he recalled. "You knew that the ship was gone. You knew when you were hit about three times that nobody was going to save that ship." Perhaps the men in the engineering spaces had a keener sense for danger knowing that three levels of decks stood between themselves and topside.

The *Helena*'s Engineering Officer, Lt. Cdr. Charles Cook Jr., was also in the after engine room during the battle. "All machinery was operating properly," he noted when the fight started. Precautions had been taken to minimize the effect of any possible damage on the power plants. "The engineering plant was spilt, as had been the invariable rule since the war commenced," Cook recorded. "The forward boilers and main engines and their auxiliaries were running absolutely independently of the after boilers, main engines, and auxiliaries, so that the possibility of damage in the forward plant affecting the after plant and vice versa, would be minimized."[7]

The engineering officer was standing in front of the main control panel in the upper portion of the engine room.[8] Directly ahead of him was an arrangement of gauges and instruments that gave him the current status of his department. From a loudspeaker system he was getting up-to-the-minute information as to course changes, target information, and other goings on around the ship. "I recall that several minutes before the engagement a number of targets were announced to port," he later wrote. The ship was moving at a speed of 25 knots with all four engines running.

Cook heard the order to open fire that signaled the start of the battle. Looking up at the after engine room clock, he noticed it was 1:57 a.m. "Thereafter Control announced that one target had disappeared from the radar screen and that there was another target at 7,000 yards," Cook remembered. "This is the last word I recall receiving from Control." The engine room suddenly shuddered from a heavy hit somewhere well forward. He presumed it to be a torpedo hit. The perforated deck grating began to shake, causing some of the men in the area to topple over. Cook immediately noticed that the firing from the forward turrets had stopped. "A quick glance at the gauge board showed steam pressure normal in both plants," he later wrote of the moment. "The after engines continued making turns for twenty-five knots." The various pieces of equipment that kept the *Helena* moving seemed to be intact and operating normally.

The engineer officer asked his talker to check if the communication circuits were still open. Just then the second torpedo hit close at hand with great force. "I saw the main steam gauges, which show the pressures in each plant, drop rapidly," he recalled. It did not take long for the engines and generators to come to a halt. Cook knew that the *Helena* had been dealt a serious blow and surmised that she had been hit somewhere in between the forward and after engine rooms. All of the communications circuits went dead, but not before the number three fire room reported that it was starting to flood. Normal lighting was replaced by the dim glow of the emergency battle lanterns.

With no power, the engineering officer could not see any reason to keep his men in place. "I ordered the forward access opened and directed that the men start out," Cook wrote. The ladder led up to an armored hatch. The men wasted no time getting out.

Before all of the men could get out of the after engine room, Cook decided to halt the evacuation. "When all but about six men had left the engine room, I directed the others to wait while I made another check and verified the fact that both plants were dead," he recalled. A quick look at the gauges confirmed that both power plants were indeed out. He also noticed that the ship was listing to port. The talker tried one last time to reach the bridge without success.

The third torpedo struck before Cook could direct the remaining men to leave the compartment. By this time the men were all on the upper grating not far from the access trunk. The blast splattered the sailors with oil and water. The sound of rushing water was immediately heard coming from the lower area of the engine room. It was pretty clear that a bulkhead somewhere close had been breached. "We evacuated the station on the double," Cook reported. "Fortunately most of the men were already out and the gangway was clear."

The access trunk led to the third deck near the scullery. Cook and the last group of men did not attempt to close the trunk hatch. They moved quickly through a watertight door into the next compartment aft. "I was no sooner through this door with the last men then water, rising in the scullery, started aft," Cook wrote of his escape. The water was coming in fast. The men immediately grouped together to try to close the watertight door behind them. Lt. j.g. David La Hue and Machinist's Mate 1st Class Cobden Hitchon helped in the action. Working against the rushing water and building pressure, the group struggled in vain to close the hatch. They came to within a couple of inches of closing the door before giving up in the face of insurmountable pressure. "We let go of the door and made a dash for the center line ladders," Cook recalled. The men found that only one escape shuttle was open. "The water hit me before I reached the ladder and sent me sprawling," Cook recounted of the perilous moment. "I don't think this crushing wave was more than a foot or two high at the very first." As it grew in depth and intensity, the water actually pushed him toward the ladder, which he was able to hook with his arm. He then climbed up to the second deck, but still had one more level to go to get topside.

Once on the second deck, Cook moved to the next compartment aft. He noticed a steady stream of men running through the area, some of whom he recognized from the engineering department; he speculated the others were from the after ammunition handling rooms. It was at this juncture that he encountered Lt. Robert Beisang, the head of repair party two. Beisang had not received an abandon ship order and was busy directing sailors back to their battle stations. Not knowing the full extent of the damage, he seemed to still be concerned with the possibility of having to repair it.[9] "I think he did a splendid job in preserving a good semblance of order and discipline under extremely difficult circumstances," Cook observed.

Beisang apparently did not immediately recognize the engineering officer in his oiled covered state. Once Cook made himself known, he told him of the situation below and asked for any recommendations. Beisang had none. "I told him I thought we would have to abandon ship, and suggested he send all men topside," Cook recounted. "This he did."

A sailor then called Cook over to look at something in a nearby compartment. It was a large flange on a ventilation exhaust trunk that was positioned a few feet from the overhead. He immediately recognized it as connecting to the main deck. A strong stream of water was squirting out of the flange. Cook knew that this could only mean one thing: the main deck was under water or close to it. He immediately told everyone within earshot to get out fast. He then directed Beisang to get all the remaining men out on the double.

Wendt was among those to escape the after engine room through the hatch. Once off the ladder and through the escape hatch, the men seemed to scatter. "Everybody knew what his route would be ahead of time if he had to get out of the ship," he said. "You had to make your own way to topside. You knew damn well that if you didn't get the hell out of there, then you would stay with the ship." Making his way through various compartments, Wendt eventually emerged on the main deck near the back of the ship. "I was just ahead of the last turret," he said. The night seemed pitch black.

After groping around in the darkness topside, Wendt came across a good friend from the engine room, Hitchon. The machinist mate had made it topside after unsuccessfully trying to close the hatch with Cook and others in the face of rushing water. Wendt surmised from the look on his friend's face that he was in bad shape mentally. "When he got up on topside, he was about done," Wendt said. Hitchon had lost his life belt and seemed at a loss as to what to do next. "It got scraped off of him trying to get through a hatch or something." Wendt was able to locate a life belt in a nearby locker and decided to put some air into it before giving it to his friend. "There [were] two hoses on the life preserver," he said. "One was the exhaust hose and you had to be sure that was closed. You could unloosen a valve there and blow air out of your lungs into that." He quickly gave the partially inflated belt to Hitchon. "He always said I saved his life," Wendt said, "but I think he would have made it all right."

The immediate concern for the two sailors now was how to get off the sinking ship. "It was closing like a jack knife," Wendt recalled. "The stern was up at a very ridiculous angle." He could see that he had better get off fast. "The back end of the ship was coming up, while the center part of what was left of the ship was heading down," he described. "It made the ship pretty untenable." Just then the men were faced with a new hazard: empty powder cases were rolling freely around the deck. "The powder cans would roll across deck and you had better darn well get out from in front of 'em when they come by you," Wendt said. Dodging the cases, the two friends made their way over to the starboard side and went into the water near turret four. "We just stepped into the water," he said. "Normally that part of the deck when you were just steaming along was about twenty-three feet above the surface of the sea." Now, it was only a short trip down.

While Wendt and Hitchon were getting off the ship, Cook climbed up a nearby ladder and came out on the port side of the main deck. He immediately saw that the stern of the ship was high in the air. There did not seem to be any sailors in the immediate vicinity. "I went over to the starboard side and noted that we had a moderate list to starboard at this time which, however, was nothing compared to the trim," Cook later wrote. He saw a few men going down a line, which he presumed led to a raft below. Returning to the port side, Cook found two men near a 20mm gun mount. He did not recognize either one. "We heard an occasional grinding noise coming from the ship's structure as it slowly pulled apart," he continued. "We could see no rafts and there were no other people in our vicinity." Cook suggested that it was time to get off and that the three of them should stay together once in the water. All were in agreement. The three men went over the rail into the darkness below.

■ ■ ■ ■

The *Helena* had a wartime complement of nearly twelve hundred officers and men.[10] On her final night, 168 sailors did not survive the sinking.[11] Most of the men lost were probably in the immediate vicinity of the torpedo hits. There must have been no shortage of acts of heroism as men desperately searched for and found ways to get off the ship.

ABANDON SHIP

In the confusion on the main deck shortly after the third torpedo hit, a junior officer came across one of the mess attendants. Yelling wildly, the man was wearing an uninflated life belt and appeared to be in bad shape mentally. The officer inflated the belt, securely fastened it to him and pushed him over the side before ordering several nearby sailors to go in after him.

Below deck in the 5-inch powder handling room, a single sailor used his body to hold up a stack of powder cases that would have otherwise blocked the escape route for others. When some of the cases fell, breaking his leg, he stayed in position until the last sailor was able to leave the compartment before departing himself.[12] An untold number of other stories of heroism will likely remain undocumented forever.

■ ■ ■ ■

Meanwhile, the Battle of Kula Gulf was not yet over. Most of the Japanese destroyers were well clear of the northern portion of the gulf by the time the American force returned to the area from the trip to the entrance of Vella Gulf. The *Suzukaze* and *Tanikaze* had moved well off to the north after the initial fight. Both reloaded torpedo tubes while keeping a safe distance from the fighting.

During the battle most ships of the two Japanese transport units had gone south after finding the northern section of the gulf blocked by American ships. Some of the Japanese destroyers had been damaged, yet most were able to successfully off load their troops and cargo. Japanese records indicate that sixteen hundred troops and ninety tons of supplies were dropped off at Vila-Stanmore.[13] Not wanting to pick another fight with the American ships to the north, many of the destroyers exited Kula Gulf to the south via Blackett Strait. The *Amagiri* and *Mochizuki*, however, both ventured north, traveling along the east coast of Kolombangara. The move would put both on a collision course with American ships.

Once he learned the fate of the *Helena*, Admiral Ainsworth immediately ordered the *Radford* to begin rescuing survivors. "When you are sure you can do no more, sink hulk [*Helena*'s bow] and rejoin," he radioed. He then directed the *Nicholas* to assist. Captain McInerney was placed in charge of the two-ship rescue operation. By 3:30 a.m. it was time for the other

American ships to head out. "The remainder of the force commenced retiring down the Slot, the *Honolulu* following the *St. Louis* in column screened ahead by the *Jenkins* and *O'Bannon*," Ainsworth later wrote. The ships had to get out of the immediate area well before daylight or tempt fate with the certain risk of an air attack.

10

A Night in Kula Gulf

Getting away from the sinking ship was the immediate concern of most of the *Helena* survivors in the water. "The *Helena* is a block long . . . she would suck you down with her," remembered one junior officer.[1] The survivors, however, also had another problem. After belching out from the *Helena*'s broken hull, a thick coating of fuel oil covered the water in the immediate area. The hazard posed a multitude of threats from burning and blinding eyes, to catching fire.

The most basic naval abandon-ship training taught sailors to congregate in large groups away from a sinking vessel once in the water. One training article tersely warned that a lone swimmer was a good candidate to end up on a missing list.[2] Accordingly, the *Helena* survivors tried to stay together. The many rafts that were hastily cut down and tossed over the side began to fill up quickly. As a general rule the wounded were put into a raft first, followed by as many able-bodied men as could fit. Others stayed in the water, grabbing onto a raft's side rope. If an officer or chief was on a raft or in close proximity, he would take charge of the group. Although the men in the water may not have known it, help was on the way.

■ ■ ■ ■

Using radar to pinpoint the position of the *Helena*'s bow, Commander Romoser turned the *Radford* toward the survivor area. At 3:41 a.m. the *Radford* reported, "We are in the mist [*sic*] of survivors now."[3] The *Nicholas* arrived in the area at almost the same time, allowing the rescue operation to get fully under way. Whether groups or individuals, in the water or on rafts, hundreds of sailors were spread out over the sea. Some had flashlights to signal their positions, while others used whistles to attract attention.

Because the *Helena*'s bow was about six and a half miles off the northeast coast of Kolombangara, it was a dangerous setup. Its position at the northwest entrance of Kula Gulf put the survivors in the likely path of any Japanese ships that still needed to leave the area. With Admiral Ainsworth's cruisers gone, the two destroyers would be on their own if the enemy was to return.

The crews of both destroyers were ready for the rescue operation. There were two possible ways to save the men: pull them up out of the water or put boats over the side to collect them. The rescue ships started the operation by hanging cargo nets over the side with sailors manning the rails above ready to help.

Many of the survivors in the water were exhausted and did not know what course the battle had taken or which side was victorious. When one of the American destroyers approached a small group, the survivors initially shouted and flashed lights to attract attention. Someone suddenly yelled for the lights to be put out, fearing that the ship might be Japanese.[4] It was only after hearing American voices that the men came forth to be rescued.

As the *Radford* slowly moved through the area, her crew began to hear the faint sound of voices in the black night. Romoser yelled through a megaphone for the men in the water to stay calm and come alongside his ship.[5] It was not long before oil-covered survivors made their way to the side of the destroyer. Soon men were either climbing up the vessel's side or being pulled aboard.

The rescue operation was not under way for very long before the *Radford*'s executive officer burst into the bridge to announce that radar had picked up an approaching enemy ship. Initially spotted at 4 a.m., the vessel was closing fast. Romoser immediately ordered his ship to prepare to attack and then yelled back down to the men in the water to stand clear because the ship was leaving to deal with an enemy vessel. He added that his destroyer would soon return. As the *Radford* sped toward the unknown target, Romoser radioed the information to both McInerney and Ainsworth. Within minutes radar on the *Nicholas* also picked up a target and the destroyer sped off at 27 knots to investigate.

Aboard the *Nicholas*, Captain McInerney noted the perilous position of his destroyers. "Both ships had to clear survivors from the sides, get boats clear, and make speed to engage enemy," he recalled. "Hundreds of men were in the water near the two ships and these had to be left there for the moment." At the same time the American captains were trying to make sense of the contact. Romoser interpreted it as two ships trying to leave Kula Gulf by hugging the northern coast of Kolombangara. McInerney thought it could be a ship coming down from the Shortland Islands or coming east from Vella Gulf. As the officer in charge, he decided that only one ship should continue toward the enemy. He directed the *Radford* to return to the survivor area, while the *Nicholas* stood between her and the approaching enemy.

The enemy target continued to move closer to the *Nicholas* as the American destroyer prepared for battle. Not knowing if he was dealing with a cruiser or destroyer, McInerney decided to close for a torpedo attack. No battle, however, took place. "The enemy ships moved in to about 13,000 yards and then reversed course and stood to the northwestward," McInerney wrote. It soon disappeared from the American radarscope. Romoser thought that the Japanese may have tried a long range torpedo attack. "It is believed that at least one of these vessels fired torpedoes inasmuch as high speed propeller noises were picked up by the sound gear," he later wrote.[6]

The mysterious targets were the Japanese destroyers *Suzukaze* and *Tanikaze* of the support unit.[7] Both had moved off to the northwest after firing their torpedoes and narrowly escaping the barrage of American gunfire in the opening round of the battle. The two apparently spent the time away from the battle reloading their torpedo tubes. Japanese records note that the destroyers returned to the scene of the battle to look for either the *Niizuki* or enemy ships. Finding neither, they headed for home. There is no mention of the destroyers launching torpedoes.[8]

Battle of Kula Gulf
Part 2

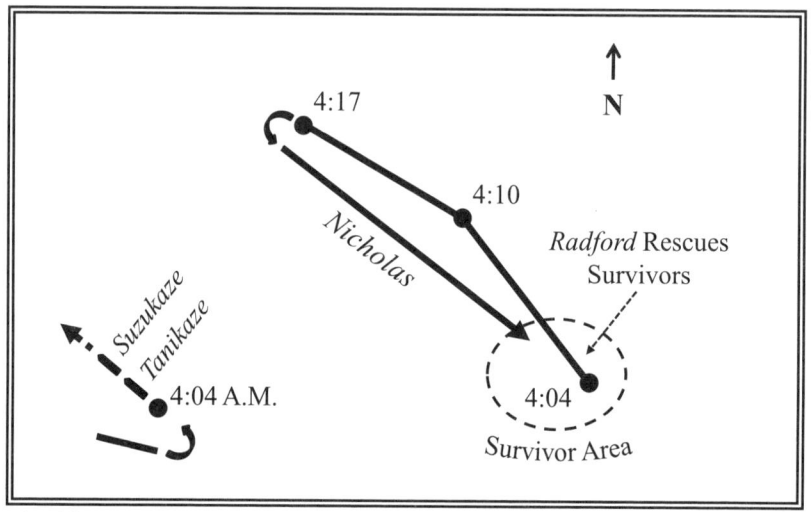

Adapted from U.S. Navy, *Combat Narrative X*, with supplemental information from Morison, *History of United States Naval Operations*.

Upon receipt of the *Radford*'s contact report, Ainsworth decided to turn his force around and head back to the gulf to support his two destroyers. All four ships made a simultaneous turn to the right, and the admiral laid a course that pointed directly toward Kolombangara. His run back to Kula Gulf, however, was short lived. After hearing from McInerney that the enemy contacts had disappeared, he again reversed course to continue the journey home. He then radioed the *Nicholas* and *Radford* to try to make the Russell Islands by daybreak. It is a good thing that Ainsworth did not return for another fight. The night battle and bombardment mission had depleted the ammunition supply of the two remaining cruisers. The *Honolulu* had only ten minutes worth of fire left for her main battery guns and the *St. Louis* was in a similar quandary.[9]

Shortly after 4:15 a.m. both destroyers were back in the survivor area. Aboard the *Nicholas*, McInerney was in a good position to oversee the rescue operation that he commanded. "The survivors seemed to be scattered over an area of one mile square," he later wrote. "This area was filled with men in life rafts and swimming separately."[10] He had no idea as to the number and condition of the survivors.

It was at this juncture that both destroyers put whaleboats into the water to aid in the rescue. The small, motorized vessels could pull individuals aboard as well as tow rafts over to the destroyer's side. The *Radford* lowered two boats, each with a crew of four.

Quartermaster 1st Class Albert Phillips was in a whaleboat as it pulled away from the *Radford* in search of survivors. He remembered that the boat soon came across four rafts. Each was loaded full of men with others hanging on to the side. Two badly burned men were carefully transferred into the whaleboat. A coxswain then connected the rafts and tied the rope to the tiller used to control the whaleboat's rudder. Pulling up alongside the *Radford*, most of the *Helena* men were able to scramble up the cargo nets. Sailors from the destroyer climbed down to assist the injured or those too tired to make the climb.[11] The operation, however, took a turn for the worse when the stress from the towline proved too much for the whaleboat's tiller and it broke off. The boat now had no way to control its rudder.

Clayton Carkin was in command of the *Radford*'s second whaleboat. As he searched for survivors in the dark water, he noticed the smell of oil and gunpowder, both lingering remnants of the battle. Water Tender 1st Class Cliff Hemstock was also in the boat. As he pulled the men aboard, he began to notice that everyone seemed to look the same. Each man was covered with a thick coat of black fuel oil.[12] As the rescue continued the whaleboat made multiple trips to and from the destroyers. At one point the boat stopped to transfer some wounded men to one of the *Nicholas*'s whaleboats, which was heading back to the ship.

Ensign John Fitch was in command of one of the whaleboats from *Nicholas*. "We could hear the men in the water," he later recalled. "They were covered in oil, so it was hard to see them. You could see the whites of their eyes."[13] Seaman 2nd Class Joe Moll grabbed a signal gun before jumping into Fitch's whaleboat. He had the foresight to hastily arrange a call signal with one of the signalmen aboard the destroyer to make finding the boat easier in the dark.[14] On the first trip out the boat quickly became filled up with survivors. Although the intention was to pick up the injured, the boat was soon full of mostly uninjured sailors. Moll signaled the *Nicholas* before heading back to drop off the passengers. The able-bodied survivors simply climbed up the cargo nets, while the few injured were lifted up.

Before shoving off for a second trip, a sailor tossed aboard a rope for a towline. The boat crew could now tie together rafts while keeping the main area of the whaleboat open for the wounded.

As the whaleboat continued to ply the area, Fitch noticed that most of the survivors were found in large groups of fifty or more, and most all were wearing life jackets. The boat crew gave up their jackets to those who were without. Only a small number of men in the water appeared to be dead or unconscious.[15]

■ ■ ■ ■

Helena survivors remained mostly calm while waiting to be rescued. In some cases they even resorted to humor. One individual was sighted swimming near the *Radford*. When he was directed by megaphone to swim toward the ship, he jokingly asked if it was going to San Francisco. He added that he would wait for the next destroyer if it was not.[16] Groups of men sang or cheered in unison to help attract the attention of lookouts on the destroyers. "Hip, hip hooray," was heard on at least one occasion by men aboard the *Radford*.[17]

Once off the *Helena*, Mason Miller stayed with a small group. He recognized a couple of them as officers. "We had a life raft which consisted of this very lightweight wood, which floats and has netting in the middle," he remembered. A group of steward mates were among those clustered aboard. "They were scared to death. I don't think that anybody tried to get them to move. I know I didn't." Miller was just happy to be with a group and a raft. "I had a place to hold on, so I could swim and I didn't bother too much about it." Miller never did inflate his life belt. "I had failed to close the valve so that it would hold air and I didn't even know it," he said. "It didn't make any difference." The sailors tried to get away from *Helena* as best possible, watching their ship go down in the process. "I said, there goes the ship, and that was it," Miller said. "There's not much you could do about it."[18]

The time on the raft seemed to go by fast. The men were soon able to make out the hazy shape of a destroyer approaching. The sighting sparked a discussion as to whether the ship was American or Japanese. "Somebody said we might as well go ahead and signal to them because if it isn't ours we are not going to make it anyway," Miller recalled. "So our signalman happened to be in our group and he had a flashlight. We gave him our number and they came back DD-446, which was the USS *Radford*." As the raft moved closer to the destroyer, Miller waited for the right opportunity to find a way to get aboard. Like the rest of the men around him, he was covered with oil. "When the opportunity presented itself I climbed aboard," he continued. "I don't know that I did a whole lot of swimming." Miller was just happy to be out of the water.

After walking into the water off the starboard side, Gene Robinson swam toward the closest raft he could see. It seemed to be about a hundred yards away from the ship. The kapok life vest made it a slow swim, but it gave Robinson a level of security. "I finally got to the life raft and turned around and saw the ship going down," he said. "And that's when you feel like you lost your home. It's the ship that you lived on for a year and you're so used to it and to see it disappear is very bad."[19] After the ship went under, Robinson focused on survival. The raft was a small one with eight or ten men huddled in the water around it. Although there did not appear to be any wounded among the group, no one sat in the raft. Robinson identified the executive officer, Cdr. Elmer Buerkle, among the group but did not recognize any others.

The raft eventually came close to one of the destroyers, but the men were not immediately rescued because the ship had to leave to do battle. Eventually, however, rescue came in the form of the *Radford*. "I was picked up in about four hours," Robinson recalled. As the raft pulled up to the side of the destroyer, Robinson grabbed hold of the cargo net and began the arduous climb. At least one set of helping hands offered assistance as he neared the top. Buerkle was the next man below him. "Just as I got off the top, the destroyer took off again to go after another target." Robinson was pulled aboard, maybe as the last man of his group, but Buerkle fell off the side as the destroyer started to pull away. "I really don't know how high he got, but he was next to me on my right, below me, and I don't remember how far down he was." The commander was never seen again. "It always bothered me," Robinson related. "If I could have reached down and could have grabbed him, I might have been able save him." Robinson felt lucky to be alive but lamented that he had been unable to save Buerkle.

■ ■ ■ ■

At 5:15 a.m. the *Radford*'s radar made contact with what appeared to be a single ship coming out of Kula Gulf. The vessel was about thirteen thousand yards away, heading northwest at a high speed. The course would have the ship pass just south of the survivor area. Radar on the *Nicholas* spotted the same target only a minute later. The contact was the *Amagiri* from the Japanese Second Transport Unit. Coming up from the south to search for *Niizuki* survivors, she had just located a group of men in the water when lookouts spotted the American destroyers to the northwest. Capt. Katsumori Yamashiro knew that he would be unable to stop for a rescue. He pointed his ship to the northwest and ordered flank speed.[20]

McInerney decided to go after the lone target. "I directed both ships to prepare to get way on and engage enemy," he reported. "Again both ships had to discontinue rescue operations, clear survivors from alongside, get boats shoved clear, and prepare to get under way." He gave both destroyers the authorization to fire torpedoes when ready. Just then the commanding officer of the *Nicholas*, Lt. Cdr. Andrew Hill, reported that his ship had a favorable firing solution and unleashed a spread of five torpedoes.

The *Amagiri* was closing fast. By 5:22 a.m. the *Radford*'s radar showed that the Japanese destroyer had closed to 9,700 yards. Just minutes later sonar operators picked up the telltale sound of torpedoes coming from the direction of the enemy. Romoser quickly made a sharp turn. "Maneuvered to avoid torpedoes, one of which observed by fan tail personnel to be running on surface and to have passed approximately fifteen yards astern," he later recalled. "Sound indicated two other torpedoes probably passed ahead." It was now the *Radford*'s turn to reply. At 5:30 a.m. she fired four torpedoes at the *Amagiri*, which was thought to be six thousand yards away moving at a speed of 25 knots.

McInerney ordered his destroyers to change course and close on the enemy. The *Radford* led the way with the *Nicholas* following about seven hundred yards behind. As the *Nicholas* moved toward the enemy at full speed, Hill muttered a comment that must have summed up the feelings of many aboard. "If the son of a bitch wants to fight, I'll give him a fight."[21]

Both American ships opened fire with 5-inch guns. The *Nicholas* fired star shells to provide illumination, while gunners on the *Radford* sent shells

Battle of Kula Gulf
Part 3

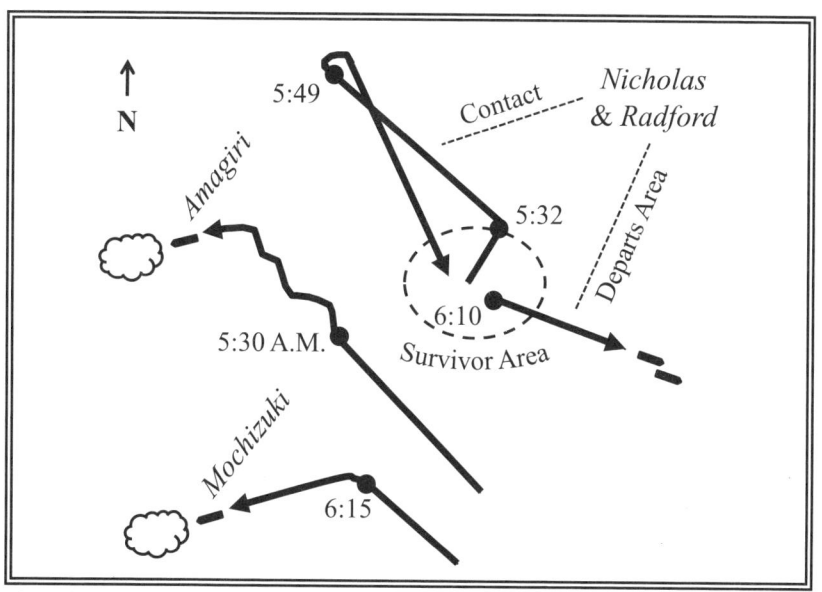

Adapted from U.S. Navy, *Combat Narrative X*, with supplemental information from Morison, *History of United States Naval Operations*.

hurling toward the enemy. It was not long before return fire came at the American ships. Men on both destroyers and survivors in the water reported shell splashes in close proximity. "It is estimated that this target returned about five [to] ten salvos of gunfire during the engagement," noted Romoser. Neither American ship, however, sustained any damage. After the exchange of gunfire a series of loud detonations were heard in the direction of the enemy vessel. Many aboard the American destroyers believed that their torpedoes had found the mark, but none actually hit the Japanese target. About twenty minutes after opening fire, the *Radford* stopped shooting to bring the short battle to a close. The destroyer had fired 240 rounds of 5-inch.

The fog of war and the confusion of night battle created many different versions of what happened during this brief firefight. Romoser believed that his shells were hitting home. "Salvos were rocked back and forth over target and hits were observed by control personnel," he reported. "Large clouds of smoke emitted from target." He thought that the enemy warship was definitely sunk, most likely by torpedoes fired from his ship.[22] The Japanese vessel was thought to have disappeared in a cloud of smoke replaced only by debris floating on the surface.

From his vantage point aboard the *Nicholas,* McInerney believed that there were actually two enemy ships. "The ship appeared to be a four stack cruiser and large black clouds of smoke could be seen pouring from the ship," he noted. "Another smaller ship, also smoking heavily appeared to be about 1,000 yards to port of the larger ship." Hill, the *Nicholas*'s commanding officer, also thought that there were two enemy ships. "The cruiser was probably sunk by torpedoes and the destroyer probably received one hit," he concluded.[23]

The *Amagiri* was in fact the only Japanese ship involved in the skirmish. After the aborted attempt to rescue the *Niizuki* survivors, she sent a spread of five torpedoes toward the American ships. These were the torpedoes that passed near the *Radford*. During the brief exchange of gunfire, an American shell crashed into her midsection destroying fire control circuits and demolishing the radio room.[24] Yamashiro had enough and withdrew under a smoke screen. The destroyer headed for home, believing that two of her torpedoes hit an American cruiser.[25] The *Niizuki* survivors were left to fend for themselves. Most of the three hundred men aboard perished at sea, although a few were taken prisoner by the Americans.[26]

Ensign Fitch and his whaleboat crew continued to search for survivors as the two destroyers intermittently departed the area to continue the battle. "We would go up to a group of men and first pick up the ones who were wounded the worst and get them back to the destroyer," he related.

■ ■ ■ ■

Growing up on a lake in Wisconsin made Walter Wendt a pretty good swimmer. "I was a strong swimmer, not a fast swimmer, but I could swim all day if I had to," he said. He was in the water with Cobden Hitchon. "Hitch wasn't a very good swimmer," Wendt said of his friend. The two quickly set out to fully inflate their life belts. "At first I didn't close the exhaust valve." When Hitchon commented that his belt was also going flat, the two realized their mistake and corrected it. There was just enough light from the stars to help the two muddle through the process. It did not take long for them to become mixed up in oil. Soon the two came upon a third man, Fireman 3rd Class Thomas Tizzard, who was in the same division as Wendt. "I can't swim a bit," Tizzard shouted. "If it wasn't for this life preserver I'd go down. I don't know how to swim."[27] Wendt assured him that he would not be left behind and then wondered what to do next. "Before we got into the water I could see an island off in the distance," he said. "It was Kolombangara, I guess."[28] Once in the water, however, he could not see land in any direction.

After drifting for some time, the group began to hear the faint sound of voices off in the distance. Moving toward the sound soon led them to a large group of survivors. The three eagerly joined the crowd. "This group was probably a hundred fifty or two hundred guys," Wendt said. "There were two rafts tied together and you couldn't get quite half of 'em all onto the life rafts. So I didn't even attempt to go onto the life raft because I was a strong swimmer." While Wendt stayed in the water, Hitchon was able to squeeze onto a small space on one of the rafts and Tizzard simply disappeared into the group. "I don't know what happened to him after that," Wendt said of Tizzard. "He got absorbed in a whole bunch of guys." Occasionally the moonlight allowed the large group to make out the big number fifty on *Helena*'s bow in the distance. "Everyone was talking and comparing notes and trying to find out who was dead and who wasn't dead," Wendt continued. It was a way to pass time.

The men soon saw a searchlight far off in the distance, but they did not know whether it was American or Japanese. They debated what to do, but the ship did not come close enough. A little later a ship closed in on the men in the water. "We had no idea if we had won the battle or not," Wendt said. As the vessel moved closer, he could make out some detail. "You knew it was an American destroyer because of the superstructure. They didn't have the pagoda-type superstructure." It was the *Radford*. Sailors manning the rail dropped down ropes for the survivors. Wendt grabbed a line only to quickly fall back into the water. His oily hands were much too slippery to get a firm grip. The rope came down for a second try. "I wrapped it around my wrist a couple of times, so they couldn't pull me loose and they pulled me up." Hitchon and Tizzard both made it aboard as well.

■ ■ ■ ■

After climbing down a cargo net into the water from the *Helena*, Remmel Dudley came across a sailor who was desperately clinging to the side of the ship. "He was holding on to the ship, I don't know [why]. I was trying to get him to let go because, you know, it would suck him under if he didn't get away from the ship," Dudley said. The sailor would not budge. "I tried to pull him away and I did not succeed and I don't know what ever happened to him." The marine immediately began to swim away from the ship. "There was a whole bunch of us [that] were leaving the ship at the same time from both sides," he continued.[29] He remembered seeing the deck crew cut down and toss some rafts over the side. He swam toward one that he spotted in the water.

There were two rafts in close proximity that were beginning to fill up with men. Dudley was one of many who jumped on the raft, but then went into the water to make room for others. He remembered that eventually only the wounded were actually put in the rafts and as many as thirty men were soon clustered around each. "We all had life preservers of one kind or another." The sailors briefly debated the merits of tying the rafts together. "If we did, there's a better chance we'd been seen and be picked up," he said. "On the other side though, if we did tie them together then there's more rafts to be fired upon by the enemy. But anyhow, we did tie them together." As the senior officer present, Lt. Cdr. Jim Baird took command of the two-raft flotilla. Between the initial swimming and later bobbing in the water next to the raft, Dudley was fully covered with oil. "I'm red headed," he later said. "I used to wonder what I'd look like with black hair and I found out."

Dudley spent several hours in the water and may have been among the first to be rescued. "I was picked up by the *Radford*," he recalled thinking that the rescue took place between some spells of gunfire. Dudley began the slow climb up the side of the destroyer. When he neared the top a sailor reached down from above to help him the rest of the way. "I still remember saying 'god bless you.' I don't know why I remember that." Dudley does not remember what the sailor said in reply.

■ ■ ■ ■

By 6 a.m. both American destroyers returned to rescuing survivors. With sunrise fast approaching, the ships would have to leave the area soon or face a Japanese air attack. The rescue had not resumed for long when both destroyers made radar contact with an unknown vessel coming north out of Kula Gulf. "This ship was sighted visually, since it was now daylight, and appeared to be a cruiser or destroyer," McInerney reported.

The contact was the *Mochizuki*. Having successfully offloaded her troops and supplies at Vila-Stanmore, Capt. Tsuneo Orita decided to leave the area by the northern route. Except for the beached *Nagatsuki*, the *Mochizuki* was the last Japanese ship to leave Kula Gulf. The American destroyers yet again pulled away from the survivors and turned to face the approaching Japanese ship. Both foes opened fire at long range in an encounter that was brief and inconclusive. Hill noted that the enemy gunfire was not close. The *Mochizuki* fired a single torpedo in the direction of the Americans that found no target. After sustaining minor damage from shell hits on a forward turret and torpedo tube, she withdrew into Vella Gulf under cover of smoke. The last skirmish of the Battle of Kula Gulf was over.

With full daylight almost at hand, McInerney was forced to make the difficult decision to end the rescue operation. "In view of unknown number and size of enemy ships which still might be in Kula Gulf (and since daylight would take away any advantage from us), reported presence of enemy submarines, and almost certain enemy air attacks at dawn, I decided to retire in order to protect the two destroyers and personnel," he later wrote. It was a wrenching decision for the squadron commander. "I regretted leaving many men still in the water, but felt that they could reach our own positions on New Georgia by using the four boats we left, together with the life rafts from the *Helena*."

Romoser did not like the decision to withdraw either, but knew that the ships could not stay in Kula Gulf without fighter cover. "When the rescue destroyers commenced retirement at daylight, it [was] felt that there were still many survivors in the area," he wrote. "If this fighter cover had been overhead it is felt that the rescuing destroyers could, and should, have remained in the area to pick up the remaining survivors." The *Radford* had aboard a fighter director group headed up by Lt. j.g. Burton Atkinson. The officer, though, was unsuccessful arranging for fighter cover to arrive over Kula Gulf at dawn. The planes instead arrived over the ships while en route to Tulagi.

Both destroyers picked up the last remaining survivors in their immediate vicinity and made preparations to get under way. Albert Phillips and his whaleboat crew had already been hauled up aboard the *Radford*. With a broken rudder, the boat had been circling helplessly in the area and was left in the water for use by any remaining survivors. The *Radford*'s other whaleboat was alongside the *Nicholas* when it came time to leave. The boat crew, Carkin and Hemstock among them, decided to stay behind with the remaining survivors. Romoser cited their actions as heroic and well above the call of duty.

The *Nicholas* was getting ready to depart the area when Fitch's whaleboat pulled up for the last time. He and the boat's crew were ordered out. The young officer wanted desperately to stay, but in the end followed orders. "So reluctantly I went up a knotted line," he later said. The boat was left for the remaining *Helena* survivors with a half a tank of fuel, four breakers of water, and four cans of provisions.[30]

Undoubtedly there were some sailors who made it off the sinking *Helena* but did not survive their time in the water. One junior officer later told of seeing a young lieutenant patiently waiting while men around him were loaded into a whaleboat. When the small vessel became overloaded, the lieutenant swam away, never to be seen again.[31]

■ ■ ■ ■

At 6:21 a.m. the *Nicholas* and *Radford* began the long journey back to Tulagi. The anchorage was almost two hundred miles southeast. The rescue operation had been disrupted on three separate occasions when the destroyers left the area to engage the enemy in battle. At exactly 7:07 a.m. a flight of American fighters appeared overhead, bringing great comfort to those on the ships below. The *Nicholas* had aboard 291 survivors, while *Radford* was crowded with another 444. A total of 735 lucky *Helena* sailors made it out of Kula Gulf alive.[32]

11

The Captain's Flotilla

Captain Cecil was thought to be one of the last men off the *Helena*. Once in the water he immediately began to move away from the sinking ship and yelled to others to do the same. "Paddle like hell straight away from the ship," he shouted to anyone within earshot.[1] He soon became intermixed with fuel oil. It was through oil-filled eyes that the captain watched as the last of the *Helena* disappeared beneath the sea.[2] Cecil came upon a raft shortly after he cleared the danger area and was later joined by three others. All of the rafts were overcrowded with men hanging onto the sides. The captain refused to take a seat in a raft due to the overcrowding.[3]

The rafts were in close proximity to the *Nicholas* and *Radford* when it came time for the destroyers to depart, but not close enough for rescue. Refusing to leave his men, Cecil elected to stay behind.[4] He was pulled up onto Clayton Carkin's whaleboat from the *Radford* where he took Cliff Hemstock's seat. The water tender moved to an uncomfortable seat on the sharp edge of the bulkhead.[5]

Cecil took command of the boat, somewhat to Carkin's relief, and began to organize the remaining men. With the departure of the destroyers, survivors were jumping into any raft or boat that could be found. Some of the vessels became overloaded, making capsizing a serious concern. Once all the men were out of the water, it became necessary to equalize the loads among the available boats and rafts. Men jumped from one boat to another as the three whaleboats clustered together.

The *Helena* sailors were grateful for the support provided by the whaleboat crews. "Their crew stayed with us," recalled Electrician's Mate 3rd Class Don Hensler. "Even though they weren't on our ship, they were still in the whaleboats."[6] It was Hensler's second dunk in the ocean, as he had already survived the sinking of the destroyer *Benham* off of Guadalcanal in November 1942.

With the balancing of the boats completed, it was time to leave. The survivors certainly benefitted from Cecil's knowledge of the general area as he had taken the *Helena* into Kula Gulf multiple times. The captain's eyes were burning from oil and salt water and his vision was somewhat impaired, but he ably led the small fleet nonetheless. "I formed a small boat flotilla, three motor whaleboats each towing a life raft, and set course to the northward with a view to getting well outside visual range from Kolombangara," he later wrote. The *Radford*'s second whaleboat with the broken rudder was left behind.

Cecil knew that many of his men were in bad shape. "I noticed among the survivors in my group that those who were not in good physical condition began to suffer," he later said. "All officers and men were greatly inconvenienced by fuel oil irritation of the eyes. Not only is one's vision dimmed, but he also suffers severe pain."[7] Cecil's goal was to reach the Kula Gulf side of New Georgia and land somewhere near friendly natives or the American positions at Rice Anchorage. He estimated that the starting point of the voyage was about four miles off the coast of Kolombangara.

Among the group was Machinist's Mate 1st Class Paul Weisenberger. He was picked up by one of the whaleboats during the rescue operation, but never made it aboard either of the destroyers. "They came close yes, but got an alarm right away and had to pull away," he said of the rescue ships. "I don't know which one it was."[8] He remembered that organizing the flotilla took some time, "At least half, three quarters of an hour, all of that." In the end things seemed to go smoothly. "We had three motor whaleboats and we ended up with eighty-eight guys," he said.

The morning sunrise brightened spirits. As the procession slowly moved through the sea, the men began to take stock of their supplies. Two cartons of cigarettes along with some dry matches were found strapped inside one of the rafts. One of the whaleboats had two rifles, but no ammunition. Cecil decided not to circulate the part about the no ammunition.[9]

Since Kolombangara was thought to be heavily occupied by the Japanese, the boats steered well clear of its coast. While still near Kolombangara they saw a Japanese plane pass in the distance near the still visible bow of the *Helena*, but it did not attack.[10] The flotilla moved north for about three miles before turning due east for the voyage across the gulf. The captain wanted to make sure that the group stayed well clear of Visuvisu Point on New Georgia as it was suspected to be a Japanese stronghold. Cecil noted that his whaleboats were, "bucking wind and tide." The voyage, however, was not without problems. "One motor whaleboat ran out of fuel and had to be towed about three quarters of the way," the captain noted. The progress was slow, but steady.

The sailors did what they could to pass the time as the hours drifted past. Many of the men were covered in oil and exhausted. A number felt ill from swallowing oil while in the water. Sailors on one of the boats used a knife to pry open some cans of fruit that were found floating past. Each sick survivor was given a small amount to eat. It caused most to vomit, but they soon started to feel better. Once clear of the fuel-covered area, some of the men dipped rags in the ocean and used the salt water to try to wipe away the oil from their eyes.

As the day dragged on, the survivors must have had a range of questions going through their minds. Would they make New Georgia? Once on land would they find friends or the enemy? How would they be rescued? The *Nicholas* and *Radford* certainly knew of their plight and would hopefully make arrangements to send help. Later in the day the group was sighted by a plane initially thought to be Japanese. Cecil told the men to make ready to jump off and get clear of the boats if it looked as if it was going to make a strafing run. The plane, however, was American. The survivors were lucky to have among them Chief Signalman Charles Flood. He had in his possession a flare gun and blinker light, both extremely useful items to have while stranded at sea. Flood fired off a flare to attract the plane's attention and then blinked a message that they were American and heading for New Georgia.[11] The plane dipped its wings in recognition as it slowly circled the boats before moving out.

The arduous trip took most of the day, with almost all of July 6 spent at sea. They sighted land just before 5 p.m. Lt. j.g. Fred Lawler, the only other officer in the group, went ashore first with a few men to scout out a landing point. He signaled back that they found a suitable beach and that there was no sign of the Japanese. The water was very shallow between the boats and the beach. The whaleboats cautiously approached the land, but were not able to make it all the way in due to undersea obstructions. "We wanted to beach there and we couldn't get the boats to the beach," recalled Weisenberger. "They hit a sand bar. So we just put them on the sand bar and started walking in." The boats were less than a thousand yards off shore when the men started wading toward the beach. Weisenberger remembered that the water was less than knee deep.

As the sailors made their way toward land, a new hazard emerged in the form of sharp underwater coral. Many of the men had either left their shoes on the *Helena* or lost them while at sea. Hensler was one of the lucky ones. "I kept mine on," he said of his shoes. "One thing I did right." He helped carry some of the less fortunate men ashore. Weisenberger did not have shoes. His walk to shore stalled quickly when his feet were cut by the razor sharp coral. A shipmate soon came to his rescue. "My friend Frank Smith, everybody knew him by Freshwater Smith," he said of his rescuer. "He saw me waving and he came out and piggybacked me ashore." The sailors helped each other get ashore safely. Much as men would pass a bucket in a fire drill, they formed a line. As an individual with shoes made it to the beach, he passed the cherished pair back through the line to be used by another. The process continued until all of the men were safely ashore.[12]

The group had made it to Menakasapa Island, although the survivors probably did not know their exact location at the time of landing. Positioned on the northwest coast of New Georgia, the u-shaped land was actually a peninsula. Visuvisu Point was northeast and American positions at Rice Anchorage were about seven miles south. "We had no information what so ever [about the immediate area] and it was pretty quiet," Weisenberger said. "The sandy beach was, I'd say, fifty yards wide. Then trees and brush next to the beach." They did not know whether friendly natives or Japanese troops were lingering beyond the tree line. But, after having their ship sunk and spending the better part of a day at sea in lifeboats, the survivors must have been happy just to be on solid land.

It was already late in the day and Cecil knew that there was probably not much that could be done until morning. He remembered that it was, "too late to permit scouting for a native guide to lead us towards Rice Anchorage. Camp was established for an overnight stop." The captain gathered the survivors together. He was exhausted and sick like many of the men, but needed to take charge if there was to be any hope of survival. Carkin remembered that Cecil's calm demeanor helped keep up morale. The captain told the group that they were in a difficult position. They needed to stay alert and keep together. The men also took action to help prevent detection by the Japanese. There was to be no smoking on the beach, but taking a puff under the cover of the adjacent jungle was all right. However, smokers later found that lighted cigarette tips quickly attracted the attention of large jungle bats. One sailor discovered this the hard way when a bat attacked his face. The captain also directed that no one was to wander too far out into the jungle, as they might get lost or could be an easy target for a Japanese patrol.[13]

Because it was too dangerous to stay out on the beach in open view, the survivors made camp for the night under some trees on the edge of the jungle. They pooled the available rations and kept the food under a watchful eye. For the evening meal each man was allowed two crackers, a minuscule portion of canned meat, and a cup of water. The meager food supply would not last long, although an abundance of coconuts appeared to be only a tree climb away. Nightfall brought about the eerie sounds of jungle creatures, unfamiliar to American ears.

Carkin was tired and scared as he thought of all the possible outcomes. As he talked with shipmates he thought of home and wondered if the group was being watched. Other survivors talked among themselves about their chances of survival. Some favored trying to make their way south toward American positions. A number of men nursed swollen feet caused by the painful cuts suffered from the sharp coral.

Hemstock dug himself a small trench about a foot deep in which to sleep. He was armed with a twelve-inch knife that he found in the whaleboat. While the weapon probably would have offered little in the way of actual protection, it provided a feeling of comfort to the *Radford* sailor. During the night, Hemstock awoke to the sound of rustling in the nearby brush. He feared the worst after immediately jumping to the conclusion that the group had been discovered. Much to his relief it turned out to be another American sailor who had gone into some nearby underbrush to relieve himself.

Weisenberger remembered that the weather was good during their stay on the island. "On the warm side," he recalled of the temperatures. He picked out a spot below a tree to sleep. "I remember I woke up real early in the morning and there's a big bird standing there looking at me." Perhaps startled, the creature took off in short order. When he woke up for good later in the morning he saw no activity in area.

■ ■ ■ ■

Unknown to the stranded sailors, help was on the way in the form of two ships sent to search for them. Whether the mission was prompted by the reports of the *Nicholas* and *Radford* or from the American plane that sighted the boat flotilla is not known. The destroyers USS *Woodworth* and *Gwin* anchored at Tulagi after returning from the July 5 trip into Kula Gulf. Both ships had been part of the screening force that provided close cover for the transports landing troops at Rice Anchorage. The night had seen plenty of activity. The *Woodworth* assisted in the rescue of personnel from the torpedoed *Strong*, while the *Gwin* joined the *Radford* in exchanging fire with Japanese shore batteries. The ships were soon pressed into service for a rescue operation.

On orders from Admiral Turner, the two destroyers pulled out of Tulagi late in the morning of July 6 for a night sweep into Kula Gulf to hunt for *Helena* survivors. During the early afternoon hours, the *Woodworth* temporarily fell behind her companion due to mechanical problems.[14] She was back on station within a few hours. The two ships were soon plying the waters of Kula Gulf looking for survivors. A night-long search turned up no *Helena* men. "We swept the whole area with a fine-toothed comb," an officer of the *Gwin* later told an interviewer on the condition of anonymity. "We hunted all night long and could not see a thing."[15]

After spending much of the night focused on the mouth of Kula Gulf, the destroyers made a sweep of the northwest New Georgia coast to search for any survivors who might have landed there.[16] As with the *Nicholas* and *Radford* on the previous morning, the rescue ships could not stay long after daybreak due to the air threat. During the last sweep of the area, lookouts on the *Gwin* spotted something unusual on the beach in the morning light. Moving closer to investigate, they discovered that the dark fuzzy shape was a group of men.

■ ■ ■ ■

The survivors awoke and ate a scant breakfast that was the same as the evening meal the night before. They had posted lookouts on the beach in the faint hope that something, anything, would be sighted. About an hour after the morning meal, two mastheads suddenly appeared on the horizon. Although they did not know if the ships were friend or foe, some of the men rushed to the beach, wildly waving their arms. Flood feverishly blinked a message on his signal lamp. Spirits among the survivors waned when the two ships appeared to be moving back out to sea. Undaunted, the chief signalman kept working his lamp.

Cecil ordered several men to take one of the whaleboats to sea in the hopes of getting the ships' attention.[17] Before the men were able to get very far, the distant ships returned, and a signal light blinked on one, indicating they had seen the men on shore. "We thought, well here they come after us," said Weisenberger. "They kept on going and going and then all of a sudden they must have seen the signals that we were putting out." The survivors and their accompanying boat crews were jubilant. They survived sinking in battle, made a perilous journey across an enemy gulf, spent a night on an island without being found by the Japanese, and were about to be rescued. Hensler was as happy as anyone. "I think they knew where we were at," he said of the rescue ships. "They just came and got us."

At 7:45 a.m. the *Gwin* moved closer to shore to begin the rescue operation, while the *Woodworth* stood out to sea to provide cover. The men ashore quickly gathered on the beach. Using their boats and rafts, it took two trips for all of the men to make it out to the *Gwin*. The rescue operation was completed just before 8:30 a.m. when all eighty-eight men were safely aboard the destroyer. Cecil was the last to leave the island. The three whaleboats, though, were not saved. The boats, which had provided a safe haven for the daylong journey across Kula Gulf, were set on fire.

Weisenberger's feet, already cut up from the underwater coral, were in for another surprise when he boarded the *Gwin*. "When I got out there on that hot deck, it was really something barefooted I'll tell you," he recalled. "Hot steel decks with bare feet." But he did feel safe and secure once aboard, especially when he felt the destroyer speed up to begin the journey home. "We went down below and changed clothes." He then went looking for something to eat.

The *Gwin* sailors were cordial hosts. They converted the destroyer's wardroom to a medical station for those who needed attention. The ship's cooks had hot coffee and food ready for the hungry survivors. The trip south was uneventful and the *Gwin* pulled into Tulagi at 3:20 p.m.

12

Return

Just after 9 a.m. on July 6, lookouts aboard the *Honolulu* sighted Russell Island.[1] Savo Island and Guadalcanal soon loomed in the background. The remaining ships of Admiral Ainsworth's force had made it out of harm's way without incident. After leaving Kula Gulf he kept in contact with the *Nicholas* and *Radford* via T.B.S. radio until the distance became too great. By noon the flagship was securely anchored in Tulagi Harbor.

The admiral believed he had won a resounding victory over the Tokyo Express. In the weeks that followed he reviewed the action reports of the individual ships under his command trying to put together an accurate picture of the night action soon to be known as the Battle of Kula Gulf. Immediately after the conclusion of the battle, Ainsworth had sent a dispatch to his superiors providing a brief summary and stating that at least six Japanese ships had been sunk.

On August 1, Ainsworth submitted his formal action report on the battle. In estimating the damage inflicted on enemy ships, he openly addressed the need for accuracy. "The Task Force Commander has been well aware of the tendency to overestimate the damage inflicted upon the enemy, especially in actions at night," he reported. "However, in this action he feels that the individual ship reports will bear out the dispatch sent immediately after completion of the action to have been a very accurate, if not an underestimate of enemy losses." In spite of these reflections, the admiral did not reduce his initial estimate of Japanese ship losses. "To date there is no information available here which would indicate that this figure should be revised in any way except upward," he noted. In support of his claim that more enemy ships may have been lost than first thought, Ainsworth included with his report a before-and-after intelligence summary of Japanese ships reported to be in the Solomon Islands around the time of the battle. "Since there were a total of seventeen [Japanese] warships available on July 5, it is indicated that eight to ten [Japanese] warships are unaccounted for," the analysis concluded.[2]

The battle report was far from accurate. Short of the beached *Nagatsuki*, the only Japanese ship that Ainsworth's force actually sank was the *Niizuki*. Although the overestimations can be attributed to a host of issues, an over reliance on radar-controlled rapid gunfire, and the belief that such could deliver early fatal blows to enemy ships, is probably at the top of the list. The ever-present confusion associated with night sea combat was certainly a contributing factor.

In terms of the *Helena*'s sinking, the report offered no clear answers. "Just how the *Helena* was torpedoed is a matter of conjecture," Ainsworth concluded. In the admiral's defense, his report was written before he had the opportunity to fully digest Cecil's report, which had been delayed due to his belated rescue.

Like most American flag officers of the day, Ainsworth was ignorant of the true range and power of Japanese torpedoes. Information gleaned from a stray enemy torpedo recovered on Guadalcanal in early 1943 should have been a warning to American naval commanders as to the weapons power. However, the facts never made it to the front lines of the South Pacific. Having heard stories of the powerful torpedo himself, Cecil had shared his concern about long range gunfire with Ainsworth before the Kula Gulf battle to no avail.[3] It would be some time before American night fighting tactics changed.

In his action report, Ainsworth did acknowledge that the *Helena* had run out of flashless powder early in the battle, making her a prime target for torpedo aim. He did not, however, believe that the torpedoes were long range. "The fact that these torpedoes seemed to be running together like a team would substantiate a short range theory either from a destroyer or a submarine," he wrote. The report concluded that the torpedoes came from a lone destroyer that closed range early in the battle. "If one enemy destroyer broke off from their formation prior to our opening fire and had closed to within 4,000 yards of the cruiser formation by 2:00 a.m., this destroyer could have fired short range high speed torpedoes and scored hits on the *Helena*."

The Japanese were also optimistic about their success in the battle. Their claims, though, were not as extravagant as Ainsworth's. Upon returning to base the Japanese ships reported sinking two American cruisers and setting fire to one destroyer.[4]

■ ■ ■ ■

The lucky *Helena* men who had been plucked out of the water by the *Nicholas* and *Radford* were safely on their way back to Tulagi by mid morning. Both ships were crowded with hundreds of survivors. After spending time in the water, no one seemed to be complaining about the accommodations.

The medical staff on the *Nicholas* did their best to help the survivors. There were, however, two serious injuries. One man suffered a broken leg and had it reset during his stay on board. Another man, Fireman 1st Class Irvin Edwards died as a result of serious burns. He was most likely well below deck on the *Helena* in close vicinity to the torpedo hits. Most of the survivors only needed routine medical care. After a quick check for any wounds, the men had to have their eyes and noses cleaned of oil.

Robert Howe was one of the survivors aboard the *Nicholas*. A trip to the shower allowed him to remove most of the oil. Crewmen gave him a set of dry clothes and he went off to get a bite to eat. It soon occurred to him that the *Nicholas*'s sailors were now doing for them what the *Helena*'s men had done for *Wasp*'s sailors less than a year ago when the *Helena* had rescued a large number of the sunken carrier's survivors.[5]

Conditions on the *Radford* were more cramped as she was carrying a larger number of passengers than the *Nicholas*. The destroyer's crew worked hard to accommodate the hundreds of unexpected guests. Commander Romoser noted that, "all facilities [were] heavily taxed by sheer numbers." There did not, however, appear to be many serious injuries among the survivors. "In this number there were less than half a dozen serious casualties and probably none that will prove fatal," Romoser continued. "There were no burn cases and only about twenty-five had cuts or superficial wounds. The majority of survivors were covered with fuel oil and principally required treatment of the eyes."

Remmel Dudley was not one to complain about the conditions aboard the ship that rescued him. "They picked us up," he said of the *Radford*'s men. "That's all we cared about." Shortly after coming aboard the destroyer, the marine found himself standing on deck topside near the forward turrets. "Then the battle resumed, the firing commenced again," he said. "We were right under those 5-inch thirty-eight guns that the destroyers were firing. Those particular guns are very, very noisy."[6] Each shot meant a sharp, loud crack to his ears.

Knowing full well the dangers of having men topside while the guns were firing and the ship was moving at high speed, Romoser ordered the survivors to go below deck. Dudley followed the line of men below, perhaps leaving a trail of oil behind him. "We went down below in the crew's quarters where we were just standing around." Dudley remembered that the hatches of the compartment were closed and dogged down. It made him feel a bit uneasy. "For the first time I started thinking about what could happen to us. I thought, my god if this ship gets hit I have absolutely no way to get out of this place." When the battle subsided, he went for a hot cup of coffee. "They didn't feed us, but we had coffee," he recalled. The food would have to wait until the ship made port.

Walter Wendt and Cobden Hitchon were having trouble walking on the slippery deck of the *Radford*. "We couldn't stand up because the deck was so slippery from all the oil that was draining off us," he recalled. "We just went on our bellies like, you know, crawled on our hands and knees."[7] The pair made it to one of the 5-inch guns, but soon found it to be a precarious position when it started firing. "Every time this thing would go off it would almost knock you out." Wendt felt that the coat of oil in his ears saved his eardrums from being blown out. The two quickly found another place to congregate.[8]

Mason Miller was among the many survivors who felt ill from having swallowed fuel oil. He went below deck and sought out help for the gunk in his eyes. "I was covered with oil. They had done the best that they could do for us," he said of the *Radford*'s sailors. "They had wiped the oil out of our eyes and tried to clean some of it off of my face. But I had a load of it in my stomach, so I was not a very happy camper."[9] The young officer then just tried to stay out of the way. "I think I went down in the area of the wardroom and found a seat," he said. "Everybody that went down there messed everything up with oil." He noted with pleasure the increase in speed when the destroyer headed for home.

Gene Robinson did not go below deck right away. Remaining topside, he and a few others were content to lean against a bulkhead in the middle part of the ship. But it was not long after the *Radford* darted out for battle that he realized his precarious position. "Pretty soon we felt a couple of swishes going over our head," he recalled. The comfortable position that the group had selected was right under the torpedo tubes. "Well that was something different," he said.[10] Robinson decided to go below deck after the gunfire started, but returned topside once the destroyer started home. "We looked overhead and there's P-38's circling around us," he recalled. He was over taken by a feeling of great comfort. After clearing the oil out of his eyes, Robinson decided to try to get cleaned up. "The crew's shower was up in the bow of the destroyer," he recalled. "I tried to take a shower. The destroyer was bouncing up and down going over the waves." He soon found it to be a difficult task, as he seemed to be jolted against the bulkhead every time the ship hit a wave. Although not hurt, Robinson gave up.

The *Nicholas* led the *Radford* into Tulagi Harbor at 12:40 p.m. on July 6, completing a long but uneventful return voyage.[11] Although he hated to leave men behind, Captain McInerney was happy with the rescue work accomplished by his two destroyers. "Words are inadequate to express the actions of the *Nicholas* (together with the *Radford*) during the rescue of the *Helena* survivors in the pitch dark of night," he later wrote. "On three occasions, with survivors in the water alongside, the ships had to clear the area and engage enemy ships emerging from Kula Gulf. The bravery, courage, and efficiency under stress of the officers and men were in keeping with the highest traditions of the United States Naval Service."[12] Admiral Ainsworth was equally pleased with the operation, writing that the destroyer men were worthy of "the highest praise."

Immediately after entering Tulagi Harbor, the *Nicholas* pulled up alongside the *Honolulu*. Six heavy manila lines were used to secure the ships together and a plank was set up.[13] The injured sailors were the first survivors transferred to the light cruiser. Once they were safely moved, *Helena* sailors began to walk across in a steady stream. Many of the survivors were barefoot, but it did not slow down the procession. The transfer to the flagship took well over an hour to complete.

The topside of the *Radford* was jammed full of sailors as the destroyer slowly glided through the harbor. Many of survivors must have wanted to get a good look at surroundings they may have thought they would never see again. Robinson was one of the faces in the crowd. "We saw all the ships in the harbor," he recalled. "Their crews were lined up against the rails and they were waving at us and saluting." It made for somewhat of a festive sight. "That was a cheer that we'll never forget," Robinson said. "That just made you feel good." After anchoring for a short time, the *Radford* moved to the portside of the *St. Louis* to transfer the rest of the survivors.

■ ■ ■ ■

The first concrete information that the American public received of a naval battle in the Solomon Islands came with a navy communiqué released on July 6. A previous dispatch had hinted that a naval action was under way in the South Pacific, but provided no details. The July 6 report announced that an American task force had engaged Japanese surface units in Kula Gulf near New Georgia Island. The release noted that while detailed results of the action were not yet available, it was believed that both sides suffered damage.[14] The fate of the *Helena* was not yet revealed.

13
Adrift

The *Helena* survivors still adrift in Kula Gulf were not forgotten. The rescue operation was ongoing and not limited to ships. Two navy PB4Y Liberator bombers under the command of Lt. Cdr. William Moffett took off from Guadalcanal at first light on July 6 for the trip up the Slot. Arriving over Kula Gulf by mid-morning, the planes evidently saw no survivors during a pass over the southern and central portions of the area. It did not take long, however, for the airmen to spot the beached *Nagatsuki* along the Kolombangara coast.

Initially thinking that it was an American ship, the airmen quickly realized their error when anti-aircraft guns on the vessel sprang to life. Concluding that the ship was Japanese, the planes closed for an attack but were jumped by a flight of Japanese Zero fighters.[1] Breaking free of the fighters, the planes made a wide turn that put them back in the Slot. As a result of the move, the airmen apparently missed the remaining *Helena* survivors, but they did find a lone Japanese destroyer slowly limping north. Turning to attack, the bombers were again intercepted by Zeros. Moffett's plane was able to slip away, but his wingman was not as lucky. The second Liberator, piloted by Lt. j.g. Howard Nopper, took a beating. One crewman was killed, two others injured, and an engine was knocked out, but the bomber escaped and headed for home.[2]

By late morning a third navy Liberator arrived over Kula Gulf. Piloted by Lt. James Nolan, the plane left Guadalcanal at 9:30 a.m.[3] Nolan's plane was the one that spotted Captain Cecil's small flotilla sailing toward New Georgia and dipped its wings in acknowledgement. After concluding that the survivors were American, the pilot radioed a contact report with the boats' location and course. He then continued into Kula Gulf.

■ ■ ■ ■

While Cecil was leading his small fleet of boats to land, another group of *Helena* survivors remained at sea. The first daylight of July 6 brought new hope for those still in the water. The men had survived the night, but were in a precarious position in enemy waters. They hoped that the American commanders knew of their plight. Perhaps help would arrive soon, but the survivors' immediate concern was the need to stay alive.

The remnants of the *Helena*'s bow had miraculously stayed afloat. Perhaps a small pocket of trapped air was just enough to keep the hulk of steel from sinking during the night. However, it was slowly settling in the water and it was only a matter of time before it sank altogether.

Almost two hundred survivors were thought to be spread out near the bow. Many had stayed clear of it during the night, with some fearing it would become a target during the ongoing battles. With the battles over and the onset of daylight, many survivors were attracted to the bow. Using some dangling lifelines, a number of sailors climbed up the side and perched on the peak. A larger number clustered in the water below.

The general area was a motley assortment of wreckage, oil, and sailors. Some lucky survivors were on or around the life rafts. Others clung to small bits of wreckage or just floated freely in their life jackets. Off in the distance Kolombangara looked lush and inviting, but those familiar with the area knew that it was a hotbed of Japanese activity. For each man in the water, it was an individual fight for survival.

The closest that Gayle Gilbert had come to being rescued during the night was getting a hand on the net of one of the destroyers. After swimming away from the sinking *Helena*, he joined a small group of men clustered together in the water. Like most of them, he was covered with oil. A nearby sailor told him to take his shoes off. "So I took my shoes off," Gilbert said. "It was a dumb thing on my part, but I did it anyway."[4] It was a decision he later regretted.

When a destroyer approached the group, Gilbert swam toward it. "They had their nets down and I was grabbing one," he said. "I had a hand on the net." Just then he noticed another sailor who was violently ill, apparently from swallowing too much oil. Gilbert motioned for the other man to climb up first. But when the destroyer suddenly took off at high speed, both men were tossed back down into the water. Gilbert was caught in the violent churning water left in the wake of the speeding ship. "I thought I was going down to the bottom of the ocean," he recalled. "It sucked me right down and the only thing that brought me up was my kapok life jacket. God bless that thing." It was the only encounter that he had with a destroyer that night.

Gilbert eventually came across a raft. It was overcrowded, but he managed to squeeze aboard. "[It] had ropes around so that you could grab ahold," he remembered. "In the middle was a lattice work of wood. It was balsa wood all wrapped with canvas, painted, and the whole works." For the remainder of the night he alternated between spending time on the raft and in the water along the side.

After daybreak, Gilbert was able to see that his raft was not alone. Several others were in the immediate area. "I got over to another one that wasn't quite so crowded," he said. "I got on it. One foot was out in the ocean and the other foot in the inside." The raft was loaded with about ten or fifteen sailors, none of whom Gilbert knew. There did not seem to be any wounded aboard. Someone who looked to be in charge ordered all of the rafts to be tied together. "We just stayed out there in a group," Gilbert said. "The one guy in charge of the whole thing says we'll stay together. If we stay together like this the radar will pick us up, which we thought would happen." It did not. "The sun started shining and first thing you know I couldn't see darn a thing. I couldn't see anything because the oil." The *Helena*'s bow was barely visible in the distance through the film of oil in his eyes.

When Jim Layton left the *Helena* he never looked back. "I started swimming with everything I had to try to get away from the ship," he said. He heard stories about a sinking ship sucking sailors down with it and wanted to avoid that fate. He never actually saw the ship sink. "Like everyone else,

I was trying to get away from it."[5] He must have swum a good distance though, because he did not feel any suction from the sinking.

At some point in the night Layton ended up on an overcrowded raft. With no officer aboard, the men worked out a rotating system that allowed a limited number to stay inside the raft while the others clung to the side. There was one wounded sailor who stayed aboard. Neither of the two rescue destroyers came close to Layton's raft during the night. Two or three other rafts eventually joined up.

Bin Cochran was no more than a hundred yards away from the *Helena* when the ship took her final plunge. Starlight provided just enough illumination for him to see the vessel's final minutes. He soon realized that he was swimming in a pool of oil. As he struggled to put air into his life belt Cochran regretted his decision not to inflate it while still on the ship. Unable to fill the tube with air, he decided to swim toward distant voices. The men seemed to be doing some type of organized cheer to attract attention. Between the aborted inflating and swimming, he swallowed a fair amount of oil. By the time he reached a raft, Cochran was feeling ill and vomiting. As he began to pull himself aboard, he heard a voice yell out to make room for the sick man. Machinist's Mate 1st Class Lawrence Flanagan voluntarily slid into the water to make space. Flanagan eventually swam away and was rescued by a destroyer later in the night.[6]

From his position on the raft, Cochran was able to see the *Helena*'s bow floating in close proximity when a destroyer illuminated it with a searchlight. Once the light went out, he could not see anything. The men aboard the raft were optimistic that they would soon be rescued. However, when it did not immediately happen, fear began to set in. Cochran ordered the men to begin paddling in an attempt to keep away from Kolombangara. With the raft going nowhere, they soon abandoned the effort. To make more room in the raft, they put a small canister of supplies over the side attached by a small string of rope.

After almost two hours in the water, Cochran's raft and several others were approached by one of the rescue destroyers. His raft was off the starboard bow of the vessel, but the cargo nets were amidships. The arrangement put the men on several of the other rafts in a position to climb up the cargo nets first. To keep Cochran's raft from floating away, a sailor aboard the destroyer threw down a rope, which Cochran grabbed and held firmly to keep his raft in position. The destroyer then began to pick up speed to clear the area. After being hit in the head by the feet of a sailor still hanging onto the cargo net as the destroyer sped past, Cochran dove off the raft to clear the ship. Someone on the destroyer yelled out that they would return.

With the arrival of daylight, the mood on the raft dropped to a low point. The canister put over the side during the night was gone, leaving the men with no provisions. Cochran's eyes were burning from oil, and the bright sunlight made the pain worse. He tried to use water to clear out his eyes to no avail. Cochran and his raft mates knew that the chances of being rescued were not good.

■ ■ ■ ■

Near the bow of the ship was the most senior *Helena* officer still in the water, Lt. Cdr. John Chew, who had been aboard the vessel since her commissioning.[7] As an assistant gunnery officer, Chew was in charge of the anti-aircraft defenses.[8] While at his battle station aft of the bridge, he was thrown against an overhead by the concussion from the torpedo hits. However, he was saved from injury by his steel helmet. Chew went overboard after helping to toss life rafts over the side from the forecastle. "After going into the water I swam away from the ship and by calling out, gradually collected a group of men, numbering fifty to seventy-five."[9] The group was loosely organized at best. Only a few men in the cluster seemed to be wounded, but others were in shock from the battle and the sinking. Like many of the *Helena* survivors, Chew was immersed in fuel oil, and his well-manicured moustache was covered with a thick coat. Every time he took a breath, it was full of an oily stench.[10] The constant movement in the sea, the smell, and the involuntary swallowing of oil was nauseating.

From his position in the water, Chew saw the *Helena* sink about fifteen minutes after he left the ship. A night rescue, however, was not in the offing. He tried to signal one of destroyers with his flashlight, but to no avail. "Later our destroyers were seen in the area, but at no time were they close enough to recover any of our group," he added. With no life rafts in the immediate area, the group tried to stay together as best possible. The men occasionally sang songs together in an effort to keep their spirits up. Some survivors yelled out into the night in the faint hopes of attracting rescuers.

The survivor group contained a number of officers, including Lt. Cdr. Warren Boles and Marine Maj. Bernard Kelly. Boles was with a cluster of about fifteen men who were staying afloat by clinging to small bits of wreckage. Kelly, who was swimming with an inflated life belt, had spent a number of hours rounding up other survivors in the immediate area.[11] The son of a Chicago policeman, Kelly was the leader of the *Helena*'s forty-one member Marine detachment and had been aboard the vessel since just before Pearl Harbor.

It proved difficult to keep the fragmented cluster of survivors together around Chew. With increasing frequency men drifted away. Some would be brought back to safety, while others were never seen again. "Lieutenant Commander Boles, time and time again, swam away from the group and brought back those who were helpless or had drifted off," Chew later wrote.

The *Helena*'s chaplain, Lieutenant John Wheaton was near Boles and Kelly. The clergyman had narrowly escaped from the flooding sickbay after the concussion of the first torpedo left him stunned and shocked. A buoy helped keep the chaplain afloat. "We all took turns during the night holding him up," Kelly remembered.[12] With the help of others the chaplain survived the night. "We did a lot of tall praying," Wheaton later said.[13]

Daylight allowed some members of the group to see the *Helena*'s bow off in the distance. Boles was able to make it out and decided to swim for it with another sailor. As he moved closer he was eventually able to clearly see the big white number fifty on the grey side. En route the pair came across a crate of potatoes and a floating can of tomato juice, which they grabbed. Boles estimated there were about a one hundred men clustered on or around the bow.[14] They welcomed the food he brought aboard. When another survivor came across a crate of tomatoes, it was eagerly pulled aboard only to find that the vegetables were spoiled.[15]

Through oil-smeared eyes, Boles could faintly make out Kolombangara in the distance. Some of the sailors thought that the island was close enough to reach with a swim. Joining a small group of others, Boles started out toward the island.

John Chew also decided to go toward the bow. Astonished to find the hulk still afloat, he reasoned that it could attract the attention of a rescue plane.[16] His eyes were now burning from the oil, but he could see enough to make his way around. When he arrived at the bow he was too exhausted to even try to join those on top. He simply grabbed of a piece of dangling chain and decided to rest.

■ ■ ■ ■

With the morning clouds beginning to scatter, Nolan brought his Liberator down to about fifty feet, allowing his crew to scan the water for survivors. The sea was calm. In a position estimated to be eight miles east of Waugh Rock, Noland spotted *Helena*'s bow. He quickly made a sketch of what he saw: men clustered on and around a large floating hulk of metal. Noticing the survivors had no life rafts, Noland decided to drop the few rafts he had aboard the Liberator. He moved the plane to a position just upwind of the bow and ordered one of the rafts be dropped into the sea below. He thought that it would drift to the position of the survivors.

Continuing the flight, the Liberator's crew took note of a large oil slick that was stretching to the northwest. There were some empty life rafts and an assortment of wreckage in close proximity. The plane next came across a cluster of survivors in life vests, perhaps ten miles northwest of the bow. Crossing near the men, the plane dropped another life raft, which inflated after hitting the water. Nolan then came across an empty whaleboat, with some empty life rafts and an assortment of wreckage nearby. He did not know whether the boat and rafts were American or Japanese.

Circling back to the *Helena*'s bow, the Liberator dropped its last two rafts. Nolan had already radioed word of the men in the water back to Guadalcanal. Ordered to return to base, Nolan and his crew had done all that they could for the survivors below. It may have not seemed like much at the time, but seeing a friendly plane dropping life rafts was a great help to the weary *Helena* sailors. On his way back to Guadalcanal, Nolan spied a glimpse of the *Gwin* and *Woodworth*.[17] The two destroyers would find Cecil's group on the beach, but not the others still afloat in Kula Gulf.

Of the three life rafts dropped near the bow, only two survived. The third sank. The rafts were relatively small in size, not like the larger versions that had been on *Helena*. Chew organized the men as best possible around the two inflated life rafts. "Two wounded men were placed in the boats and men were gradually collected until about twenty-five surrounded each boat," he later wrote. "Chaplain Wheaton was embarked in my boat; Lt. j.g. John Anderson with the two wounded men was placed in charge of the second boat." Boles had been swimming toward Kolombangara when the Liberator overflew the area, but decided to turn back. He ended up with a place around one of the rafts.

During the daylight hours of July 6, there seemed to be no shortage of planes in the sky above Kula Gulf. "Nothing but planes, both friendly and enemy, were sighted," Chew recalled. "Zeros passed close aboard, but we were not strafed." All of the survivors remembered the close overfly by the enemy planes.

Layton was not in the immediate vicinity of the bow when the enemy Zeros arrived. "There were three Japanese planes," he said. He remembered that they appeared at the same time and flew low as if to make a strafing run. "They circled over us two or three times and then they left. They pulled out and left and never opened up."

Although his eyes were still giving him problems because of the oil, Gilbert had no trouble seeing a single enemy plane drop low near his raft. "He was down that low and that close to us. A lot of the guys got up and waved." Gilbert was not one of them. He chose to jump into the water as a precaution. The plane did not attack, but let loose a few machine gun rounds as it headed away toward Kolombangara. "And that was it," Gilbert recalled. "The good lord was looking after me."

When two Zeros approached his raft, Cochran was certain it meant trouble. "I was sure it was a strafing run," he later wrote. "I yelled for everybody on the raft to scatter, and we hit the water swimming in all directions." Cochran soon found that he was not under attack. He noticed that men on a nearby raft had not abandoned ship, but rather were standing up and waving. Perhaps the Japanese pilots could not determine if the oil covered faces were friend or foe.

When the planes left the area, Cochran swam back to a raft. With several rafts in close proximity, and many men in the water to avoid the Zeros, it turned out to be a different raft than the one he had left. Cochran was one of thirteen men to jump onto the new raft. On board were two junior officers that he knew, Lt. Sam Hollingsworth and Ensign Lee Spaulding.

As the day turned to afternoon Chew began to have second thoughts about staying around the bow. Originally thinking it was a safe haven, he now began to worry it might attract the attention of the Japanese and decided it was time to leave.[18] He reckoned that Kolombangara was less than ten miles away. Although well aware that the island was occupied by the Japanese, he thought it offered the only real hope for rescue. The number of men in Chew's group was now down to about fifty. The two rafts were tied together and men pushed away from the bow to begin the trip. They were, however, moving against the current; it was a journey to nowhere. "Tuesday evening an attempt was made to reach Kolombangara, but no headway could be made in that direction," Chew later wrote. With no provisions and not sure what to do next, the men remained adrift in the gulf.

■ ■ ■ ■

Route of *Helena* Survivors
July 6–8, 1943

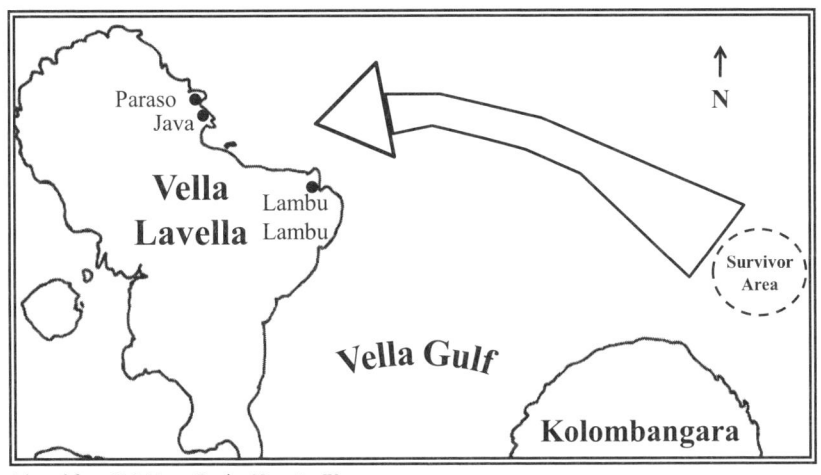

Adapted from U.S. Navy, *Combat Narrative IX*.

The prevailing wind and ocean currents were slowly pushing the *Helena* survivors out of Kula Gulf. Drifting north and west the men were heading toward the Slot, even further into Japanese territory. By the late afternoon of July 6, most of the remaining survivors were either on or around a raft. The attempts to keep groups of rafts together, however, began to falter.

Such was the case with Cochran's raft. "The rafts became more and more scattered and finally drifted completely out of sight of each other," he later wrote. When a raft later drifted into sight, he nervously wondered if it was full of American or Japanese. The end of July 6 certainly must have brought the realization to many of the survivors that they were not going to make landfall on Kolombangara.

As the time at sea lengthened and the hope for rescue faded, so did the will of some of the men to survive. Whether by choice or through delirium, some survivors simply did not make it. One was the *Helena*'s popular bandleader, John Simpson. As a bugler, Gilbert frequently hung around with the band members. He saw Simpson remove his life jacket and jump off a raft on the first day at sea. "He just took it off and then he was gone," he remembered. "I wouldn't believe that he would do that. I wasn't about to give in, but he just [gave] in and just let it go." Simpson was never seen again. "It was so sad to see him do that," Gilbert concluded.

■ ■ ■ ■

Adrift on his original raft, Layton's hope for a rescue ship was starting to fade. "I don't remember having a lot of fear on the raft and I don't know why not," he later recalled. "I don't remember anyone else displaying a lot of fear. Maybe we more or less accepted what was happening." In the interim, he just had to pass the time. "There isn't much you can do," he said. The men had no food. "There were some emergency supplies, but [when] the raft fell in the water it fell upside down." At least one man tried unsuccessfully to swim underwater to fetch the provisions. All that Layton and his raft mates could do was to hope for the best.

Water partially filled up the inside of Cochran's raft, but it did not seem to be in danger of sinking. He and his raft mates just sat in silence as the hours drifted past. There was no good way for them to relax. "The moment a man would doze, he would fall forward into the water and be awakened," he later wrote. "There was a constant noise of someone flopping over from the waist, hitting the water, reviving, and straightening back up." Cochran finally put his arm in front of the man next to him to prevent the sailor from slumping into the water. The spirits of many *Helena* survivors fell with the setting sun.

Morning brought new hope. The *Helena* survivors had made it through another night. A full day had now passed since the cruiser sank, and the men would spend July 7 entirely at sea. Gilbert never left his raft. "We stayed together that night and nothing happened," he recalled. "The next day we started splitting up and I ended up with one life raft." Chief Water Tender Ken Green was in charge of the raft, which contained about a dozen men. There was no need to shift men on and off the new raft. "I happened to be on a life raft where I could straddle the raft all the way," Gilbert added. "I don't remember there being any rotation at all."

Gilbert was lucky to be on a raft that had some supplies. The provisions were carefully rationed. "We had a cup of water that day and some malted milk tablets and some biscuits. The chief took care of all that; he made sure that everybody got some." In addition to having supplies aboard, the new raft was equipped with a set of paddles. "So we started paddling with the darn thing[s]," Gilbert said. The effort did not seem to be substantially helping the movement of the raft. "But we paddled anyway, just to pass off the time."

Having previously studied charts of the area, Chew knew that Vella Lavella was the next island up the Slot from Kolombangara. "It was decided to attempt to make Vella Lavella as the wind and sea were setting in towards that island, and I had read that the natives were friendly," he later reported. He also hoped that there were less Japanese on Vella Lavella than some of the other area islands.

The men used good old American ingenuity to help Chew's raft along. Some of the men tied together two paddles in the form of a cross and then took off their shirts to create a sail. While it must have looked like an odd assemblage, the survivors welcomed anything to get the raft closer to land. In the end, however, it was unclear if the improvised sail actually helped the raft move any faster. A case of potatoes floating near the raft was quickly corralled and enjoyed by the sailors. The surprise provisions helped to quench hunger and thirst. The raft also lost some men during the course of the day. "One man died in my boat and a few others swam away and were not seen again," Chew later wrote. During the previous night a seriously wounded man with two broken arms and two broken legs died. The survivors conducted a makeshift burial at sea that included a prayer and removing the deceased sailor's life jacket.[19]

Although no longer tied together, Chew's raft was still traveling in close proximity to the one under the command of Anderson. As July 7 faded into night, the two rafts continued into the Slot, heading in the general direction of Vella Lavella. "Our course was continued but unfortunately more men were lost having strayed from the boat and either gone to sleep or just given up," Chew wrote of the time. "Their identity was unknown as all of us were covered with oil and suffering from periods of exhaustion and mental relapse." Seaman 1st Class Jose Mora and Coxswain Paul Foster were later identified as two who were lost from the raft. Mora had told a raft mate that he did not think that he would be able to continue. When morning came, he was gone. Foster suddenly announced that he was going below deck, took off his life jacket, and disappeared into the sea. It happened so fast that none of the other men were able to intervene.[20] There was no alternative but for Chew and Anderson to press forward.

■ ■ ■ ■

Initially around one of Chew's rafts, Kelly fell asleep during the second night at sea and drifted away. The next morning he woke up alone. He started to swim but soon stopped after realizing that he was going against the current. Kelly's life belt provided enough buoyancy to keep him upright, but he could not see or hear any other survivors. He shouted out, but did not get a reply. Shortly after dawn, he felt something hit his foot. "Looking down I saw two sharks, each of them, however, only about four feet long," he said of the incident. "I kicked them a couple of times and they went away."[21] He later reasoned that the oil on his skin was not an appetizing target for the sharks.

After drifting alone for several hours, Kelly saw a raft in the distance. When he yelled for help two men swam out and brought him back. It was Anderson's raft. As the senior officer present, Kelly took charge and implemented a rotating system so that every non-injured man could spend some time in the raft. Sailors were also assigned one-hour watches.[22]

■ ■ ■ ■

The conditions at sea were nothing less than brutal for the survivors. Exhaustion was coupled with meager or no rations and no shelter from the elements. The hot tropical sun beat down on the men during the day. "As I can recall it was sunny all the way," Gilbert said of his time on the raft. "Of course we were pretty suntanned anyway from being out there all that time." After dark the temperatures plummeted. "At night I was freezing," Gilbert continued. "You know it was a glory just to wet your pants to warm your legs up." Each night brought renewed hope that a rescue destroyer would appear. After being adrift for two days, hope was about all that the *Helena*'s survivors had left.

14

The Island

When the periscope of the American submarine *Grampus* poked above the ocean's surface on October 13, 1942, Cdr. John R. Craig found himself staring at a Japanese destroyer. The submarine was off the northwest coast of Vella Lavella in the Central Solomons. The island was about fifteen miles northwest of Kolombangara, separated by Vella Gulf. The submarine had pulled out of Brisbane, Australia, about a week earlier to conduct her fourth war patrol. Aboard was a group of four coastwatchers, two of which were to be stationed on Vella Lavella.

Comprising British, Australian, and New Zealand servicemen, the coastwatchers lived a meager existence on various islands of the Solomons chain. From their jungle hideouts, they secretly reported the movements of Japanese planes and ships. Often delivered in a timely manner, the intelligence was invaluable to the war effort in the South Pacific. Coastwatchers often worked closely with local natives, many of whom despised the Japanese, to create a network of lookout posts on a particular island.[1]

By forming a new lookout station on Vella Lavella, Sub Lts. Henry Josselyn and John Keenan would be able to keep a watchful eye on a portion of the Slot. A native of England, Josselyn had spent time in Africa, before coming over to the South Pacific. He was on Tulagi prior to the Japanese occupation and returned to the region after the American invasion of Guadalcanal to assist in the offensive.[2] After the visit to Vella Lavella, the *Grampus* was to drop the two other men off on Choiseul Island directly across the Slot.

After first sighting the Japanese destroyer, Craig felt that the circumstances were favorable for an attack. As he silently stalked his prey, however, the conditions changed. Darkness started to set in, making it difficult to see the target. With the specter of uncharted reefs in the immediate area making the possibility of an attack even less favorable, Craig took his submarine deep. Soundings soon indicated that the enemy destroyer was moving away. While on the deep submerge Craig met with Josselyn and Keenan to discuss the situation. "If the destroyer previously stalked had landed personnel, they could hardly have come south to our proposed landing place by the time we landed," Craig later wrote. "To delay the landing would jeopardize our chances of success even more."[3] The result of the conference was that the landing of the coastwatchers would take place as planned.

The *Grampus* rose to the surface during the early morning hours of October 14 and slowly began moving into position off the coast of Vella Lavella. At 1:42 a.m. Josselyn and Keenan left the submarine in a collapsible canoe and two small rubber boats for the three-quarters-of-a-mile trip to shore. Among the coastwatchers' supplies were three months worth of food, some arms, and a radio.[4] The small flotilla did not get far when one of the rafts sprung a leak. It kept Josselyn busy for the remainder of the trip, trying to keep the raft afloat while Keenan continued to paddle toward shore. The pair finally made it to land just before dawn. Hurriedly moving their boats and supplies ashore, the two exhausted men found a good hiding place and fell asleep.

The coastwatchers found a place to set up camp on the edge of the jungle near an abandoned plantation. They got the radio up and running about a week later, and made their first communication with Guadalcanal on October 22.[5] Josselyn and Keenan soon made contact with a native chief from a local village, which turned out to be friendly. The coastwatchers learned from the locals that the Japanese had just landed a small party on the island, perhaps from the same destroyer that the *Grampus* had hovered near. They also learned that a minister was on the island.

Reverend Archie Silvester had arrived on Vella Lavella before the war started. The Methodist minister from New Zealand had set up a missionary camp on the far southern portion of the island to teach the natives Christianity. After the attack on Pearl Harbor, Silvester and a nurse decided to stay put after other workers were evacuated.[6] By the end of 1942, the nurse was ordered out and Silvester remained on his own. The minister had a loyal cadre of friendly natives who offered protection and acted as scouts. Silvester and his scouts soon became part of the coastwatching mission. Josselyn, Silvester, and the fate of a large group of *Helena* survivors would soon become dangerously intertwined.

■ ■ ■ ■

Sunrise of July 8 marked the beginning of the third day at sea for the remaining *Helena* survivors. The morning hours found the scattered clusters of rafts heading across the top of Vella Gulf and toward the island of Vella Lavella. Most of the survivors were able to see the distant land later in the day, but were unsure if the ocean current would carry the rafts to the island or past it. Many survivors concluded that the unknown island offered the last possible hope for survival. Everyone, it seemed, wanted to somehow make it to the island.

By this time Bin Cochran arrived at the harsh conclusion that rescue ships were probably not going to find the remaining survivors. He wondered what would happen next. His last letter from home had brought the news that he now had a baby sister, born in early June. "My thoughts often went to home and this little girl, and I wondered if I would get to see her," he later wrote.[7] Lee Spaulding was one of many aboard the raft who began to hallucinate, most likely from extreme fatigue. He jumped out of the raft under the belief that he was heading toward a bunk. Cochran and others quickly pulled him back aboard. Some men were too fatigued to help.

A day earlier the men on Cochran's raft implemented a rotating system to paddle. Using four paddles the men took turns trying to coordinate the effort. When the morning light brought the welcome sight of distant land, the paddling continued in earnest. As exhaustion mounted, however, the number of able volunteers slowly dwindled. Eventually only Cochran and one other man were still able to paddle. When the other sailor could no longer continue, Cochran gave up. To his relief the current seemed to be carrying the raft directly toward the island.

With the land getting closer, Sam Hollingsworth made an unusual statement to Cochran. "Bin, we've got some men here who badly need medical attention. As soon as we get ashore we want to get them to a doctor as soon as possible," Hollingsworth said.[8] Cochran agreed, knowing full well that his raft mate was probably hallucinating.

As the raft neared the island, a few men mustered up the strength to resume paddling. The determined effort yielded results when the bottom of the raft soon dragged on something solid. Spaulding was straddling the side of the raft when his foot suddenly hit a coral reef.[9] It was close enough to land that the men were able to wade ashore. The name of the island was unknown and it was probably Japanese occupied, but it was solid land. "Whatever lay ahead, we had made it," Cochran later recalled of the moment.

Gazing out from his raft at distant Vella Lavella in the early morning daylight, John Chew estimated that the island was about two miles away. In reality, it was probably much farther.[10] Warren Boles was among those on the raft who were concerned that the current would push them past the island. Chew felt if a swimmer could reach the island, then perhaps friendly natives could be found to help the rest of the men. Chew asked for volunteers. Warren Boles and Boatswain's Mate 2nd Class Ted Blahnik agreed to join him. The trio set out during the morning hours for the long swim. Those who stayed behind diligently paddled in the hopes of getting the raft to land.

By all accounts it was a long and arduous journey. Suffering from severe fatigue, almost no food, and little sleep, the swimmers became disorientated. The three were soon separated. Chew discarded his waterlogged life jacket, but kept his inflatable belt. He later felt that he spent some of the time swimming in the wrong direction or swimming underwater. Slipping in and out of consciousness, Blahnik thought he heard a female voice calling him over for a Coke. Chew had a similar experience, believing that he was meeting someone who would be taking him to a cocktail party.[11]

After swimming almost the whole day, all three men eventually made it to the island. Finally coming near land, Chew suddenly spotted a canoe with two natives heading directly toward him. When it pulled up next to him, one of the natives asked if he was American. After hearing that he was, a native examined his dog tags and then pulled Chew aboard for the short trip to the beach. The natives found Chew's raft and brought the remaining sailors to land. Blahnik was also picked up. Boles reached land on his own.[12]

Late in the day on July 7, the men on Gayle Gilbert's raft were able to see something on the distant horizon. Though they thought it was clouds, the shape of an island slowly materialized. "We tried to stay away from it," Gilbert said. "We [didn't] know what island it was." Some of the men were fearful of landing on a Japanese-held island, but the current was carrying the raft directly to the beach. During the night the raft crossed over some coral. "You could actually see the coral there; it was real sharp," Gilbert recalled. "At that time I did see a little shark. He was a little small thing, the only shark I ever seen in the whole area."[13]

By morning the island was much closer and in clear view. A canoe suddenly appeared a short time later, heading directly toward the raft. Gilbert could make out that it was homemade and had been whittled out of a log. The men inside were clearly natives, not Japanese. Eventually moving close to the raft, one of the natives motioned for the men to follow him. The sailors did not know if the natives were truly friends or if it was a Japanese trap.

Ken Green had somehow managed to bring a pistol off the *Helena*. He volunteered to go with the natives back to the island. "I'll go in and see what's going on," he told the rest of the men. "If you hear a lot of shots, you guys keep paddling and getting away from this island."[14] The others waited with trepidation for the sound of gunfire, but none came. Instead more canoes came out from the island and natives started hauling the weary sailors to land. "I think they had to make two or three trips to get us all in because they didn't have that much room," Gilbert recalled. "I was the last one off." With the raft now almost to the beach, the canoe ride spared the *Helena* men from walking across razor sharp coral. As a final move the natives pulled the raft ashore. Gilbert did not notice any other rafts or survivors in the immediate area.

Not having any paddles, the ocean current provided the only real movement for Jim Layton's raft. "We could see the island, but we didn't know what it was," he recalled. One sailor from the navigation department thought the island was Vella Lavella, but that did not mean much to the other men who were not familiar with the area. They were going to the island whether they wanted to or not. "No matter what you did, tried to do with the raft, you still went with the current," Layton said.[15] The raft drifted until it reached a coral reef just short of land. With most of the survivors lacking shoes, it was a painful experience walking across the sharp coral to the beach.

It was an arduous final night at sea for the men on Bernard Kelly's raft. Suffering from extreme exhaustion, hunger, and thirst, many of the sailors were on their last legs. It was a common occurrence for men to lose their grip and drift away during the evening hours. Marine Ken Hiatt pulled many back to safety, but he could not save everyone. Kelly estimated that the raft lost ten men during the night.[16] With land in sight the men used whatever strength they had left the next day to paddle and push the boat toward the island. Late in the day, the raft finally ran aground on a coral reef just short of land. In a move that he now regretted, Kelly had taken off his shoes before leaving *Helena*. Although he now had to endure a painful walk across coral to the beach, he had survived the long ordeal in the water.

■ ■ ■ ■

By the middle of 1943, the coastwatching operation on Vella Lavella was working like a finely oiled machine, with Josselyn and Silvester working closely with the natives. All of the native chiefs had agreed to lend help to the effort. A network of fourteen lookout points were established along the coast and manned by natives in shifts. Keenan left the island for Bougainville and was replaced by Australian Sub Lt. Robert Firth. The movement of Japanese ships, planes, and anything else that seemed unusual was immediately reported to Guadalcanal. In the course of operations the group also rescued a few downed Allied airmen.

The number of Japanese on the island was growing and so were their activities. The Japanese had established a base on the northwest coast of the island at Iringila. Not only was the number of enemy foot patrols on the rise, but so was barge activity along the coastal regions. The coastwatchers regularly reported enemy barge positions to their headquarters, which often resulted in attacks by American aircraft.[17]

Earlier that year Josselyn and Firth had moved to a more secure interior hideout, near the village of Toupalando. The Japanese, apparently, had never learned of the coastwatchers' presence on the island.[18] The natives were not as lucky as the coastwatchers. Japanese destroyers bombarded the coastal villages, in what may have been an act of retribution for the mounting barge losses.[19] The episode caused the natives to abandon the villages for the interior jungle, bringing with them a great hatred for the Japanese.

The first sign of unusual activity on Vella Lavella arrived at the coastwatchers' hideout in the form of a messenger on the afternoon of July 8, 1943. The native reported to Firth that many Americans were arriving on the island and produced a set of American dog tags as proof. Suspicious that it could be a Japanese trick, Firth decided to do some further investigating. He radioed down to Guadalcanal, relaying the name and serial number on the dog tags. About an hour later he received a reply that it belonged to a sailor from the American cruiser *Helena* that sank a few days ago in Kula Gulf.[20] Firth now knew that it was not a Japanese trick and notified Josselyn as to what was happening.

Not knowing how many survivors were already ashore and how many more might be coming, Josselyn put in motion a plan to help. A messenger was immediately sent off to the native chief of the coastal area where the survivors were coming ashore. He was asked to get the men ashore as quickly as possible and to provide for their safety, shelter, and food. Time was of extreme importance, lest the Japanese find out what was happening. A second messenger was dispatched to make contact with Reverend Silvester.

The *Helena* survivors were coming ashore in scattered places along the northeast coast of the island. The ocean current had carried the men into the Slot and across the entrance, but not into Vella Gulf. The men were making landfall in a roughly ten-mile stretch of coast from Lambu Lambu Cove northwest to Paraso Bay.

Josselyn directed Firth to stay behind at the hideout, while he traveled east to direct the effort of saving survivors in the Paraso Bay area. Staying behind to assist Firth was Lieutenant Eli Ciunguin, a downed American aviator who was himself awaiting rescue. Josselyn directed Silvester to take charge of the men coming ashore near Lambu Lambu Cove. Josselyn,

Silvester, and Firth kept in contact with walkie-talkies. None of them knew the number or condition of the *Helena* survivors.

■ ■ ■ ■

Arriving ashore late in the day, the men from Gilbert's raft slept near the beach for the night. The next morning he awoke to see the natives fishing in the ocean off the beach. The islanders soon warned that it was time to go. Whether they had been somehow notified that a Japanese patrol was on the way is unclear. What was very clear was that there was no time to waste. As the group moved out Gilbert wondered what had happened to the raft. "I don't know what they did with it," he said, assuming the natives disposed of it. "They probably chopped it up and used it for something."

Marching quickly, the group left the beach area and went up a nearby hill. Moving into the interior of the island, they came across a small church that served as a stopping point. The natives provided some provisions for the break. "We hit the church and that's where we ate our dinner. They had fresh water there," he remembered. Gilbert had forgotten how good it tasted.

The group was soon on the move again, having increased in number as more survivors washed up on shore. The men passed near a small village and were able to catch a brief glimpse of some native women. The route seemed to have both highs and lows. "We walked on up, quite a ways up and then we dropped down a ways." Gilbert recalled. "We dropped down into an area that had sulfur there and I would say at one time it was an active volcano. You could smell the sulfur." At one point a Japanese plane flew almost directly overhead forcing the marchers into the brush. The walk resumed up the side of a small hill.

At the top of the hill was a small lean-to, which marked the end of the journey for the day. Gilbert was one of the lucky ones to get a space under the structure for the night. He shared a woven mat with another sailor. "Something like a blanket," he remembered. Made of leaves it provided warmth and comfort when the evening temperatures dipped. It was his first night spent on dry land in several weeks.

At the time of making landfall, the men in Layton's raft did not seem to be in bad shape like many of the other survivors. "We were all in amazingly good physical condition," he recalled. "I don't know why we should have been, but we were." Pulling the raft with them out of the water, the weary survivors could only think of sleep. The small group moved into a brush area just off the beach, which appeared to be well hidden. The men discussed the idea of posting a guard, but no one actually stood watch.[21] The sailors quickly collapsed and slept through the night.

A flight of Japanese Zeros woke the men up early the next morning. One of the first problems that the survivors had to address was footwear. "None of us had shoes," Layton remembered. "I cut that life belt up [and] wrapped it around my feet. And the ones [who] didn't have a belt on cut their kapok and wrapped it around their feet." It was rudimentary footwear at best, but it seemed to suffice.

The men were still working on their makeshift shoes when natives suddenly appeared. "We didn't know it [but] we were surrounded by natives," Layton said. The individual who appeared to be in charge asked, "American or Jap? American or Jap?" When someone in the group said that they were American, the lead islander smiled and began to shake the hands of the *Helena* men. "We had to shake hands with each native," Layton added. The men later found out that only the lead native spoke English.

When he motioned for the Americans to follow him into the jungle, some of the survivors became apprehensive. The sailors knew that the natives were not Japanese, but did not know on which side their loyalties lay. "Some of [the men] were against following because they didn't know what was going to happen," Layton said. "Their theory was we don't know who they are; we don't know where they're taking us. You couldn't argue that point." Layton, however, was among those in favor of going with the natives. He was willing to take the chance because he knew that the group could not stay where they were without eventually being spotted by the enemy. Layton's group won out and they all disappeared with the natives into the jungle.

After arriving on the beach, several of the men in Cochran's group worked together to pull their raft ashore. With everyone safely on dry land the attention turned to sleep. "Every individual looked for a dry spot to get precious sleep that had been impossible for three to four days," Cochran later recalled. He soon found a small patch of tall grass that offered some protection and appeared to be just high enough above sea level so that he would not get wet. He quickly collapsed and fell asleep.

The sound of voices woke Cochran early the next morning. He did not know where he was other than on an island somewhere in the Solomon chain. "I noticed that we had landed at the mouth of a little shallow bay, no more than a hundred yards deep and thirty yards wide," he later wrote. A few men from his raft were frolicking around in the shallow water. Given that there was no gunfire, it appeared there were no Japanese in the immediate area.

Looking over to the other side of the bay, Cochran noticed several men talking with a young native boy. He thought the islander was about twelve years old. Joining the group, Cochran soon found that the boy could not speak English but was trying to communicate. The boy pointed in one direction and said, "Japs." He then pointed to the opposite side of the island and said, "Mericans." The group of *Helena* sailors had no problem figuring out what it meant. They all pointed toward the "Mericans" side of the island.[22] The boy motioned for the men to follow him in that direction. "Then we started single file following the boy along a path that paralleled the beach, but which was mostly in the trees," Cochran continued. "The thirteen of us didn't have any trouble keeping each other in sight." The men later learned that it was a widely used trail. In addition to the natives, the path was also used by Japanese patrols and downed airmen. "Luckily, this day the trail was ours to use," Cochran recalled.

Boles arrived ashore at an isolated beach. While still swimming at sea, he thought that he saw an area where other survivors were landing. But as he looked in different directions, he was unable to see anyone. Finding a coconut, he used his knife to break it open so that he could drink the milk and eat the meat. Moving to an area just off the beach he slept for the night. The next morning he entered an abandoned native village and stayed for the remainder of the day.

When Chew arrived ashore he immediately noticed that he was not alone as there were other rafts and numerous men from the *Helena* in close proximity. Chew thankfully drank some coconut milk from a shell that a native offered. It was the officer's first nourishment in days. He then dipped into some nearby fresh water in an attempt to clean off some oil. When it came time to leave the beach area, however, Chew found that his legs could not support him. Days in the water had made him too weak to walk. Carried by natives in a rudimentary litter, the group headed inland. Like the rest of the *Helena* men, Chew was on his way into the jungle. Where he was going, however, he did not know.

15

Hideouts

In the span of only a few short days, the *Helena* men survived the sinking of their ship and an ordeal at sea. They were now on an island, the name of which was unknown to many. The survivors were being helped by friendly natives, but only a few spoke broken English. Although none of the Americans actually saw any Japanese, most of the *Helena* men knew that they were well behind the front lines and thus in great danger.

■ ■ ■ ■

It was a difficult trek through the jungle for the men of John Chew's group. Those carried in litters were fine, but the others trudged through hard conditions. The journey included crossing through a swampy area where some of the men sank to their knees before navigating a rough path up the side of a small mountain. The group eventually arrived at their destination: a secret, well-hidden house in the jungle.

To Chew the house looked like a summer vacation home on the East Coast.[1] It was, however, no villa. The house belonged to Chinese trader Sam Chung and was located about two and a half miles inland from Lambu Lambu. Chung went into hiding after the Japanese landed on the island and lived in the house with his small family. The isolated structure and grounds were soon transformed into an encampment for what would become a large group of *Helena* survivors.

The house was situated on the top of a hill and surrounded with a thick jungle growth. Many of the trees were more than a hundred feet tall and had large leaves. The vegetation blocked out much of the sun and protected the hideout from planes. There were only two narrow clearings in the growth where the survivors could look directly out at the sea. It was a restricted view at best. Come nightfall the jungle was completely dark and echoed with the strange sounds of unknown animals.

Jim Layton and Bin Cochran eventually arrived at Chung's house, too. "When the natives picked us up we kind of marched all that day, marched through the jungle and sometimes in the swamps," Layton said. "We ended up on the top of a tall hill or a small mountain, which ever you want to call it."[2] It was a meeting point for all of the survivors in the area.

As he walked through the jungle, Cochran hoped he would be meeting up with some Marine raiders who would take him off the island. Unfortunately, this would not be the case. A number of men near him were having a hard time walking. Those without shoes had endured painful cuts on their feet from the sharp coral when the group came ashore. Their feet continued to bleed as they slowly walked along. "I may have made a bad decision by not blowing up my life belt before leaving the ship, but I realized now what a good decision it had been to leave my shoes on," Cochran recalled.[3] When the pain became too much for some of the men to endure, the party stopped so that makeshift shoes could be cut out of life belts. "These didn't stop the hurting, but they did make mobility possible again," Cochran remembered of the homemade shoes.

An occasional plane passed overhead as the men walked along. Not wanting to take any chances of been seen, they dropped to the ground each time a plane came near. The group eventually arrived at a small lagoon about two hundred yards wide. Thick trees surrounded the area on all sides and the water was too deep for wading. The native boy leading the group had left a canoe in the underbrush. The small boat could only carry about four men, but it was the only way to get the survivors across. Cochran was in the last group ferried across the water. When the canoe was in the middle of the lagoon, a plane suddenly passed overhead. "There was no place to hide, so the two of us survivors bent over as far as we could hiding our faces while the boy kept paddling," Cochran recalled. Although the plane passed low, it continued on, showing no signs of having spotted the activity below.

With all men safely across the lagoon the unrelenting hike went on. "The coral continued to torture the men without real shoes, and I continued to be thankful that I had kept mine on," Cochran wrote. After a lengthy hike on a rough and winding trail, the group stopped at a small cluster of huts. The men were now deep inside the jungle. Much to Cochran's surprise an American was waiting among the huts. "Instead of a well equipped Marine, however, he looked like one of us, his clothes black with oil and his equipment no more than a sheath knife such as most of us were carrying." Cochran did not recognize him. Not knowing if the *Helena* was the only ship sunk in the area, he asked the American his ship. "The same damn ship you came from," was the sharp reply.[4]

In a subsequent conversation, Cochran began to learn the details of the situation. He was told that they were on the island of Vella Lavella and that survivors from the *Helena* were the only Americans. A coastwatcher, missionary minister, and friendly natives were helping round up the survivors to get them to an inland hideout. Now armed with a somewhat fuller understanding of the predicament, Cochran's group continued on their journey. Presumably walking on the same rough trail that was used by Chew's group, they eventually arrived at Chung's house late in the day.

Bernard Kelly's men shared a similar experience. After making landfall the group was later met by natives who took them on a jungle trek, terminating at Chung's house.

After sleeping in the abandoned village, Warren Boles came across a native carrying a large machete. He approached with some uneasiness and threw his own knife to the ground in a gesture of friendliness. Boles soon found the man to be friendly. Speaking pidgin English, the islander offered to take him to a place where there were "plenty Mericans."[5] The two set off in the opposite direction than Boles had been considering. He was the last survivor to arrive at the house.[6]

■ ■ ■ ■

Further up the coast to the northwest, Gayle Gilbert's group was experiencing their own long hike. After spending the night in the jungle, the survivors awoke to something that they had not experienced in many long days: breakfast. The natives had swiped some rice from the Japanese and somehow came across a can of Spam. "We were all starving," Gilbert said. "We hadn't had anything to eat for three or four days. We happened to have a cook in our group."[7] The cook used the meager ingredients and an empty five-gallon square can to make a fine meal. The natives added some coconuts to the feast. "We took a coconut, half a coconut and that was our dish," Gilbert said. "Those natives took care of us." The walking then resumed.

The men were hiking through a dense jungle. The group went up the side of a steep hill before stopping in a flat area. "We must have been up pretty high," Gilbert said. He later speculated that they hiked all the way across the island. The group, however, likely only went a few miles inland from the coast. The flat area was to be the stopping point. It was here that the survivors would hide out from the Japanese. The natives immediately set about making the area somewhat hospitable for the island guests. "The natives whipped us up a lean-to," Gilbert said. "It seemed just like an hour or two and he had a lean-to there for us." The frame of the structure was made out of tree poles. Vines were used to lash the poles together and leaves acted as roof shingles. "It was beautiful. It was really something to see 'em do that." The area would be Gilbert's home for the rest of his time on the island.

■ ■ ■ ■

Having a large number of widely scattered sailors unexpectedly arriving on their island posed a serious problem for the coastwatchers on Vella Lavella. If left in the beach area, it was only a matter of time before the survivors would be spotted by the Japanese. Through the diligent efforts of Henry Josselyn, Archie Silvester, and their cadre of natives, all the *Helena*'s survivors were eventually rounded up and organized in three different groups, and each was moved to a secure location in the interior of the island. Equally important was the need to dispose of the various rafts. There could be no visible traces left in the open to show that the Americans were on the island. The natives took care of that problem.

The largest of the three groups contained the 104 men who came ashore in the general vicinity of Lambu Lambu Cove. These were the men who were taken to Sam Chung's house. The senior American officer of the group was Lieutenant Commander Chew, but it also contained Boles and Kelly. The large cluster was under the direct control of Reverend Silvester. A second group of fifty survivors was organized further up the coast near Java, just southeast of Paraso Bay. The senior officer of the group was Ensign George Bausewine. A third group was positioned about eleven miles northwest of Bausewine. It contained only eleven men, including Chief Warrant Officer William Dupay.

■ ■ ■ ■

Sam Chung's house was a typical jungle variety. The structure had a bamboo floor, porch, and one large room. The roof was made of galvanized metal. The inside of the house was barren of any modern conveniences. The furnishings were few and very basic. In the large room were two beds (one large and one small), a table with a couple of chairs, a few eating utensils, and a working clock. A cot sat on the porch. Chung and his family vacated the house so that it could be used by the survivors.

Chew and his men met their guardian when Reverend Silvester arrived in the company of a walkie-talkie-carrying native on the first day. Dressed in an old pair of khaki shorts and a short-sleeved shirt, Silvester sought out Chew as the senior officer present. He told him that he had access to a radio and that American headquarters would be notified of their existence.[8] Silvester also said that he would be sending over some natives to build another building.

By late in the day of July 9, all of the survivors from the Lambu Lambu area had been safely moved to Chung's house. The next step was to establish some basic organization. The survivors were going to have to live a very barren existence, so their focus had to be limited to the most basic survival needs, including food, shelter, and protection. As the senior officer Chew spearheaded the task. However he, along with all of the other survivors, was heavily dependent on the coastwatchers and natives. "The total collected in the camp consisted of eleven officers and ninety three men. Medical supplies and emergency rations from some of the ship's rafts were assembled and the wounded were given beds," Chew later reported of the group.[9]

One way of looking at the survivor's hideout was to consider it a village. In these terms, Chew was clearly the mayor. It was up to him to make rules to provide order and organization. Being the senior marine present made Kelly the police chief. With the help of the natives, he was to provide protection. The rest of the survivors were citizens. Reverend Silvester must have been considered the highest authority, perhaps deserving the title of governor. Chew put into effect a few basic rules. Movement out of the camp area was limited. He did not want anyone wandering off to be found by the Japanese. Fires were only for cooking.

Kelly addressed the sanitary situation. Selecting a location away from the camp, he set about the task of digging a latrine. The only tool available for the work was a steel helmet worn by one of the survivors during the entire time in the water. Knowing that many of the sailors might not find the job appealing, Kelly made a good example by taking his turn digging. After some hard work the camp had a latrine that was almost thirty feet long. A large log was moved to the edge to be used as a seat.[10] An emergency latrine in the form of an empty can lined with leaves was set up in the middle of camp for those too weak or otherwise unable to walk. Any able-bodied man caught using the emergency facility would be subject to the punishment of having to empty the can on a daily basis.

Chew found a pair of shorts inside Chung's house that fit him almost perfectly. He decided to ditch his oily uniform. Other men replaced their oily clothes as well. Some optioned for makeshift attire fashioned from old burlap sacks, which may not have looked pretty but were workable under the conditions.

The house offered a good starting point for shelter. Next door was an odd-looking structure with an open front and bamboo floors, which resembled a chicken house. Shortly after the survivors arrived, a group of natives appeared and began work on a third structure. Cutting down tree limbs, leaves, and vines, the workers put together a lean-to. Chew thought that the construction arrangement was odd. The natives seemed to work for specific periods of time before stopping, as if they were members of a labor union.[11] Notwithstanding, the structure was completed with relative ease.

The pole building was almost fifty feet long and featured woven palm leaves for the walls and grass for a roof. The three buildings provided all the shelter needed to comfortably accommodate the survivors each night.

When Cochran arrived at the house, he had only two things on his mind: food and sleep. A small amount of thin soup helped to hold off the hunger. He then went inside the house, fell asleep on the bamboo floor, and slept soundly through the night. "I woke up with the marks of the spilt bamboo floor deeply embedded in my body," Cochran later wrote. "I received that first morning one of my most cherished possessions of the stay on Vella Lavella: a large burlap bag from a stack that Sam Chung had used in his trading. That bag became my mattress and security blanket. At all times of the day I either, carried it, wore it, or slept on it." The burlap bags were very popular among all of the survivors.

Finding enough food to feed an army of sailors was not going to be an easy task. Having been chased into the interior of the island by the Japanese, the natives themselves were surviving on meager food supplies. The survivors collected whatever food they could find themselves, including paltry rations from the rafts. Some additional food supplies, possibly from the *Helena*, washed up on the beach. It did not amount to much, but it was a start. Chew remembered that coffee was the one item that was not in short supply. "Fortunately about five twenty-five pound cans of coffee were washed up on the beach, so we had an ample supply of good coffee," he later wrote.

To help address the food problem, Reverend Silvester sent groups of natives out to scour the area for supplies. The effort soon paid off. "Food consisting of potatoes, tapioca, yams, pau pau, bananas, etc, was brought daily by the natives," Chew reported. Cochran remembered the regular visits by natives bearing food. "They showed up periodically always with a round of shaking hands bringing local root vegetables, canned foods that had washed up on the beaches from sunken ships, and a few fruits which were reserved for the injured," he recalled.

The supplies soon allowed for the preparation of two meals per day. The group was lucky to have two seasoned cooks at their disposal. Seaman 1st Class James Johnson and Marine Bert Adam were both experienced in the culinary arts. The latter was a bartender from New Orleans who dreamed of opening a restaurant after the war.[12] In order to feed everyone, stew soon became the dish of necessity. The locals provided a large metal pot. It reminded Chew of something that he had seen in cartoons years ago that showed wild natives boiling missionaries.[13] Every day the cooks filled the pot with a variety of strange vegetables, sometimes adding a Spam-like canned meat. The concoction was not totally without flavor. A small amount of salt and some herb leaves that the men found in Chung's house were put to good use. The end result was a watery stew that often varied in color from day to day.

The stew was served first as breakfast and then as a late day meal. Empty coconut shells served as dishes. Homemade wooden spoons that the men carved with their knives filled the need for utensils. Since there were not enough bowls and spoons to go around, meals were served in shifts. Everything was washed only after all the men had eaten.

Layton remembered that the stew was dominated by roots. "I would say our main meal was swamp root," he said. "It's kind of like a long narrow sweet potato, but it's slimy." He thought that it was something that the natives regularly ate. Like the others he had no complaints. "If you get hungry enough, you'll eat most anything." Sam Hollingsworth noted that the stew tasted much better after the oil left his system.[14]

Maintaining a suitable fresh water supply was not a concern for the survivors. The main house had a gutter system that deposited all of the rainwater into a large barrel. Given the frequent rain, usually several times a day, the barrel was almost always full. Additionally, a stream ran at the base of the hill below the hideout. The survivors filled barrels, taken from the rafts, for an additional water supply. It was, however, a strenuous effort for some of the still weak men to haul the full barrels the mile-and-a-half journey from the stream back up to the camp. One who looked forward to water duty was Cochran. "I did this a couple of times, and getting into the cool water after filling the containers was the nearest thing to pleasure we would have," he recalled.

The wounded were cared for as best as possible. A few first aid kits were available from the rafts and served as the starting point for medical supplies. Some of the officers carried small canisters of morphine shots. The Reverend Silvester arranged for some sulfa and painkilling medicine to be sent over from the missionary supplies. Collected together, the meager medical supplies at least provided some help for the wounded.

As the senior medical man among the group, Layton cared for the wounded. Another pharmacist's mate at the encampment, Vic Walker, provided assistance. They placed the wounded in the house's few beds. Three or four seriously wounded men were not able to walk. "One guy had a broken leg," Layton recalled. "There was a guy with a fractured hip. One guy had shrapnel in his leg." Layton also remembered a man with a fracture in his lower leg. "I set that fracture. I was the senior medical officer," he noted, laughing. Although ranking low while aboard the ship, he was now the leading medical authority on the island. Layton also treated wounded feet that had been cut up by coral and cases of shock.[15]

Seaman 1st Class John Ewing was among the seriously wounded, having suffered a compound leg fracture. Layton tirelessly tended to Ewing, keeping his leg packed with sulfa powder. The remedy seemed to work and the leg did not have to be amputated, which would have been a difficult undertaking with the lack of medical resources on the island.[16]

In addition to the seriously wounded, Layton and Walker tended to a variety of smaller injuries. Salt water sores were among the most common of ailments confronting the two men. The painful sores occur when broken skin is exposed to saltwater for an extended period of time.[17] After cleaning the open sores as best he could, Layton covered them with sulfa powder.

Ensign Don Bechtel was typical of the walking wounded whom the medical men encountered. "I was in fairly good shape," he later said. "I had some trouble from salt water sores that developed under the backs of my legs and [in] the fold of the knees so I couldn't walk so very well. Otherwise, I was in good health."[18]

One of the men recovering in the house was Chaplain Wheaton. "He had really a bad case of saltwater sores," Layton remembered. "He could not walk." The chaplain seemed to get better after a few days of convalescing.

Although the hideout was deep in the interior of the jungle, there was no guarantee that the Japanese would not find it. The enemy still did not have a large contingent of troops on the island, but their numbers and activity were increasing. Foot patrols were common and growing in number.

The job of providing security fell to Major Kelly. His resources were limited, but he was determined to make it work. Kelly had five marines among the survivors, along with a small assortment of junior officers and chiefs. The result was a small security force that was soon dubbed, "Kelly's Irregulars."

Manpower was not the main problem facing Kelly—it was weapons. Many of the survivors had knives, but these offered little protection against a well-armed Japanese foot soldier. The men needed guns if they were to have a fighting chance at surviving any type of encounter with the Japanese. The group initially only had two guns, both pistols carried ashore by survivors, one of which was Cochran's.[19] Chung's house contained a shotgun with only one shell. However, the variety and number of weapons soon grew. Knowing that the survivors needed protection, Silvester sent over a small assortment of rifles, many of which were quite old.

Marine Cpl. Molloy Frisbee had the duty of overseeing all of the weapons. He soon learned that it was an odd assortment of mismatched gunnery with a wide variety of ammunition. Both pistols had clips, but none of the rifles had more than thirty rounds of ammunition. One of the Japanese rifles Silvester sent over only had three bullets. As with just about everything else at the hideout, the weapons were meager, but had to be made to work.

The men in the security detail had various tasks. Sentry posts were set up at points around the encampment. "Our guards were established nightly," Kelly later reported. "Plans were prepared to guard against any contingency arising from the proximity of Japanese patrols."[20] Many believed that the enemy would not venture too far into the jungle at night out of fear of the natives.[21] No one, however, could be certain. The contingency plan in case of a serious Japanese threat was to move the camp deeper into the jungle. Two men were often assigned to each gun, so that if one took a hit then the other could immediately pick up the weapon.[22] There simply were too few weapons to risk any one gun being idle.

The natives provided their own form of security. They knew the island much more thoroughly than the Japanese. Their large machetes and ability to move with stealth through the jungle provided some amount of equalization to the heavily armed enemy. Shortly after the hideout was established, Reverend Silvester made arrangements to post native guards at various key points. Every time the Japanese made a move, Silvester knew about it in short order.[23] Between Kelly's men and the natives there was not much firepower, but most of the sailors felt somewhat safe in their surroundings.

Maintaining order and discipline did not seem to be a problem at Chew's camp. One of the few breakdowns came when someone stole food. "One morning it was discovered that one or two pieces of native fruit that was being held for the wounded had been stolen," Cochran later related. "All of us who were aware of this were upset and angry, but the culprit was never known." One day Kelly's police force caught an able-bodied man using the emergency latrine. The stated punishment was dished out and the offending individual was soon seen regularly carrying the heavy can of human waste out of the camp for emptying.

■ ■ ■ ■

The men in George Bausewine's raft were helped ashore by natives who pulled up in canoes. The number of men on the junior officer's raft had declined during the days spent adrift at sea. He later attributed the loss of a few men to hallucinations. "Aboard ship they had to go below deck to smoke," he later explained. "Of course we had no decks and had no smokes, but so overpowering was their instinctive discipline that, wanting to light their imaginary cigarettes, they stepped into what they thought to be a hatch and never reappeared."[24] Like all of the survivors, the sailors did not know what was going to happen next.

Boatswain's Mate 2nd Class Paul Kavon was part of a small group helped ashore further up the coast. He soon joined Bausewine's group near the beach. A member of the master at arms group while aboard the *Helena*, Kavon had narrowly missed being rescued by a destroyer the first night in Kula Gulf. "Everyone with the help of the natives was busy cleaning up," he later wrote. "Oil was extracted from coconuts and used to sooth our tired and burning eyes, while some of the men were washing the fuel oil from their bodies in a nearby stream. It made everyone feel better to be scrubbed up."[25]

The natives prepared some fish and a stew that contained an assortment of roots and fruit for the men. It was not food that the Americans were used to eating, but there were no complaints. The group spent their first night ashore sleeping in huts near the beach at Java. Kavon remembered it passing quickly. "It seemed only a few minutes, but it was next morning and we were being shaken by the natives and gestured at to get up," he recalled. Using broken English, Kavon remembered the lead native trying to explain that the men had to leave the area because a Japanese patrol was nearby.

No sooner had the message been understood than a white man suddenly appeared out of the jungle. He was slim and had long hair. It was coastwatcher Henry Josselyn. He took Bausewine, the senior officer present, aside and explained the situation. He told the ensign that the men were in great danger at their present location. Japanese activity on the island was increasing and the coastal area was alive with patrols and barges. The survivors had to leave at once, but they were too far up the coast to join Chew's group. Although still exhausted, Bausewine and his band of men followed the natives into the jungle.

The men faced many of the same challenges experienced by those farther to the south. Kavon remembered that a lack of shoes was a major issue. "The majority of the men had kicked off their shoes in the water and were now barefoot," he recalled. "Some cut up their life jackets to wrap around their feet, others used wide leaves, and some of them had nothing to wear at all." During the hike the group met an English-speaking native named Daniels. He told them that they were on Vella Lavella and gave them some basic information about the island. "Finally, Daniels told us he was to be the runner between our group and [the] underground headquarters on the island which was operated by a British naval officer," Kavon later wrote, having apparently not seen Josselyn earlier in the day. The group eventually arrived at a makeshift hideout.

It is most likely that Gilbert was among the group of fifty men who eventually came under the direction of George Bausewine. The only time Gilbert recalled seeing Josselyn was after the makeshift camp was set up.

There was not much that Gilbert could do but to settle into the camp. "I slept in there for four or five nights," he recalled. He always had a spot under the lean-to. "I'll tell you, it never rained on us." Gilbert was fascinated when he saw how the natives scaled the large trees to cut down coconuts. "They wrapped their toes right around that thing with their hands and they'd go right up that tree," he said. "It was their way of life." Gilbert did not try to replace his clothes while on the island, but kept his oily uniform. He never attempted to fashion any homemade shoes. "I never could make 'em. I don't know why. I just didn't know how to do it, I guess." He ended up walking barefoot during his stay on the island. "My feet were getting pretty tough at last. I could do pretty good."

The survivor group was not totally isolated. "There was one native [who] could speak English and he kept us informed as to what was going on," Gilbert said. He was so focused on the possibility of being rescued that he was not overly worried about the chance of being captured by the Japanese. "They just kept telling us that someone was going to come and get us," he remembered. "That's the only thing that was on my mind."

■ ■ ■ ■

Gunner's Mate 2nd Class Frank Cellozzi was among the many weary sailors arriving at Chew's hideout. The days at sea were akin to a nightmare for him and he was happy to be on dry land after the experience. His raft had made it to about four hundred yards off the beach before becoming entwined in coral. The barefooted men aboard had to walk to reach the beach. "We watched our blood rising to the surface as the razor sharp rocks cut through our skin like knives," he later wrote of the ordeal that had lasted about an hour. By the time Cellozzi reached the beach his feet were bloody and raw. The trip ashore notwithstanding, his first thoughts of the island were good ones. "Our first impression was of paradise—lush, rich jungle forest and cool, green palm trees," he recalled.[26]

After completing the arduous trek to Sam Chung's house with the assistance of the locals, the first person that Cellozzi saw was Chew. Cellozzi knew him from the ship because Chew was one of the officers that he served under in the gunnery department. Cellozzi immediately noticed that Chew looked somewhat emaciated, an obvious outcome from the days lost at sea. The exhausted gunners mate soon joined the others in settling into the new home.

■ ■ ■ ■

The days on Vella Lavella began to blur together. After the initial time spent organizing, the sailors slowly fell into a routine. While not easy, life seemed to be progressing at a normal pace; at least as normal as could be under the circumstances.

The unwounded men of Chew's group performed the routine chores that were needed to keep up the living arrangements. Sailors took turns maintaining the latrine. Some were assigned to make repairs as needed. The cooks prepared two meals a day. Guard duty was ongoing and shared by many.[27]

The daily routine did not vary much. The men rose early with the sun, usually about 6 a.m., and ate breakfast a few hours later. The morning typically included some type of basic stretching to keep the men limber. Everyone was required to exercise by walking laps around the camp.[28] The men learned to wash up without soap. Lime peel was found to be effective for keeping teeth clean.

The shipwrecked sailors occasionally heard a nearby air battle. The men never really could tell which side was victorious, but many assumed it was the Americans. When a plane passed near the hideout, it was not uncommon for everyone to take cover out of sight. It was, however, unlikely that any pilots would be able to see them through the thick jungle canopy.

Beyond the normal routine there was not much for the men to do. They often passed the time talking. "On board ship the conversation would most likely have been about dates and women in general, but now hunger had completely eliminated sex drives," recalled Cochran. "The topic ninety-nine percent of the talking, was talking about food." It was not uncommon to overhear men talking about the meals they desired once they made it home. Some of the survivors also worried about how their families back home would react when the navy sent word that they were missing.[29] Reverend Silvester occasionally forwarded news about the two other survivor groups on the island.

"The stew wasn't very tasteful," recalled Bechtel.[30] Remembering the days spent at sea with little or no food, however, the men had few complaints. One day, the natives treated the *Helena* survivors to a feast.

The event started inconspicuously when a group of natives butchered a stray cow some distance from the hideout. However, Japanese patrols prevented them from getting the fresh meat to the camp in a timely manner. By the time the natives arrived, the meat was close to spoiling. Just when it appeared that the catch would have to be discarded, Machinist's Mate 2nd Class Grady Atkinson came to the rescue. An older man, Atkinson had mined gold in Alaska and experienced survival in rough conditions. He claimed to know how to save the meat. The problem, though, was that the meat had already been buried. With Chew's permission, it was dug up, cleaned, and turned over to Atkinson who boiled it for days.[31] Once the preparations were complete, it was enjoyed by all. Layton remembered indulging in the onetime treat. "Of course that didn't go far with a hundred people," he said.[32]

One luxury the sailors missed was cigarettes. While a few packs may have survived the time in the water, the supply was quickly depleted. They found some cigarette paper inside Chung's house. When a native later brought over some homegrown tobacco, a few sailors made what turned out to be very powerful smokes. To remedy the problem in the future the tobacco was mixed with coffee.[33]

■ ■ ■ ■

Having been on Vella Lavella for the better part of a week, the *Helena* men developed an intrinsic friendship and bond with the natives. The Americans understood that to a large extent they owed their lives to these people. Gilbert remembered the natives' dark skin and bushy hair. Others recalled their flat noses that often contained a spike. Many had pierced ears. "I wouldn't say that they were big guys, maybe over five feet all of them," Gilbert said. "There was one native that seemed to take a liking to me." The native had assisted Gilbert on his first day ashore. "He took a liking to me, I don't know why. It was funny." The islanders appeared to be very civilized and far from the common stereotypical image of wild savages. A few natives spoke broken English, although it was often of a diluted form.

For the men of Lieutenant Commander Chew's group, the bond extended to Archie Silvester. In the course of the stay on the island, Layton became friends with the minister. "I got to know him well," he said. "He was the type of guy that you would want to be your father or your best friend. He was just a great guy." Layton saw the missionary almost every day and developed a great appreciation for his help. He remembered Silvester taking many measures to ensure the safety of the camp. "He never would use his walkie talkie with us," Layton recalled. "He would go out into the jungle somewhere and use his walkie talkie, then come back because he did not want the Japanese to pick it up and be able to pinpoint it."

Many survivors believed that Silvester was deserving of a title greater than minister. Some began to call him Bishop. The nickname soon took hold, but was eventually shortened to simply Bish.

Silvester held a religious service for Chew's group early in the stay on the island. It was partially done to celebrate the completion of the third building near Sam Chung's house. Attended by both survivors and locals, the event included an abundance of singing. At one point the survivors joined Silvester in singing "Onward, Christian Soldiers."[34] Cellozzi remembered the service. "As the evening progressed, we became louder and louder," he recalled. "We were all laughing and had our arms around each other."[35]

Before long a well-attended evening prayer service became commonplace. One song that both the survivors and natives knew was "Rock of Ages." In what must have appeared to be an odd arrangement, the two groups often ended up singing together, each in their native tongue.[36] As the survivors were getting accustomed to their temporary home on the island, others far away were trying to figure out how to get them out.

16

Rescue Operation

True to his word Henry Josselyn made radio contact with the district officer on Guadalcanal to notify him of the *Helena* survivors on Vella Lavella.[1] It did not take long for the information to reach Admiral Turner's headquarters. It presented the admiral with the difficult problem of how to rescue such a large group trapped far behind enemy lines.

Small-scale rescue operations were now commonplace in the South Pacific. Picking up a downed airman or a few trapped sailors could easily be accomplished in a variety of ways, none of which worked for a large group. An early conclusion among the headquarters officers was that any rescue probably had to be done in one swoop.[2] Trying to pull out the survivors in small groups was too risky and invited a Japanese trap. A potential operation with submarines or PT Boats was quickly ruled out as neither could meet the size requirement.

■ ■ ■ ■

As Turner's men grappled with the problems, daily life continued for the *Helena* men trapped on Vella Lavella. Frank Cellozzi recalled one of his four-hour stints of guard duty in John Chew's camp. Alone on a moonlit night, he hid near a fallen tree a few hundred yards from the camp in a position overlooking the main trail. Likely the first line of defense if the

Japanese arrived, he prayed diligently that the enemy would not come. As the night dragged on, his mind began to wander. He thought of the sea battle, the sinking of the ship, and friends who did not survive. "I thought of my home and family in Ohio and wondered if I would ever see them again," he later wrote of the time. Much to his relief the shift passed without incident.

Bin Cochran remembered an episode when he was on night guard duty. He was stationed on the porch of Sam Chung's house. One of the old rifles was loaded and positioned within easy reach near his side. "They've found us," said a voice that suddenly cried out from the night. "In the black dark I grabbed for the rifle, but instead of my fingers closing around it I knocked it to the floor," Cochran recalled.[3] In the process of trying to find the rifle, he tipped over an adjacent chair before falling to the floor himself. He regained both his footing and weapon in time to see Reverend Silvester emerging from the darkness.

However, danger was never far away, and other potential security breaches were not as humorous. The first serious crisis came when a four-man Japanese foot patrol started down a path that would take them dangerously close to the camp. Whether it was just a routine patrol or if the enemy actually knew of the camp's existence was not known. A group of native guards ambushed the unsuspecting Japanese soldiers, killing three.[4] The fourth enemy soldier was taken alive and brought back to the hideout.

The survivors were now confronted with a difficult situation and many questions. How could they possibly take care of a prisoner when they themselves were surviving on meager resources? What if the captive were to somehow escape? As soon as he made it made back to base, the survivors' days would be numbered. While the decision of what to do ultimately rested with Chew, he also asked others in the group for recommendations. The consensus was that they simply could not keep the prisoner, so he had to be executed. Chew agreed, but asked that it be merciful.[5] It was a difficult decision, but it had to be done for the group's safety. In one quick movement a native struck the prisoner on the back of the head with a machete, killing him instantly.[6]

The immediate danger was over. The Japanese patrol did not get close enough to do any harm to the survivors. However, a missing four-man patrol would certainly be noticed by Japanese authorities. How the enemy would react and what type of response would come could only be a matter of speculation.

Late in their stay on the island, the men received an abrupt warning that a Japanese barge had landed on the coast in the vicinity of Lambu Lambu Cove. The location was the closest sea point to Chung's house. Native scouts reported that twenty heavily armed soldiers had started up a trail leading to the hideout. Cochran remembered the urgency of the situation. "All fires had to be extinguished and care was taken not to make any sounds that might carry," he recalled. "That meant the soup pot fire went out and things got tedious." The survivors would very possibly be facing a fight to the death.

Lieutenant Commander Chew made immediate preparations to move the men further into the jungle, while Bernard Kelly organized his defense force to meet the threat. The marine knew that his group would probably be outnumbered and definitely outgunned. He selected a position that gave his men good cover and the chance to ambush the enemy when they came up the narrow mountain trail single file. The tension must have nearly reached a breaking point as the irregulars moved into position. The distant sounds of the approaching Japanese soon could be heard, with boots carelessly hitting rocks and voices talking in casual tones. The noises seemed to carry freely through the jungle. Just as the first enemy soldier could be seen coming up the trail at a distance, the sound of airplanes suddenly filled the air, immediately followed by the rattle of heavy machine gun fire. A flight of American Corsair fighters seemingly appeared out of nowhere. Diving toward the barge, the American planes riddled it with machine gun fire, creating a small mushroom cloud of black smoke.[7] Although many of the survivors were not in a position to view the action, they easily heard the sounds.

The attack sent the Japanese soldiers scurrying back down the trail to the beach. Their voices were no longer calm. In all probability the planes were most likely on routine patrol, and spotting the barge, the pilots decided to attack. It was an event that was likely repeated many times over in the general area. Whether the Japanese were on a routine mission, searching for the missing four-man patrol, or perhaps trying to return from another island, may never be known. The danger had passed.

As their days on the island mounted, the *Helena* men must have wondered if they were going to be rescued and how. Although harboring fears of what could happen, many seemed optimistic. Cellozzi felt a little of each. "I had survived until now and I fully believed that we would be rescued," he wrote. "We knew that if we weren't rescued soon, discovery was inevitable." Among those confident of a rescue was Don Bechtel. "We thought we might be there for a good long time though before they finally got us out," he later said. Josselyn felt that the survivors were living on borrowed time. He feared that the Japanese were getting closer by the day.[8]

The stranded survivors were by no means forgotten. Admiral Turner was determined to find a way to get the men home.[9] An idea soon emerged involving the use of destroyer transports, which seemed workable. The *Dent* and *Waters* began life as four-stack destroyers. Built at the very end of World War I, the ships were antiquated well before America's entry into the Pacific War. The vessels, however, found new life after being converted to fast troop transports for use in amphibious operations. The conversion necessitated removing some armaments to make room for troop quarters and landing boats. With the modifications the ships assumed the designation of APD's. Both had recently participated in landings at New Georgia and were now in the Guadalcanal area.

The rescue idea essentially amounted to an amphibious operation in reverse. American planners felt that if these fast ships could dash up the Slot under the cover of night, the survivors could be quickly picked up by landing craft in time for a safe return before daylight. An escort would be needed in case of enemy interference.

Admiral Turner tapped Captain McInerney to lead the operation. A seasoned veteran, the destroyer commander had directed the rescue operation in Kula Gulf the night the *Helena* went down. Three groups of ships, all destroyers, were to be involved in the operation. In addition to leading the overall mission, McInerney would command Destroyer Squadron Twenty-One. The unit was comprised of the *Radford*, *Jenkins*, *O'Bannon*, and *Nicholas*, with the *Nicholas* still serving as McInerney's flagship. Capt. Thomas J. Ryan would lead the four ships in Destroyer Squadron Twelve, which included the flagship *Taylor*, along with the *Maury*, *Gridley*, and

Ellet. Transport Division Twelve, the *Dent* and *Waters*, operated under Cdr. John D. Sweeney.

The mission orders were outlined in a dispatch from Turner. Admiral Ainsworth met with some of his destroyer captains aboard the *Nicholas*. He used the conference to outline the basic plan for the rescue operation.[10] The overview of the mission was simple. Ryan's four destroyers were to escort the transports north with all six ships operating together. McInerney's force was responsible for providing distant cover and his vessels were to be ready to tangle with any Japanese ships that might happen on the scene. The plan called for the survivors to be picked up by landing craft from two locations along the northeast coast of Vella Lavella, first near Paraso Bay and then at Lambu Lambu Cove.

The mission was fraught with danger. The penetration would be the deepest ever attempted up the Slot, bringing the rescue ships to within sixty miles of large Japanese naval and air facilities.[11] If the American ships were sighted coming up the Slot, it was possible that heavy Japanese naval forces could be brought into play in short order. Moving close to Vella Lavella meant navigating through hazardous waters that were not well charted. There was also the potential for communication problems between the landing ships and coastwatchers on shore. As with the Battle of Kula Gulf, the force had to be out by daylight due to the threat of enemy air. Speed and surprise would be the keys to success.

■ ■ ■ ■

Coordinating the rescue effort from Vella Lavella had its own set of challenges. The *Helena* sailors were divided among three groups. All were hiding out well inland, with the two northern groups some distance from Chew's group. The men had to be able to get to the water's edge without being spotted by the Japanese. Arrangements had to be made for American ships and landing craft to find the survivors at the landing points.

Sub Lieutenant Josselyn was responsible for coordinating the land portion of the operation. Combining his efforts with those of Reverend Silvester, he was able to develop a workable plan. The fifty men in George Bausewine's group would combine with the eleven sailors under William Dupay. Josselyn was to lead them to the coast near Paraso Bay and signal for the American ships at the appointed time. The coastwatcher would board with the survivors and then guide the rescue ships through the reef-infested waters to the next pick-up near Lambu Lambu Cove. Further south, Silvester and native guides were to bring the 104 men of Chew's group to the water's edge. If all went as planned the marooned sailors would be snatched to safety from right under Japanese noses.

Josselyn and Silvester notified the stranded sailors of the planned rescue operation. "We got information back that the navy would pick us up," said Bechtel. "Some of us had been on the island a week; others had been there eight days."[12] All that the survivors could do was to wait and hope for the best. "We learned there was actually a plan to rescue us," Cellozzi later wrote. "We waited day after day in anticipation." It was not long before the final hours arrived.

The initial plan called for the rescue to take place over two nights, with the first pick up at Paraso on July 12.[13] The operation was postponed when it became clear that Japanese ships were on the move. On the night of July 12–13 American naval forces and the Tokyo Express again clashed in the vicinity of Kula Gulf in an inconclusive fight known as the Battle of Kolombangara.

From his hiding place on Vella Lavella, Cochran awoke in the middle of the night to the distant sounds of naval gunfire. A few rumbles were powerful enough to shake the ground below him. He concluded that another American night bombardment of Kolombangara was taking place.

The original plan for a pick up on July 12–13 had brought the men of the two northern groups to the beach near Paraso Bay. Gayle Gilbert walked to the coast near a native with a large machete. "I was right behind that native," he recalled. "We stepped over a log and there was some kind of a snake."[14] Using his machete the native instantly chopped up the snake with ease. The event reassured Gilbert that he was in the right place.

Paul Kavon learned of the rescue plan from the English-speaking native, Daniels. He told the sailors that they had to be at a spot on the beach at a certain time. "We waited for darkness and then started out for the beach," Kavon later wrote. "Although we got to the beach alright, and were well covered, something went wrong."[15] The men had no way of knowing at the time that the operation had been postponed. A short time later a

Japanese plane passed in the vicinity and dropped a flare that lit up the immediate area. "Whispers were passed along to be as still as possible and to pull the tall grass around us so we couldn't be spotted from the air," Kavon recalled. The men stayed hidden near the beach until just before dawn when they moved back into the jungle. "Everyone was tense and a little disappointed because the attempt had failed." Daylight brought the need for the sailors to move further inland. "We were on the move once more and tension began to build; when would we be able to try it again?"

The men soon learned that another rescue attempt would take place in the near future. "So we went back up," Gilbert said. "Up to our camp and we stayed there." He remembered it being about a three-hour hike from the coast back to the hideout.

■ ■ ■ ■

The rescue of the *Helena*'s sailors had already been pushed back several days. Time was now of the essence to get the operation moving as the Japanese could discover the stranded survivors at any time. "Since the escorting group was at Guadalcanal and the covering group at Tulagi there was no opportunity for a conference," McInerney later wrote.[16] However, to better coordinate the efforts of the transports and close cover force, Ryan met briefly with Sweeney off Koli Point, Guadalcanal on July 15. The latter brought to the conference a memorandum from the mission leader. "This memorandum set out Captain McInerney's intentions and coordinating measures between APD's, screening destroyers, and covering force," Ryan later wrote. "Captain McInerney's suggestions provided an excellent modus operandi between the two groups . . . but allowed Sweeney and me complete and necessary latitude in carrying out our respective tasks."[17] During the conference the two worked out a range of details including projected courses and code words to be used between the ships. Ryan knew that his role was to protect the transports. "In the event of contact with snoopers or other Japanese, the APD's were not under any circumstances to open fire without direct orders from me. They were to get clear, hug the beach if possible, and let us do the fighting."

The transports and escorts pulled out of the Guadalcanal area at noon on July 15 to begin the journey northwest. The cover force left Tulagi at about 3 p.m. In accordance with operational plans, the two groups took different routes. Traveling west of Rendova, Ryan's group passed south of Kolombangara, entered the bottom of Vella Gulf through the narrow Gizo Strait, and moved to the rescue points. The cover force went the more traditional route straight up the Slot to a position north of Vella Lavella. The maneuver was designed to put McInerney's force in a position to block the most likely route of Japanese ships coming down from the northwest.

McInerney knew that the ships were venturing into unknown waters. "As far as is known this is the first time that any of our ships had gone through Gizo Strait," he wrote. "It was anticipated that enemy forces might be encountered near Gizo Strait as well as in Vella Gulf." He was well aware of recent reports that Japanese warships were active in both areas, but each group proceeded without incident as the last hint of daylight faded from the sky.

Banyetta Point at the far west end of Rendova was the last point of familiarity for Captain Ryan. Just days ago he had led a group of destroyers through the area to bombard Munda. "Beyond Banyetta Point the route was through new territory, but the night was clear with bright moonlight and the *Taylor*'s SG [radar] was in excellent working order," he reported. The flagship was to serve as the guide ship through the dangerous waters ahead. The moonlight also meant that Japanese search planes were likely to be out in force.

Passing south of Kolombangara late in the evening on July 15, Ryan exercised extreme vigilance for the approach to Gizo Strait. A handwritten note of caution was printed across one particular area of his outdated map, perhaps to warn of an uncharted reef. He was trying to keep his ships clear of the hundred-fathom curve line, but the available maps were imperfect and unreliable. The *Taylor*'s radar soon got a navigational fix on a point on the west coast of Gizo Island. "At about the same time, fathometer registered fifty fathoms," he wrote of the moment. "Course was changed ten degrees to the left."

The ship went to general quarters just before midnight as it approached Gizo Strait.[18] The moonlight allowed lookouts on the destroyer to see an array of islands. Off the starboard side was Gizo Island with Kolombangara towering in the background. To port was Gonongga Island and Vella

Lavella. The ships proceeded through the strait with no sign of the Japanese. At 12:40 a.m. two aircraft flares were sighted by lookouts. A third was seen just minutes later. By 12:55 a.m. the force was cautiously proceeding up the east coast of Vella Lavella.[19]

The covering force moved up the Slot at 25 knots, apparently undetected, until about 9 p.m. when the ships began to be shadowed by a Japanese plane. "Our exact position was known and we could not shake off the snooper," McInerney reported. He knew that the gun flashes would give away his position and ordered his anti-aircraft guns to stay silent. At 1 a.m. the covering force arrived at the appointed station ten miles north of Vella Lavella.

■ ■ ■ ■

As the rescue ships journeyed into Japanese-held waters, the *Helena*'s sailors spent the day getting ready to meet them at the water's edge. After the false alarm a few days ago, the northern group once again prepared for the march to the coast. "Before going to the beach we bid our friends, the Melanesian natives good [bye.] Some of the sailors had knives which they left as an expression of thanks," Kavon wrote. He did not have a knife, but gave the natives a few dimes that were still in the pocket of his dungarees. The natives took a great interest in the coins. "They were in a huddle like a football team and were passing the coin back and forth to look at it. I approached them and tried my best to tell them in words and gestures that the coin was ten cents in American silver." He did not know if the natives understood what he was trying to communicate. Kavon was then astonished when one of the men, whom he did not think spoke English, suddenly asked him how much of a dollar the coin was worth. "One tenth," Kavon replied. "I don't know if he understood or not for he never said anything more, but mingled with the others."

Further south the men of Chew's group were also moving toward the coast. Getting the large number of men to the beach was a big undertaking. Chew had a number of concerns about the journey. The coastal plain near Lambu Lambu offered little in the way of protection during the daylight, and all possible precautions had to be taken to avoid detection by the Japanese. Chew was also concerned about navigating the jungle trails at night. As a result, the group left at 3 p.m. for the long walk to the coast in the hope of arriving at dusk.[20] Joining the *Helena* men for the evacuation were Sam Chung and a number of Chinese. Native scouts acted as guides for the group and Major Kelly's men provided a screen.

■ ■ ■ ■

By 1:15 a.m. the main body of the rescue force completed its journey through Vella Gulf and was traveling along the northern coast of Vella Lavella. Somewhere ahead in the darkness lay Paraso Bay and the mouth of the Ngawkosoli River. As a precursor to the final leg of the journey, Captain Ryan directed the *Maury* to lead the *Ellet* and *Gridley* to a position about five miles off Paraso Bay. The three destroyers were to remain on patrol in the area until the pick-up of survivors was complete.

Using her modern radar and sound gear, the *Taylor* continued to lead the *Dent* and *Waters*. "Although the mouth of the Ngawkosoli River could not be clearly distinguished on the SG scope, the contours of Vella Lavella in this vicinity were so well defined that we believed we were heading approximately for the center of Paraso Bay," Ryan wrote. When the small formation was thought to be about four thousand yards off the entrance, the *Taylor* took a depth reading that showed five fathoms of water. "I directed the captain of the *Taylor* to back clear, and immediately after, directed Sweeney to feel his own way in leaving the *Taylor* on his starboard hand." The destroyer moved about three thousand yards back and the destroyer transports slowly nosed their way into Paraso Bay. It was about 1:30 a.m.

Wary of the shallow water, the *Dent* and *Waters* were moving at 5 knots toward the pick-up point. Neither ship, however, saw the expected signal from the men ashore. "We felt certain that our navigation was correct, but in view of the very short distance to the beach, and the failure of the coastwatcher to make the prescribed signals, we began to have doubts," Ryan recalled.

Aboard the *Dent* Sweeney gazed intently out into the darkness. A tree line began to emerge out of the murky night as the ship moved closer to shore. The signal suddenly came at exactly 1:55 a.m. in the form of a small flash of light. Sweeney quickly moved to the side of the bridge in time to see a canoe emerge from the darkness. On the water below, William Dupay was still not entirely sure that the ship he was approaching was American. "I am the gunner of the *Helena*," he bellowed out much to the relief of the anxious men aboard the *Dent*.[21] "Exchanged recognition signal with small boat in accordance with previously arranged procedure," the War Diary of the destroyer transport recorded of the moments that followed.[22] The vessel immediately lowered three Higgins landing craft from davits. The *Waters* did the same. To lessen the chance of detection by the enemy, the engines on the boats were muffled.

Ensign Rollo Knuckles was in command of the three boats from the *Dent*. Each craft was thirty-six feet long, typically carried a crew of three, and was equipped with two .30-caliber machine guns.[23] The boats had a moveable ramp at the front. The murky coastline of dense trees was visible in the distance as the first boat moved away from the *Dent*. Sailors manning the machine guns pointed each toward the coastline, while others checked their rifles. A lookout posted at the front of the ship carefully scanned the water for any sign of coral reefs.[24] The moon silhouetted each landing craft as it slowly moved farther away from the *Dent*. As the small ships disappeared into the night, tense lookouts aboard the destroyer transport kept binoculars trained toward the shore.[25]

Ensign Knuckles soon found the guide canoe and followed it at a slow speed to the pick-up point, making drastic turns as dictated by the guide. The two other boats from the *Dent* followed the lead craft, while the three boats from the *Waters* stayed behind. As the boats were en route to the beach, the *Dent* drifted to a stop before slowly turning to point her bow seaward. Ryan was relieved when he received word that a connection with the coastwatcher was finally made. "Our worries were over," he reported.

Just after 2:10 a.m. the *Gridley* made contact with the covering force by radar and TBS. Some distance away in the *Nicholas*, McInerney listened intently as the operation progressed. His destroyers seemed to be under the watchful eye of Japanese planes as numerous aircraft flares were sighted in the immediate area. "On two occasions sticks of bombs were dropped near the destroyers," McInerney reported. "There was no damage." He again had his ships hold fire.

Reaching the designated point, the *Dent*'s three Higgins boats pulled up to shore. When the front ramps dropped, the weary survivors marched aboard. In addition to the *Helena* survivors waiting to be taken away was a downed Japanese pilot. The aviator had been captured by natives and brought to Ensign Bausewine's group. He was tied up and blindfolded as a precaution after the decision was made to allow him to live. Downed P-38 Pilot Eli Ciunguin was also among the group.

As he made ready to board the landing craft, Boatswain's Mate 2nd Class Kavon thought about those who were staying behind. "I could not help but think of the missionaries who had been there and the fine job they had done and also what could have happened if they would have never been on the island," he recalled. He was soon on his way out to the rescue vessel.

Fully loaded with *Helena* survivors, the three landing craft pulled alongside the *Dent* at 3:18 a.m. Within minutes the small boats were hoisted aboard and the transport was making 5 knots toward the entrance of the bay. All of the survivors were picked up by the *Dent*, including Josselyn. His mission was now to guide the rescue ships on their journey south to Lambu Lambu Cove.

By 3:30 a.m. the *Taylor*, *Dent*, and *Waters* joined the three patrolling destroyers and began to move out of the area under Josselyn's guide. "The run to Lambu Lambu was short and uneventful," Ryan reported. The formation arrived at the second rescue point just before 4 a.m. Both of the destroyer transports slowed to 5 knots for the final approach. Higgins boats from both ships were soon on the way toward the land. All of the small craft were needed to accommodate the large group of survivors.

The transports came close to being spotted a short time after embarking the landing craft. Lookouts aboard the *Waters* sighted a single unidentified float plane at 4:16 a.m.[26] Captain Ryan believed that the ships were not seen, noting that the Japanese plane "went on without knowing of the beautiful target over which he had passed, or of the nearness of screening [destroyers]."

■ ■ ■ ■

The exact pick-up point was not the beach itself, but rather a small dock at an abandoned trading post on the Lambu Lambu River. The location was about a mile inland.[27] It was a risky gamble. If the Japanese were to spot the operation and be able to bring troops in quickly, it could end badly.

Jim Layton did not remember having much advance notice that the rescue ships were coming. "A day or so, no more than that," he said. He had spent much of his time on the island diligently working to care for the wounded. Now he made preparations to get the injured men down to the sea. "I think we had three we had to carry out on stretchers," he recalled. "We made makeshift stretchers." Parts of trees were used for the poles. The rest of each stretcher was made with clothing or anything else that could support the weight of a person. The strongest men were assigned to carry the stretcher cases.

To better organize the procession, many of the officers were given the responsibility to watch over a small group of men. Lee Spaulding oversaw the Chinese who were making the journey. The group included a pregnant woman and a baby. "My job in that evacuation plan was to be in charge of ten men," remembered Cochran. The trek started without incident. "Each group kept close to the group ahead. Mine was about two-thirds back in the column." Cochran remembered the procession stopping at about the halfway point to better time the arrival to the coast with darkness. Another disruption occurred later when the line was suddenly told to turn around based on a report that men with guns were seen down near the coast. "We didn't get disorganized, but we turned around and jogged several hundred yards in the direction of the camp thinking that a Japanese patrol was too close for comfort," Cochran recalled. It turned out to be a false alarm. The men ahead with guns were members of Major Kelly's security force.

Aside from the few glitches, the trek to the coast went without major problems. Arriving at the end of the trail, Cochran took stock of the immediate area. He saw the wharf that was to be the pick-up point and noticed an assortment of native houses. There seemed to be no activity. Remaining in small groups, the survivors, natives, and Chinese guests waited in darkness and silence. "I believe an unsuspecting person could have walked through the area and never known that anybody else was around," Cochran remembered. The silence was suddenly broken by the wail of a crying baby. It was enough to put many of the sailors on edge, with one later commenting that it seemed like one of the loudest sounds he ever heard.[28] The baby was quickly quieted and no Japanese appeared.

An essential part of the operation was for someone on land to make contact with the landing craft and then guide the small ships down the river estuary to the dock. Warren Boles was designated to venture out in a canoe with a native guide to signal the rescuers. He left camp ahead of the main group and arrived at a deserted village near the beach, where he waited in the company of some natives. At the appointed time Boles and a native paddled out down the river and eventually made contact with the landing party. Pulling up alongside Knuckle's boat from the *Dent*, he climbed aboard. Then six Higgins boats slowly moved up the river.

Hiding in the brush back near the dock, the sailors waited for any sign that their rescuers were approaching. Fears soon surfaced among the men that the appointed time had come and gone. Some were worried that the group would have to start walking back to Sam Chung's house. Their apprehensions began, however, to fade when they heard noise coming from down the river. From his vantage point in the brush Cochran could not see the approaching landing craft, but the soft sound of motors soon told him that the rescuers had arrived. Cellozzi was also waiting patiently among the nervous group of survivors. He was relieved when the faint sounds became audible. "After what seemed like an eternity, but which was probably only an hour at the most, we could hear their motors approaching," he recalled.

The landing craft pulled up to the dock and it was time for the *Helena* men to depart. The injured were the first to board. "I took the wounded on the first boat," Layton said.[29] He did so with the assistance of Vic Walker.

Under Chew's direction each small group was directed toward a boat. The senior officer made note of each cluster as it boarded so that no one would be left behind. "Finally it was our turn, and we moved up to the wharf," Cochran recalled. Standing near the dock he saw Kelly and Reverend Silvester. Josselyn was in close proximity. Cochran introduced himself as the latter approached. Standing with the others was a stranger who was definitely not one of the survivors given his clean clothes and helmet. It was Rollo Knuckles.

It seemed that every survivor stopped to say goodbye to Silvester. Before Cochran boarded the ship one of Major Kelly's guards returned his pistol as promised. "I took off my sheath knife and handed it and the .45 to either

Bish or Josselyn; shook Bish's hand for the last time and followed my ten men into the Higgins boat," he later wrote of his final moments on the island. The gun and knife were parting gifts for the men who saved his life. Cochran also remembered an officer giving Silvester a watch back at the camp, and many others leaving knives behind as parting gifts.

Layton also went back on the dock to say goodbye to the missionary who helped save him. "I was standing alongside Silvester and I was begging him to go with us," he recalled. "He had tears in his eyes." But it was not his time to leave the island yet. "I can't leave," Silvester replied. "I may be able to help someone else like I've helped you guys."[30] The boat was loaded and ready to depart. Layton could not help but think about the missionary who was staying behind. "When we pulled off he was still standing on the dock." The image of Reverend Silvester slowly faded into the darkness as the boat pulled away from the shore.

With all the others safely loaded aboard the rescue boats, John Chew was the last man to leave the island. He paused for a short moment to say an emotional goodbye. Bidding Reverend Silvester a final farewell, Chew gave him a prized possession: his lucky silver coin.[31] He then stepped aboard a Higgins boat from the *Waters* and told the boatman it was time to go.[32]

All of the Higgins boats now moved down the river toward the open sea. Perhaps expecting it to be a noisy ride, Layton could not believe how quiet the landing craft were running. "It was just gliding through the water," he recalled. That was about to change. "Come to find out they had their motors muffled. They could come in quietly, but they couldn't get any speed with the muffles on." Once the boats reached the open sea, Layton saw the ensign in charge motion for the mufflers to be removed from the engines. "They did something and [the mufflers] just fell off into the water." They immediately started to move fast. "The bow went up and it was flying." Pulling up alongside the *Waters*, Layton remembered the Higgins boat being immediately pulled aboard. "They come down with . . . something that hooked onto the boat and they lifted us right up and set us on deck," he said. In one swift movement, Layton was firmly aboard a U.S. Navy warship.

The first three landing boats arrived at the *Dent* at 4:32 a.m. and were quickly hoisted aboard. Ten minutes later the *Waters*'s Higgins boats returned. Once all were accounted for, the transports wasted no time in getting under way, joining up with the escort destroyers. The force was soon making 25 knots as it sped out of the area.

17

Home

As the saga for the *Helena*'s survivors was playing out in Kula Gulf and Vella Lavella, the American public learned about the warship's fate. After previously noting that a naval action was under way in the South Pacific, the navy released a communiqué on July 7 announcing the results of the battle. It stated in part that "six Japanese ships were probably sunk and several damaged, the light cruiser *Helena* was sunk." The release concluded with a statement that the next of kin of casualties from the *Helena* would soon be notified.[1] With those simple phrases the world knew that the *Helena* was gone.

More detailed information began to disseminate once war correspondents filed their stories from the front lines. The tale of the *Helena* soon appeared in newspapers across the United States. The announcement of the sinking was made before relatives were officially notified by the navy. All across the United States, wives, mothers, fathers, and siblings waited for more information about their loved ones.

■ ■ ■ ■

Although Gene Robinson was safe after being pulled out of Kula Gulf the night of the sinking, he had no way of notifying his wife back in Ohio. Mae Robinson was working at the Standard Oil Company in Cleveland at the time. After hearing the news, Mae's mother rushed to meet her at the rapid transit station after work. "She was afraid that my wife would see the newspaper headlines on somebody's paper there that our ship was sunk," Robinson recalled. "Her mother met her at the train station and told her that the ship was sunk. So when she found out about it, of course she was shocked."[2]

Robinson wrote his wife a letter as soon as time permitted. The two-page note was dated July 9, 1943. "I am very sorry that I could not have written you sooner to let you know I'm safe. I know you must be worrying yourself sick." He expressed his anger that the sinking was made public so quickly and his hope that he would soon be home. Robinson concluded by explaining that the only items that had survived the sinking were his wallet and watch. The letter arrived home before the telegram sent by the navy. After days of grief and anxiety, Mae Robinson finally knew her husband was safe.

■ ■ ■ ■

When the morning of July 16 dawned, the rescued sailors from Vella Lavella were not yet safely back to an American base. Captain McInerney's four destroyers joined the other rescue ships at 6:40 a.m. and took position in a large circle around the two transports. Operating together for the first time, the combined force moved swiftly through the Slot. Four American fighter planes arrived over the formation just after 7 a.m. Within half an hour "many friendly planes" were in sight and on radar.[3]

As it turned out the *Helena* survivors were not the only ones to be rescued. On the journey home the *Radford* picked up two Japanese sailors who were found floating in a U.S. Navy whaleboat. "These prisoners stated that they were survivors of the Japanese light cruiser *Jintsu*," McInerney wrote. The ship had been sunk in the Battle of Kolombangara a few days earlier. A number of other Japanese sailors were encountered who refused rescue. McInerney had no time to delay and continued the journey home, leaving the unwilling survivors to their fate.

Once safely aboard the *Dent*, many of the survivors were sent to the galley. In anticipation of a hungry crowd, the cooks had prepared large pots of soup, sandwiches, scrambled eggs, chocolate, and coffee. Cigarettes were also available.[4] It was the first solid meal that the rescued sailors had in over a week. Gayle Gilbert remembered the busy mess hall. "We crowded in there and that was early in the morning," he said. He still had on his oil-soaked clothes.

"The first thought of everyone was food," recalled Bin Cochran.[5] Finding the mess hall jammed, he and Lee Spaulding headed for the *Dent*'s wardroom. There Cochran found an old roommate from the Naval Academy. In the course of conversation, the two rescued officers ate several rounds of toast and coffee. Cochran later returned to the mess hall for something more substantial. Many of the men started to get cleaned up after their meals, while others were only interested in sleep.

An equally receptive crew waited to assist the survivors who boarded the *Waters*. Pea soup, coffee, and cigarettes were waiting in the galley for the passengers. A limited amount of clean underwear, pants, and socks were also available.[6] After filling up with soup and coffee, John Chew did something that he could only dream about while on the island: he took a shower. His next stop was the medical department, so a doctor could treat the sores on his ankles. He then headed to the *Waters* wardroom. Much too wired to sleep, Chew spent the rest of the night talking with others about his adventure and catching up on the progress of the war.[7]

By early afternoon the rescue ships were in friendly waters. Just short of 1:30 p.m. the *Dent* passed Savo Island.[8] Within an hour the *Dent* and *Waters* were securely moored in Tulagi Harbor and both ships began offloading *Helena* survivors. Three war correspondents aboard for the rescue mission also departed the *Waters*.[9] They would surely have a good story to tell.

Within a few days the successful rescue operation was reported around the United States. A July 19 article in the *New York Times* carried the headline, "161 *Helena* Survivors Quit Enemy-Held Isle: Naval Units Daring Exploit Effects Rescue."[10] Other article headlines included, "Wild Dash Saves *Helena* Survivors" and simply, "Survivors of *Helena* Saved."[11] In coming months, articles about the rescue appeared in *Life* and the *Saturday Evening Post*.

McInerney could not have been happier with the outcome of the mission. "The entire operation was carried out exactly on schedule and as planned," he later wrote.[12] His report included words of praise for Captain

Ryan and Commander Sweeney for their skillful handling of the ships off Vella Lavella. Machinist's Mate 2nd Class Ken Schank, a *Helena* sailor plucked from the island, directed his praise toward the landing craft operators. "The boys who brought the landing boats into shore were the real heroes," he later said.[13] Schank noted that when those navy men hit land they did not know if they would find survivors or Japanese gunfire. It is likely that few of the *Helena*'s men would disagree with Schank's comments.

The survivors were well taken care of once safely ashore on Tulagi. Frank Cellozzi remembered the warm welcome. He recalled seeing a photographer from *Life* and numerous war correspondents interviewing survivors.[14] The men were able to take showers and get a brief examination by a doctor.[15] Gilbert liked the surroundings. "There was a regular base there," he said. "They had the whole works."[16] He remembered getting food and new clothes. Given his sweet tooth, he could not keep away from the bread and jelly. "We had other food, but that was the main thing for me. I couldn't get enough of that."

Many of the sailors received a small Red Cross bag that contained basic toiletries. "The Red Cross was very generous," Gilbert said. "They didn't have enough to go around, so I had to share a toothbrush with a guy and shaving . . . I had to share that with another guy."

The damaged New Zealand light cruiser the *Leander* was also in port. She was awaiting departure for more permanent repairs to torpedo damage suffered a few days earlier off Kolombangara. Cochran boarded her, and was welcomed into the wardroom where he stayed for a few drinks.

Cots were available on Tulagi to the delight of many. The first night of sleep ashore, however, was interrupted by the wailing of an air raid siren. The stay at Tulagi was not a long one—Layton only remembered being there for about three days—most of the survivors were soon sent south to New Caledonia.

In addition to being the location of the navy's main headquarters for the South Pacific, New Caledonia was home to a survivors' camp. It was nothing more than a temporary way station where sailors from sunken ships waited for their next assignment. The men from Vella Lavella were reunited with many of their shipmates after arriving at the camp.

Having lost most everything with the sinking of the ship, many of the *Helena*'s survivors still did not have much more than the clothes on their backs. "My total possessions consisted of what I wore and the little bag with my razor and soap in it," remembered Cochran. "I would start acquiring things, but for a time I experienced a feeling of unencumbered freedom that was exhilarating."

Like Cochran, Seaman 1st Class Robinson lost almost everything when the *Helena* sank. "The only thing I saved was my wallet and my wrist watch and the clothes I had on," he said. "The wrist watch stopped, I think it was ten minutes after two." Robinson recalled living out of tents, although a few permanent buildings had been constructed at the camp. "I think it was about a six man tent," he recalled of the living quarters. He remembered walking around the camp at night and smelling a variety of foods being prepared. "You could smell eggs going on in one, steaks frying in another one," he said. "The food was just given to us. They had regular mess time, but anytime we wanted anything to eat we'd just go get it."

Remmel Dudley was among the officers at the survivors' camp. Upon arrival he wrote a short note to his mother. "I couldn't go into details," he said of the letter. He just wanted her to know that he was all right and would write again soon. It took about a week for the letter to arrive in Arkansas. Having read about the *Helena*'s sinking in the newspaper, she did not know if he was alive or dead. "One advantage of living in a small town, that letter came into the post office there at night," Dudley said. "Instead of being delivered the next morning in the usual mail, the fellow who worked in the post office was a neighbor of ours down the street. He took it to my mother's home, knocked on the door at about ten o'clock at night and said, here's a letter from your son."

During his stay on New Caledonia, Layton had a chance meeting with an old friend. "I was just killing time in the master of arms shack," he recalled. A familiar looking figure came walking in and simply said, "I'm going home." It was Reverend Silvester. American forces had landed on Vella Lavella about a month after the *Helena* men were rescued and the missionary decided it was time for a trip back to New Zealand. "It was just a coincidence and something I was glad that happened," Layton said.

One of the main problems facing the survivors was the lack of any type of records. "We had no health records, we had nothing," Layton recalled. With the help of an officer he made contact with a friend at a nearby field hospital. "We conned two doctors and a dentist to come over and make us up some skeleton health records. They come over and spent a whole day doing quick health exams. [Then we had] some stuff to at least prove that we existed, I guess," Layton concluded.

The basic records opened the way for the men to leave the survivors' camp when transportation allowed. For most, the destination was the United States, as it was common for the navy to grant a thirty-day leave for the survivors of a sunken ship. Individually and in small groups, the *Helena* men began to depart the camp. Many would not see their shipmates again during the war.

A large number of survivors, including Walter Wendt and Dudley, made the trip to San Francisco aboard the Merchant ship *Lew Wallace*. Others returned home through a variety of means. Cochran took a plane to Pearl Harbor, followed by a cargo ship to San Francisco. Layton and Gilbert went to San Diego on the merchant ship *Dashing Wave*. The vessel was originally bound for San Francisco, but collided with another ship in the Pacific and was re-routed. Robinson traveled in two stages—he first took a freighter to the Fiji Islands and then boarded a troop ship to San Diego.

Wendt recalled the slow trip back to California aboard the *Lew Wallace*. "We plied the Pacific for twenty-three days," he said.[17] He fondly remembered going into San Francisco harbor because the ship's rudder jammed just before passing under the Golden Gate Bridge. The homecoming was delayed, but the problem was eventually corrected. "That Golden Gate looked pretty damn good," he remembered. "Everybody was happy."

Not all of the survivors went to New Caledonia. Mason Miller was with a small group that ended up at a Seabee camp on Espiritu Santo. "The gunnery officer on our ship had a friend who was a colonel in the army," Miller recalled. The officer told them to go to the army base to get new clothes. "We went over and got shirts, pants, shoes, and everything from him. That worked out very well." A short time later Miller ended up getting new clothes from the navy as well.

During his stay at the camp, Miller sent a V-mail (short for Victory Mail) to his wife that he was safe and hopefully on his way home soon. "It was just a sheet of paper that you could fold," Miller described of the letter. "It was supposed to move through the mail system real fast. It has to go the same way a letter does, but it's supposed to go really fast." Many of the survivors did not take any chances and wrote multiple letters. "What everybody did was write a V-mail, a regular letter, and an air mail letter," Miller said. He hoped that at least one arrived home in a timely manner.

Miller found the accommodations at the camp to be more than hospitable. "We slept in a long building, which had bunks set up in it evenly on one side," he said. "It was boarded up and about three fourths of the way up it was screened in. It was just perfect in there day and night for sleeping." He stayed at the camp for about two weeks before learning that he was to return to the United Sates. He was soon aboard a transport for a three-week voyage to San Francisco.

A bottle of whiskey from Admiral Halsey was waiting for John Chew at Tulagi. Chew was soon on a flight to New Caledonia. While en route the plane flew too close to an American carrier and was intercepted by fighters. Fortunately the transport was recognized as a friendly plane.[18]

■ ■ ■ ■

Most of the *Helena*'s survivors returned to the West Coast, either to San Diego or San Francisco. After making landfall some had the opportunity to be interviewed by reporters and their stories eventually appeared in newspapers. Most were bearing orders for new assignments, but were first granted leaves. Returning stateside was a time for farewells and a chance to say goodbye to friends and shipmates.

After arriving in San Francisco, Dudley briefly crossed paths with Bernard Kelly. The two had not seen each other since the sinking, owing to Kelly's time on Vella Lavella. "He had turned grey in just that three week period," Dudley recalled. He then checked in with the local Marine headquarters. "I was able then to go to a uniform store and buy a regular uniform," he said.

The Marines were trying to reconstruct his pay records, but Dudley needed some money to buy a plane ticket home. Someone directed him to a local bank and called ahead to let them know that he was coming. "I went down there, had on my Marine uniform, brand new uniform and walked up to this fella behind the window and introduced myself." The teller said that he had been expecting him and asked how much money he wanted. He then unexpectedly stepped away and soon returned with a wanted poster. Apparently, someone dressed in a new military uniform was robbing banks all along the West Coast. According to the information on the poster, it seemed that Dudley was a close match for the main characteristics of height, weight, and hair color. "And finally [the teller] said that his front teeth are widely spaced," Dudley said. "I opened up my mouth really fast and showed him my teeth were all together." Dudley was able to get his money and went home for a thirty-day survivor's leave.

Upon arriving in San Diego, Gilbert immediately set out to let his family know that was safe. "I was missing in action for eleven days," he said. He went to his brother's house in Long Beach before going home. "I had a thirty-day survivor's leave," he recalled. "I went back to Kansas. Stayed in Kansas for those thirty days and it was all over." He then proceeded to his next assignment.

Before leaving the South Pacific for the West Coast, Miller sent a letter to his wife letting her know that he was on his way home. Helen Miller traveled across the country and stayed with her aunt in San Francisco to wait for her husband to arrive. The two went back to Virginia together to enjoy his thirty-day leave.

Cochran went home to Mississippi to spend some time with his parents before reporting for new construction. "With us on the island . . . they couldn't get any word if I were a survivor or not," he said of his parents. "So they had kind of a hard time for a while." Cochran, however, was careful only to share some of his story. He purposely left out the part about the coastwatchers. "That was top secret. I never mentioned that until the war had progressed far beyond the Solomon Islands."

Robinson and Layton went home before reporting to their next assignments. Robinson caught a train to Cleveland and was reunited with his wife. Layton went home to Texas to visit his aunt and uncle. "I lived in a small town," Layton said. "When I got home everyone was very pleased to see me."

Wendt also used his survivor's leave to go home. Wearing a new set of clothes and carrying just a small ditty bag, he stepped off the train in McNaughton, Wisconsin. The sun was just starting to rise as he began the five-mile walk home. At about the halfway point he came across a young man in his late twenties walking along the side of the road. Wendt recognized him as Victor Sereyko, an area resident whom he did not know well. "Who are you?" asked Sereyko. "I'm Walt Wendt," was the reply. "That's good news," exclaimed an excited Sereyko. "They said Walt Wendt was killed in the Pacific!" "No, I'm okay," Wendt said as he continued his walk home.[19] It was the end of a long journey that had started thousands of miles away in Kula Gulf.

EPILOGUE

Splitting up the *Helena*'s crew after the sinking meant that each officer and enlisted man followed a different path as the war progressed. Some sailors never saw each other again. Many of them were assigned to new ships and saw more combat. Most survived the war, eventually left the navy, and settled into civilian life.

Capt. Charles Cecil was assigned to the Pacific Fleet Service Force and was later promoted to rear admiral. He tragically lost his life in a non-combat-related plane crash on July 31, 1944. He was fifty-nine years old.[1]

Widely regarded as a hero for his leadership on Vella Lavella, John Chew spent much of the remainder of the war as an instructor at the Naval Academy. In September 1945 he became part of the initial crew of the new heavy cruiser *Helena*, serving as her executive officer. Chew went on to serve a long navy career, ultimately attaining the rank of vice admiral.[2] He retired from active duty in 1970. Vice Admiral Chew died in 1999 at the age of eighty-nine.[3]

Captain Cecil wrote of Jim Layton's courageous conduct on Vella Lavella, noting that "by his exceptional skill, and devotion to duty [he] was largely responsible for saving the lives of three wounded men." Never again given sea duty, Layton was assigned to the dental clinic at the Oakland Naval Hospital. In a twist of fate, the officer in charge at Oakland Naval Hospital had been on the crew that put the recently sunk *Helena* in commission. "When I reported for duty, he thought we were blood brothers since I put it out of commission," Layton recalled.[4] He spent the rest of the war working in a laboratory that made false teeth and dental pieces. During that time, he met a young lady, whom he later married. After he was discharged from the navy in September 1945, he moved back to Texas and settled in Dallas.

Layton found work in the field of dental prosthetics and dental research before spending about twenty years in plastic surgery research. He retired from the Southwestern Medical School in 1976, but returned to work on a part-time basis about a year later. "If I wanted to take off a month I didn't have to ask anybody," he said of returning on his own terms. He was fully retired when I spoke with him about his *Helena* days and still happily married and living in Dallas.

Bin Cochran was among the many *Helena* survivors assigned to new construction ships. He reported to the Philadelphia Navy Yard to become part of the initial crew of the cruiser *Miami*. "I was there about a month or so while it was being built," he said. "I put her in commission." He spent the rest of the war aboard the vessel. The light cruiser arrived in the Pacific in mid-1944 and conducted carrier escort duty for the next year. With his ship in San Francisco for an overhaul, Cochran was home on liberty when the war ended.

Continuing in the navy after the war, Cochran served on the cruiser *Oklahoma City* and spent time as an instructor in San Diego. He got married and worked as a sales representative for a manufacturing company after leaving the navy. In 1951 he was recalled to active duty for three years to work with the the Office of Naval Intelligence in Washington, D.C. Eventually settling in Marietta, Georgia, he worked at a power company until he retired in 1985. Bin Cochran passed away in January 2009.[5]

The escort carrier *Kasaan Bay* was the next ship for Gayle Gilbert. The vessel operated in both the Atlantic and Pacific during the remainder of the war. During his time aboard, Gilbert successfully changed his rating from bugler to quartermaster. When the war ended he stayed in the navy to fulfill his six-year term of enlistment. He decommissioned the *Kasaan Bay* at Boston and was honorably discharged from the navy on September 30, 1947.[6]

While in the Boston area Gilbert met the love of his life. "I met a girl in Medford and I fell in love with her and we got married," he said. "Right after I got out."[7] The couple settled outside of Boston. "I'd go back to Kansas about every five or six years," he recalled. Gilbert worked in the nursing home industry until retiring in 1985. In 2008 his family took him on a cruise to Hawaii. Although he had previously flown to the island, the trip was his first on the Pacific Ocean since his navy days. As of this writing, he is enjoying life as a senior citizen in Massachusetts.

A large contingent of *Helena* survivors, including Mason Miller, Gene Robinson, and Walter Wendt, were part of the initial crew of the new light cruiser *Houston*. The men soon found themselves back on the front lines. The *Houston* was nearly sunk by Japanese aerial torpedoes in October 1944 while on carrier escort duty near Formosa. The badly damaged vessel was towed out of harm's way and eventually returned to the United States for repairs.

Mason Miller rode the damaged ship all the way back to the East Coast and left the vessel when it reached New York City in March. But it was not long before he was back in the Pacific, this time aboard the escort carrier *Nassau*. "We were about two days out of Pearl Harbor. We were moving from San Francisco to Pearl Harbor and the war ended," he said. "We turned around and came back to the West Coast."

After the war Miller returned home to Roanoke and began working for a paper company. After a few years he joined the Noland Company where he worked for thirty-four years before retiring in 1983.[8] Miller spent the rest of his life in the Roanoke area and was actively involved with a variety of church and civic groups.[9] Mason Miller passed away in December 2008.

Gene Robinson was among the large number of the crew that left the damaged *Houston* after she was put under tow. "We just went into the water and swam the best we could to a nearby destroyer," he said. "It was pretty close." Robinson was on the East Coast aboard the new cruiser *Providence* when the war ended. He was discharged from the navy and moved back home to Cleveland in September 1945. "I moved in with my wife's folks because we didn't have a home of our own yet," he recalled. "I got a job as an apprentice in a machine shop." He later went to work for the railroad and moved to Roanoke. He retired from the railroad in 1979.

Robinson still lives in Virginia and is in his early nineties. He still has the oil-soaked two dollar bill that was in his wallet the night the *Helena* went down.

Walter Wendt was in the engine room when the *Houston* was torpedoed, and he stayed aboard the ship until it reached a drydock in the Admiralty Islands. He was in the United States when the war ended. Wendt returned to Wisconsin after being discharged in September 1945. "If I had to do it over I probably would have stayed on in the navy as a career," he later wrote.[10] He worked as a logger and in a sawmill before taking over his family's resort in the late 1950s. At the time of this writing, Wendt still lived on his family's property near McNaughton, Wisconsin.

Remmel Dudley's next assignment was to fight on land. "I eventually joined the Fifth Marine Division," he said. "I was back in artillery."[11] Dudley landed on Iwo Jima during the first day of the invasion. "When the war ended we were sent out to Japan on occupation duty," he said. Dudley was discharged from the Marines in January 1946 and got married a year later. "When the war was over, there was no great rush of people trying to hire me," he said. In a twist of fate he ended up back in the military. "I was out for about six months and got this letter from the Marines saying that they were going to be giving regular commissions to people who were selected. I put in for a regular commission and got it." Dudley went on to fight in the Korean War before he retired from the Marines in 1963.

Dudly got a job with Metropolitan Life after leaving the Marines and stayed with the company for almost twenty years before retiring in 1983. When I spoke with him about his time aboard the *Helena* he was enjoying retirement in Virginia. Remmel Dudley passed away in February 2010.

■ ■ ■ ■

There is a lasting memory for each sailor who participated in the final voyage of the *Helena*. For some the recollection is of the ship itself, while for others it is of an individual or specific event. Bin Cochran's greatest memory was of abandoning ship.

Gene Robinson remembered the rescue from Kula Gulf and the loss of the executive officer. "I often wondered if I could have reached down and grabbed him, but I really don't know," he said. "I think about that quite often."

EPILOGUE

Remmel Dudley recalled the efficiency of the ship. "She was a very competent fighting organization," he said. "Every man knew his job and did it well."

For Jim Layton, it is the image of a friend who did not survive the sinking. "He was a pharmacist's mate," Layton recalled, telling me that in the years since the war his name has slipped out of his memory, but he can see still his face. A few years after the war Layton started receiving phone calls from the man's family who believed that he might still be alive and stranded on some Pacific island. But Layton knew that the sailor did not survive and the family eventually came to the conclusion that he was gone.

■ ■ ■ ■

During the last days of August 1989, the *Helena* survivors began to converge on the city of Helena, Montana, the host city of the Helena Reunion Association's bi-annual gathering. It was forty-six years since the light cruiser sank in Kula Gulf. The weekend event was open to all veterans who served on one of the four U.S. Navy ships named *Helena*. The reunion program included a message from then President George H. W. Bush, a fellow World War II veteran.[12]

On the afternoon of August 26, the *Helena* men gathered in a downtown Helena park for the dedication of the new USS *Helena* Memorial. It includes a propeller and anchor from the heavy cruiser *Helena* that entered service just after World War II ended.[13] The president of the reunion organization and Kula Gulf survivor Bill Bunker served as the master of ceremonies. Bernard Kelly was on hand to lead the Pledge of Allegiance. Dignitaries included Montana's lieutenant governor Allen Kolstad and Helena mayor Russ Ritter. The memorial serves as a small, but lasting tribute to the men who manned the light cruiser during her final voyage and to those who served on later fighting vessels bearing the same name.

NOTES

1. Heading North

1 *Helena* War Diary, January 8–21, 1943.

2 United States Navy, Office of Public Relations, *History of the U.S.S. Helena (CL-50)* (Washington, DC: United States Navy, Office of Public Relations), 5 (hereafter cited as "*History of the U.S.S. Helena*").

3 Al Adcock, *U.S. Light Cruisers in Action* (Carrollton, TX: Squadron Signal Publications, 1999), 20.

4 Samuel Eliot Morison, *The Two-Ocean War: A Short History of the United States Navy in the Second World War* (Boston: Little, Brown, 1963), 199–205.

5 *Helena* War Diary, January 21–22, 1943.

6 "Biographical Sketch of Rear Admiral Charles P. Cecil," Washington, DC: Naval Historical Center, August 1, 1946.

7 Gayle Gilbert, interviewed by the author and misc. documents sent to author, November 24, 2008, and June 10, 2009 (hereafter cited as Gilbert, Interview and Documents).

8 Walter Wendt, interviewed by the author and misc. documents sent to author, November 5, 2007 (hereafter cited as Wendt, Interview and Documents).

9 United States Navy, *The Bluejackets Manual* (Annapolis, MD: Naval Institute Press, 1946), 92.

10 Jim Layton, interviewed by the author, February 25 and March 18, 2008, and June 8, 2009 (hereafter cited as Layton, Interview).

11 Mason Miller, interviewed by the author, October 29, 2007 (hereafter cited as Miller, Interview).

2. Voyage to the Unknown

1 John Miller Jr., *Cartwheel: The Reduction of Rabaul* (Washington, DC: Office of the Chief of Military History, Department of the Army, 1990), 11.

2 Richard B. Frank, *Guadalcanal* (New York: Random House, 1990), 572.

3 Eric M. Hammel, *Munda Trail: The New Georgia Campaign* (New York: Orion Books, 1989), 5–6.

4 CO Task Force 67 to CinCPac, "Vila-Stanmore Bombardment," January 28, 1943, 3 (hereafter cited as TF 67, "Vila-Stanmore Bombardment").

5 Ibid., 4.

6 Frank, *Guadalcanal*, 573.

7 Bin Cochran, interviewed by the author and narrative sent to author. October 8, 2007 (hereafter cited as Cochran, Interview and Narrative).

8 Layton, Interview.

9 CO USS *Helena* to CinCPac, "Vila-Stanmore Area - Kolombangara Island - Bombardment of 1500 Zebra, 23 January, 1943," January 28, 1943, 1–2 (hereafter cited as *Helena*, "Vila-Stanmore").

10 Samuel Eliot Morison, *History of United States Naval Operations in World War II Volume VI: Breaking the Bismarcks Barrier, 22 July 1942–1 May 1944* (Edison, NJ: Castle Book, 2001), 108.

11 *Helena* War Diary, January 23–24, 1943.

12 James D. Horan, *Action Tonight, the Story of the Destroyer O'Bannon in the Pacific* (New York: G.P. Putnam's Sons, 1945), 61.

13 "U.S.S. *Helena* Radio Log 23 January 1943," enclosed in *Helena*, "Vila-Stanmore."

14 Flag Aviator, Task Force Sixty-Seven to CO Task Force Sixty-Seven, "Night Bombardment of Vila-Stanmore Area - Spotting and Observation of," January 27, 1943, enclosure D in TF 67, "Vila-Stanmore Bombardment."

15 United States Navy, Office of Naval Intelligence, *Combat Narrative IX: Bombardments of Munda and Vila-Stanmore* (Washington, DC: Office of Naval Intelligence, United States Navy, 1944), 26 (hereafter cited as *Combat Narrative IX*).

16 Miller, Interview.

3. Escape to Espiritu Santo

1. Eugene Robinson, interviewed by the author and misc. documents sent to author, December 4, 2007, and January 3, March 26 and June 8, 2009 (hereafter cited as Robinson, Interview and Documents).
2. Frank, *Guadalcanal*, 573.
3. TF 67, "Vila-Stanmore Bombardment," 6.
4. CO USS *Helena* to CinCPac, "Action Report - Attack by Japanese Aircraft - January 24, 1943," January 28, 1943, 1.
5. Frank, *Guadalcanal*, 573.
6. *Helena* War Diary, January 24, 1943.
7. Gordon L. Rottman, *World War II Pacific Island Guide: A Geo-Military Study* (Westport, CT: Greenwood Press, 2002), 78–79.
8. Lt. Robert E. Beisang, "Big H Drops In on Sydney, Then Heads for Last Battle," in undated newspaper articles provided by Eugene Robinson (hereafter cited as Robinson articles).
9. James J. Fahey, *Pacific War Diary, 1942–1945* (Boston: Houghton Mifflin, 1963), 49.
10. Gilbert, Interview and Documents.
11. "A Mother Awaits Word of Two Sons Serving on Helena," in undated newpaper articles related to Clifford Casey in USS *Helena* Web Page, accessed on various dates, http://www.usshelena.org/caseyclipsindex.html (hereafter cited as Casey Articles).
12. Hugh B. Cave and Lt. C. G. Morris, USNR, *The Fightin'est Ship: The Story of the Cruiser "Helena"* (New York: Dodd, Mead & Company, 1944), 128.
13. Layton, Interview.
14. Cochran, Interview and Narrative.
15. Miller, Interview.
16. Wendt, Interview and Documents.

4. Down Under

1. Beisang, "Big H Drops."
2. Cave and Morris, *The Fightin'est Ship*, 126.
3. Ray J. Casten, *U.S.S. Helena: The Machine-Gun Cruiser* (Martinsville, TN: Airleaf Publishing, 2006), 94.
4. Wendt, Interview and Documents.

NOTES

5 Gilbert, Interview and Documents.

6 Cochran, Interview and Narrative.

7 Layton, Interview.

8 Remmel Dudley, interviewed by the author, January 21 and December 18, 2008 (hereafter cited as Dudley, Interview).

9 *Helena* War Diary, March 1943.

10 Cave and Morris, *The Fightin'est Ship*, 127.

11 *Combat Narrative IX*, 54.

12 *Helena* War Diary, April 7, 1943.

13 *Combat Narrative IX*, 55.

14 Robinson, Interview and Documents.

15 Wendt, Interview and Documents.

5. Return to Kula Gulf

1 *Honolulu* Deck Log, July 1, 1943.

2 Gilbert, Interview and Documents.

3 Miller, *Cartwheel*, 92.

4 CO Task Group 36.1 to CinCPac, "Action Report, Night Bombardment of Vila-Stanmore and Bairoko Harbor, Kula Gulf, 4-5 July 1943," July 30, 1943, 2 (hereafter cited as TG 36.1, "Night Bombardment").

5 Morison, *Breaking the Bismarcks Barrier*, 158.

6 "Operation Order No. 10-43." Enclosure A in TG 36.1, "Night Bombardment."

7 Miller, *Cartwheel*, 85.

8 Japanese Self Defense Force: War History Office, *Senshi Sosho (War History Series) Volume 83: Southeast Area Naval Operations, Part II* (Tokyo: Asagumo Shibunsha, 1975), 226, and Paul S. Dull, *A Battle History of the Imperial Japanese Navy, 1941–1945* (Annapolis, MD: Naval Institute Press, 1978), 274.

9 CO Task Unit 36.1.4 (Commander Destroyer Squadron Twenty-One) to CinCPac, "Action Report - Shore Bombardment of Enemy Positions on Kolombangara Island and New Georgia Island (Kula Gulf) on the Night of July 4–5, 1943," July 12, 1943, 1.

10 CO USS *Helena* to CinCPac, "U.S.S. Helena - Shore Bombardment-Kolombangara Island and Bairoko Harbor, New Georgia Group, Night of 4-5, July 1943," July 30, 1943, 1.

11 TG 36.1, "Night Bombardment," 3–4.

NOTES

12 Miller, Interview.

13 Gilbert, Interview and Documents.

14 United States Navy, Office of Naval Intelligence, *Combat Narrative X: Operations in the New Georgia Area* (Washington, DC: Office of Naval Intelligence, United States Navy, 1944), 20 (hereafter cited as *Combat Narrative X*).

15 Robinson, Interview and Documents.

16 JSDF, *Senshi Sosho*, 226, and Dull, *Battle History*, 274.

17 Communication Log. Enclosure B in TG 36.1, "Night Bombardment."

18 Commanding officer, USS Strong Contingent to CinCPac, "Report of Material Damage Sustained by USS Strong (DD 467)," July 6, 1943. Enclosure F in TG 36.1, "Night Bombardment."

19 *Honolulu* Deck Log, July 5, 1943.

20 Morison, *Breaking the Bismarcks Barrier*, 157.

21 *Combat Narrative X*, 20.

6. Turnabout

1 Dudley, Interview.

2 Cochran, Interview and Narrative.

3 USN, *Bluejackets*, 88.

4 John Campbell, *Naval Weapons of World War Two* (Annapolis, MD: Naval Institute Press, 1985), 134.

5 Dudley, Interview.

6 Franklin Sears, EM2c, Edwin J. Rick, SF 3/c, "The Sinking of the U.S.S. Helena in Kula Gulf," Washington, DC: United States Naval Historical Center, NRS 1971–16, 16–17 (hereafter cited as Sears and Rick, "Sinking of the U.S.S. Helena").

7 *Honolulu* Deck Log, July 5, 1943.

8 CO Task Unit 36.1 to CinCPac, "Action Report - Night Engagement off Kula Gulf during the Night of 5-6 July 1943," August 1, 1943, 1 (hereafter cited as TG 36.1, "Night Engagement").

9 CO USS *Nicholas* to CinCPac, "Action Report," July 7, 1943, 1 (hereafter cited as *Nicholas*, "Action Report").

10 Cave and Morris, *The Fightin'est Ship*, 146.

11 CO USS *Radford* to CinCPac, "Night Surface Engagement off Kula Gulf During Night of July 5-6, 1943; Action Report of," July 11, 1943, 1 (hereafter cited as *Radford*, "Action Report").

12 Casten, *Machine-Gun Cruiser*, 111.

13 Robert M. Howe, "By the Grace of God," unpublished narrative, 44.

14 "Lieutenant W.L. McKeckney, USNW, USS Helena, Sinking of," Washington, DC: United States Naval Historical Center, November 2, 1943, NRS 1971-16, 1.

15 Cave and Morris, *Fightin'est Ship*, 147–48.

16 JSDF, *Senshi Sosho*, 227, and Morison, *Breaking the Bismarcks Barrier*, 162.

17 TG 36.1 "Night Engagement," 2–5.

18 "Japanese Torpedoes," Imperial Japanese Navy Page, accessed on various dates, http://combinedfleet.com/torps.htm.

19 *Nicholas*, "Action Report," 2.

20 Dull, *Battle History*, 275.

21 *Honolulu* Deck Log, July 6, 1943.

22 *Combat Narrative X*, 23.

23 Ibid.

24 JSDF, *Senshi Sosho*, 227 and Dull, *Battle History*, 275.

25 Dull, *Battle History*, 274.

7. Gunfight

1 "TBS Log," 1. Enclosure B-2 in TG 36.1, "Night Engagement," (hereafter cited as TG 36.1, "TBS Log").

2 CO USS *Helena* to CinCPac, "U.S.S. Helena - Night Action against Japanese Surface Forces off Kula Gulf, New Georgia Group, Night of 5-6 July, 1943 - Report of," July 30, 1943, 1 (hereafter cited as *Helena*, "Night Action").

3 CO Task Unit 36.1.4 (Commander Destroyer Squadron Twenty-One) to CinCPac, "Surface Engagement with Enemy (Japanese) Forces off Kula Gulf, New Georgia Group, Solomon Islands on the Night of July 5-6, 1943; Report of," July 20, 1943, 2 (hereafter cited as CO Desron 21, "Surface Engagement").

4 Morison, *Breaking the Bismarcks Barrier*, 163.

5 Cochran, Interview and Narrative.

6 TG 36.1, "Night Engagement," 7.

7 Anthony J. Watts and Brian G. Gordon, *The Imperial Japanese Navy* (New York: Doubleday, 1971), 124, 126, 139, 143, and 152.

8 TG 36.1, "Night Engagement," 7, and JSDF, *Senshi Sosho*, 227.

9 Morison, *Breaking the Bismarcks Barrier*, 166.

10 *Helena*, "Night Action," 2.

NOTES

11 *Radford*, "Action Report," 2.

12 Dull, *Battle History*, 275.

13 "IJN *Hatsuyuki*: Tabular Record of Movement," Imperial Japanese Navy Page, accessed on various dates, http://www.combinedfleet.com/hatsuy_t.htm.

14 TG 36.1, "TBS Log."

15 "IJN *Nagatsuki*: Tabular Record of Movement," Imperial Japanese Navy Page, accessed on various dates, http://www.combinedfleet.com/nagats_t.htm.

16 *St. Louis* Deck Log, July 6, 1943.

17 *Radford*, "Action Report," 3.

8. Fatal Damage

1 Bureau of Ships, "U.S.S. *Helena* (CL-50) Loss in Action," September 15, 1944, 15 (hereafter cited as Bureau of Ships, "Loss").

2 Ibid., 5.

3 Sears and Rick, "Sinking of the U.S.S. Helena," 17–21.

4 "Transcript of Recording by Captain C. P. Cecil, U.S.N., 7 August 1943, Intelligence Center," U.S. Navy World War II Interviews, College Park, MD: National Archives II, August 7, 1943, 3–4 (hereafter cited as "Cecil Transcript").

5 CO USS *Helena* to Chief of the Bureau of Ships, "U.S.S. *Helena* (CL50) - War Damage Report," July 31, 1943, (Preliminary War Damage Report), 3 (hereafter cited as *Helena*, "Preliminary Damage").

6 *Helena*, "Night Action," 3.

7 "Cecil Transcript," 7–8.

8 *Helena*, "Preliminary Damage," 4.

9 Casten, *Machine-Gun Cruiser*, 119.

10 Cave and Morris, *Fightin'est Ship*, 158.

11 Bruce Petty, *At War in the Pacific: Personal Accounts of World War II Navy and Marine Corps Officers* (Jefferson, NC: McFarland & Company, 2006), 111.

12 Bureau of Ships, "Loss," 16.

13 *Helena*, "Preliminary Damage," 1–2.

9. Abandon Ship

1 Gilbert, Interview and Documents.

2 Dudley, Interview.

3. Cochran, Interview and Narrative.
4. Layton, Interview.
5. Miller, Interview.
6. Wendt, Interview and Documents.
7. Engineering Officer, USS *Helena* to CO USS *Helena*, "Events that I observed during and After the Action of 6 July, 1943, 1," enclosure D in *Helena*, "Night Action."
8. Russell Sydnor Crenshaw Jr., *South Pacific Destroyer: The Battle for the Solomons from Savo Island to Vella Gulf* (Annapolis, MD: Naval Institute Press, 1998), 146.
9. Lt. Robert E. Beisang, "This is it Boys - Helena Hit by Three Torpedoes," in Robinson articles.
10. *History of the U.S.S. Helena*, 5.
11. "Dictionary of American Fighting Ships," Naval History and Heritage Command, accessed on various dates, http://www.history.navy.mil/danfs.
12. Beisang, "This is it Boys."
13. JSDF, *Senshi Sosho*, 228.

10. A Night in Kula Gulf

1. Ted Purcell, "He Saw the Helena Go Down," in Robinson articles.
2. William C. Chambliss, "How to Abandon Ship," United States Navy: Bureau of Personnel Information Bulletin, September 1943, 12.
3. TG 36.1, "TBS Log," 6.
4. John B. Penfold, "The Amazon of Kula Gulf," *Our Navy*, September 1943, 13.
5. Thomas J. McLoughlin, "Heroic Rescue of Helena's Survivor's," *World War II*, July 2001, 45.
6. *Radford*, "Action Report," 4.
7. Morison, *Breaking the Bismarcks Barrier*, 171–72.
8. JSDF, *Senshi Sosho*, 228.
9. TG 36.1, "Night Engagement," 11.
10. CO Desron 21, "Surface Engagement," 5.
11. McLoughlin, "Heroic Rescue," 47.
12. Cliff Hemstock, "The Rescue of the U.S.S. Helena Survivors at Kula Gulf," accessed September 28, 2009, http://bellsouthpwp2.net/e/a/ea_herr/BoatTrip.htm.

NOTES

13 "Interview with Lieutenant John C. ("Jack") Fitch," by Ronald E. Marcello, Denton, TX: University of North Texas Oral History Collection, March 19, 1995, 50.

14 Joe Moll, "Rescue at Kula Gulf," accessed on October 21, 2009, http://ussnicholas.org/fletcherclass.asp?r=44905&pid=44934.

15 J. C. Fitch, "Memorandum for the Commanding officer, U.S.S. Nicholas (DD 449)," accessed November 24, 2008, http://ussnicholas.org/fletcherclass.asp?r=44905&pid=44934 (hereafter cited as "Fitch Memorandum").

16 William Heald Groverman, "I Like Destroyers," *Popular Science Monthly* (July 1944): 200.

17 "600 on Helena Rescued; First Story of Sinking," in Casey Articles.

18 Miller, Interview.

19 Robinson, Interview and Documents.

20 Morison, *Breaking the Bismarcks Barrier*, 173.

21 CO Task Unit 36.1.4 (Commander Destroyer Squadron Twenty-One) to CinCPac, "Action Report," July 21, 1943, 2, enclosed in *Nicholas*, "Action Report" (hereafter cited as CO Desron 21, "Action Report").

22 *Radford*, "Action Report," 5.

23 *Nicholas*, "Action Report," 5.

24 Morison, *Breaking the Bismarcks Barrier*, 173–74.

25 JDSF, *Senshi Sosho*, 228.

26 "Introduction: The *Niizuki*," Imperial Japanese Navy Page, accessed on various dates, http://www.combinedfleet.com/niizuk_o.htm.

27 Wendt, Interview and Documents.

28 Ibid.

29 Dudley, Interview.

30 Fitch, "Memorandum," 2.

31 "Perfume of Isle Blossoms Omen of Death for Helena," in Casey Articles.

32 Ibid.

11. The Captain's Flotilla

1 Penfold, "Amazon of Kula Gulf," 13.

2 "Cruiser Helena Set Firing Mark at End," *New York Times*, July 13, 1943.

3 John Henry, "Helena Skipper Tells of Ship's Battle to Death," in undated newspaper articles, courtesy of Bill Bunker.

NOTES

4. Gilbert Cant, *The Great Pacific Victory from the Solomons to Tokyo* (New York: The John Day Company, 1946), 45.
5. Hemstock, "Rescue of the U.S.S. Helena Survivors," 3.
6. Don Hensler, interviewed by the author, September 18, 2007.
7. "Cecil Transcript," 2–4.
8. Paul Weisenberger, interviewed by the author, January 9, 2009.
9. Clayton Lee Carkin, "Whaleboat Odyssey," in *Escape from the Sea*, ed. William Henderson Jr. (Los Altos, CA: Henderson & Associates, 2001), 253.
10. Cave and Morris, *Fightin'est Ship*, 173, and Hemstock, "Rescue of the U.S.S. Helena Survivors," 3.
11. Paul Weisenberger, "Kula Gulf and Beyond," in *Escape from the Sea*, 73.
12. Carkin, "Whaleboat Odyssey," 254.
13. Cave and Morris, *Fightin'est Ship*, 174, and Carkin, "Whaleboat Odyssey," 254–55.
14. *Woodworth* Deck Log, July 6, 1943.
15. B. J. M'Quaid, "Life and Death of Gwin, A Scrap-Happy Destroyer," in Casey Articles.
16. Gilbert Cant, "They Live to Fight Again," *Sea Power*, April 1944, 21.
17. Carkin, "Whaleboat Odyssey," 256.

12. Return

1. *Honolulu* Deck Log, July 6, 1943.
2. TG 36.1, "Night Engagement," 11.
3. Morison, *Breaking the Bismarcks Barrier*, 196.
4. JSDF, *Senshi Sosho*, 228.
5. Howe, "Grace of God," 49.
6. Dudley, Interview.
7. Wendt, Interview and Documents.
8. "Walter Wendt Still Remembers Every Minute of his Naval Career," *Lakeland Times Newspaper* (Minocqua, WI) in USS *Helena* Web Page, accessed on various dates, http://www.usshelena.org/wendt.html.
9. Miller, Interview.
10. Robinson, Interview and Documents.
11. *Nicholas* Deck Log, July 6, 1943.

12 CO Desron 21, "Surface Engagement," 11.
13 *Nicholas* Deck Log, July 6, 1943.
14 "Communiqué No. 435, July 6, 1943," in "Navy Department Communiqués and Pertinent Press Releases, December 10, 1941 to May 24, 1945," accessed July 2, 2009, http://www.ibiblio.org/pha/comms/1943-07.html.

13. Adrift

1 Cant, "They Live to Fight Again," 20.
2 Howard E. Freeman, "Above Kula Gulf," in *Escape from the Sea*, 237–38.
3 Cant, "They Live to Fight Again," 20.
4 Gilbert, Interview and Documents.
5 Layton, Interview.
6 Cochran, Interview and Narrative.
7 "Biographical Sketch Vice-Admiral John L. Chew," Washington, DC: Naval Historical Center, July 10, 1970, 1.
8 "Reminiscences of Vice Admiral John L. (Jack) Chew, U.S. Navy Retired," Annapolis, MD: United States Naval Institute Oral History Collection, 76.
9 "Statement of Lieutenant Commander John L. Chew, U.S. Navy, to Commanding Officer, U.S.S. Helena, regarding rescue of his party from Vella Lavella Island," 8, in *Helena* "Night Action."
10 Commander John L. Chew, and Charles Lee Lewis, "Some Shall Escape," *United States Naval Institute Proceedings*, August 1945, 889.
11 "Shipwrecked Sailors put on Show in the Sea," *Chicago Tribune*, August 8, 1943.
12 Sergeant Pete Zurlinden, "Chicago Marine Major Tells of Helena Sinking," *Chicago Tribune*, October 25, 1943.
13 "Survivor Tells How Helena Sank," *New York Times*, October 23, 1943.
14 Samuel E. Morison, "Conversation with Lt. Comdr. Warren Boles of Marblehead, Late Gunnery Officer of U.S.S. Helena, Now Gunnery Officer of new Vincennes. Fore River, 23 September 1943," Washington, DC: United States Naval Historical Center, NRS 1971-16, September 23, 1943, 1.
15 Morison, *Breaking the Bismarcks Barrier*, 191.
16 Chew and Lewis, "Some Shall Escape," 889.
17 Cant, "They Live to Fight Again," 21.
18 Chew and Lewis, "Some Shall Escape," 891.
19 "Survivor Tells How Helena Sank."

20 Ted Blahnik, "A Swim to Shore," in *Escape from the Sea*, 100.
21 "Kicks Sharks Off as He Waits Rescue," *New York Times*, August 8, 1943.
22 Bernard Kelly, "Kelly's Irregulars," in *Escape from the Sea*, 200.

14. The Island

1 D. O. W. Hall, *Coastwatchers* (Wellington, New Zealand: Department of Internal Affairs, War History Branch, 1951), 4.
2 Chandler Whipple, *Code Word Ferdinand: Adventures of the Coast Watchers* (New York: Putnam, 1971), 114–15.
3 CO USS *Grampus* to Commander Task Force Forty-Two. "U.S.S. *Grampus* (SS 207) - Report of Fourth War Patrol - August 30 to November 23, 1942," 8.
4 Eric A. Feldt, *The Coast Watchers* (Melbourne: Oxford University Press, 1946), 102.
5 Ibid., 103.
6 Archie Wharton Ellesmere Silvester, "Papers, 1908 – 1997," Auckland War Memorial Museum Library, MS 2006/53, accessed November 18, 2008, http://muse.aucklandmuseum.com/databases/Muscat/69648.detail.
7 Cochran, Interview and Narrative.
8 Ibid.
9 Lee Spaulding, "Sky Spy," in *Escape from the Sea*, 153.
10 Chew and Lewis, "Some Shall Escape," 892.
11 Blahnik, "A Swim to Shore," 11, and Chew and Lewis, "Some Shall Escape," 892.
12 "Conversation with Boles," 2.
13 Gilbert, Interview and Documents.
14 Ibid.
15 Layton, Interview.
16 Kelly, "Irregulars," 200.
17 Feldt, *Coast Watchers*, 109.
18 Whipple, *Ferdinand*, 120.
19 Feldt, *Coast Watchers*, 109.
20 Walter Lord, *Lonely Vigil: Coastwatchers of the Solomons* (New York: Viking Press), 1977, 198.
21 James Layton, "Island Medic," in *Escape from the Sea*, 108.
22 Cochran, Interview and Narrative.

15. Hideouts

1. Chew and Lewis, "Some Shall Escape," 894.
2. Layton, Interview.
3. Cochran, Interview and Narrative.
4. Ibid.
5. "Conversation with Boles," 2.
6. Ibid., 2, and Cochran, Interview and Narrative.
7. Gilbert, Interview and Documents.
8. Lord, *Lonely Vigil*, 201.
9. *Helena*, "Night Action," 9.
10. Frank Cellozzi, "The Death of a Lady: The Aftermath of the Sinking of the Light Cruiser Helena CL 50," unpublished narrative, 13.
11. Chew and Lewis, "Some Shall Escape," 894–95.
12. Cochran, Interview and Narrative, and Lord, *Lonely Vigil,* 203.
13. Chew and Lewis, "Some Shall Escape," 895.
14. Cave and Morris, *Fightin'est Ship*, 185.
15. Ibid., 184.
16. Frank Hewlett, "Helena's Rescued Crew Ready to Fight Japs Again," in Casey Articles, and Pat Robinson, "Wild Dash Saves Helena Survivors," in undated newspaper articles provided by Howard Kavon.
17. "Sea Survival," Discovery Survival Zone, accessed December 9, 2009, http://dsc.discovery.com/convergence/survival/guide.
18. "Ensign Donald Charles Bechtel. Sinking of the U.S.S. Helena and Rescue from Vella Lavella," Washington, DC: United States Naval Historical Center, NRS 1971-16. November 2, 1943, 6.
19. CO Marine Detachment to Commandant, U.S. Marine Corps, "Report of Marine Detachment, U.S.S. Helena, subsequent to loss of ship in operations of war," July 27, 1943, 2.
20. Ibid., 2.
21. Chew and Lewis, "Some Shall Escape," 898, and Layton, Interview.
22. Kelly, "Irregulars," 202.
23. "Helena Survivors Camp on Jap Isle," in Casey Articles.
24. J. Norman Lodge, "Rescue 157 of Helena's Crew Form Jap Isle," *Chicago Tribune*, July 20, 1943.
25. Paul Kavon, untitled narrative, 15.

26 Cellozzi, "Death of a Lady," 10.
27 Ibid., 14.
28 Chew and Lewis, "Some Shall Escape," 898.
29 Ibid., 899.
30 Bechtel, "Sinking and Rescue," 4.
31 Lord, *Lonely Vigil*, 204, and Chew and Lewis, "Some Shall Escape," 895.
32 Layton, Interview.
33 Chew and Lewis, "Some Shall Escape," 896.
34 Lord, *Lonely Vigil*, 203.
35 Cellozzi, "Death of a Lady," 13.
36 Chew and Lewis, "Some Shall Escape," 899.

16. Rescue Operation

1 Whipple, *Ferdinand*, 122.
2 Morison, *Breaking the Bismarcks Barrier*, 193.
3 Cochran, Interview and Narrative.
4 Lord, *Lonely Vigil*, 205.
5 "Reminiscences of Vice Adm. Chew," 109.
6 Cellozzi, "Death of a Lady," 14–15.
7 Lord, *Lonely Vigil*, 205–6; Kelly, "Irregulars," 202; Whipple, *Ferdinand*, 121; and Cellozzi, "Death of a Lady," 15.
8 Lord, *Lonely Vigil*, 207.
9 *The Four Stack APDs: The Famed Green Dragons* (Paducah, KY: Turner Publishing Company, 1999), 21.
10 Horan, *Action Tonight*, 122.
11 Morison, *Breaking the Bismarcks Barrier*, 193.
12 Bechtel, "Sinking and Rescue," 4.
13 Lord, *Lonely Vigil*, 206–7.
14 Gilbert, Interview and Documents.
15 Kavon, Narrative.
16 CO Destroyer Squadron Twenty-One to CinCPac, "Rescue of Survivors of U.S.S. Helena from the Island of Vella Lavella (New Georgia Group); Report of," July 24, 1943, 1.

NOTES

17. CO Destroyer Squadron Twelve to CinCPac, "Rescue of Approximately 165 Helena Survivors from Vella Lavella, Solomon Islands, 16-17 July, 1943," July 25, 1943, 1.
18. *Gridley* War Diary, July 15, 1943.
19. Ibid, July 16, 1943.
20. Lord, *Lonely Vigil*, 206–7, and Chew and Lewis, "Some Shall Escape," 899.
21. Lord, *Lonely Vigil*, 21.
22. *Dent* Deck Log, July 16, 1943.
23. "Specification for the Higgins Industries 36-Foot LCVP," Higgins PT305 restoration project, accessed January 12, 2010, http://www.higginsboats.com/html/eureka.html.
24. Gilbert Cant, "Rescue in the Pacific," *Saturday Evening Post*, January 29, 1944, 17.
25. *Four Stack ADPs*, 94.
26. *Waters* War Diary, July 16, 1943.
27. Lord, *Lonely Vigil*, 207.
28. Spaulding, "Sky Spy," 155.
29. Layton, Interview.
30. Ibid.
31. Lord, *Lonely Vigil*, 211.
32. Cant, "Rescue in the Pacific," 93.

17. Home

1. "Communiqué No. 436, July 7, 1943," in "Navy Department Communiqués and Pertinent Press Releases, December 10, 1941 to May 24, 1945," accessed July 2, 2009, http://www.ibiblio.org/pha/comms/index.html.
2. Robinson, Interview and Documents.
3. *Gridley* War Diary, July 16, 1943.
4. Lodge, "Rescue of 157."
5. Cochran, Interview and Narrative.
6. Cant, "Rescue in the Pacific," 93.
7. Chew and Lewis, "Some Shall Escape," 903.
8. *Dent* Deck Log, July 16, 1943.
9. *Waters* War Diary, July 16, 1943.

10. "161 Helena Survivors Quit Enemy-Held Isle: Naval Units Daring Exploit Effects Rescue," *New York Times*, July 19, 1943.
11. Pat Robinson, "Wild Dash Saves *Helena* Survivors," and Frank Hewlett, "Survivors of *Helena* Saved," in undated newspaper articles provided by Howard Kavon.
12. CO Desron 21, "Rescue," 3.
13. "Survivors of Sunken Helena Believe Rescue Was Miracle," in undated newspaper articles provided by Howard Kavon.
14. Cellozzi, "Death of a Lady," 18.
15. Cochran, Interview and Narrative.
16. Gilbert, Interview and Documents.
17. Wendt, Interview and Documents.
18. "Reminiscences of Vice Adm. Chew," 110.
19. Wendt, Interview and Documents.

Epilogue

1. "Cecil Biographical Sketch," 1–2.
2. Ibid., 1–3.
3. "Adm. John Chew, 89, Dies; Officer on WWII Cruiser," *Washington Post*, June 8, 1999.
4. Layton, Interview.
5. "Marietta: Deale Cochran, Wartime Experience Defined his Life," *Atlanta Journal-Constitution*, January 15, 2009, accessed January 19, 2010, http://infoweb.newsbank.
6. Gilbert, Interview and Documents.
7. Ibid.
8. Betsy Biesenbach, "Celebrating Survival," *Roanoke Times & World News*, July 15, 1993.
9. "Miller, Mason Jr.," *Roanoke (VA) Times*, December 12, 2008, accessed October 10, 2009, http://infoweb.newsbank.
10. Wendt, Interview and Documents.
11. Dudley, Interview.
12. Miscellaneous information from the 1989 *Helena* reunion, accessed November 20, 2008, http://www.usshelena.org/reunion1989.html.
13. Kevin Twidwell, "500 in Town to Celebrate Helenas," *Independent Record* (Helena, MT), August 25, 1989.

BIBLIOGRAPHY

Books

Adcock, Al. *U.S. Light Cruisers in Action.* Carrollton, TX: Squadron Signal Publications, 1999.

Campbell, John. *Naval Weapons of World War Two.* Annapolis, MD: Naval Institute Press, 1985.

Cant, Gilbert. *The Great Pacific Victory from the Solomons to Tokyo.* New York: The John Day Company, 1946.

Casten, Ray J. *U.S.S. Helena: The Machine-Gun Cruiser.* Martinsville, TN: Airleaf Publishing, 2006.

Cave, Hugh B., and Lt. C. G. Morris, USNR. *The Fightin'est Ship: The Story of the Cruiser "Helena."* New York: Dodd, Mead & Company, 1944.

Crenshaw, Russell Sydnor, Jr. *South Pacific Destroyer: The Battle for the Solomons from Savo Island to Vella Gulf.* Annapolis, MD: Naval Institute Press, 1998.

Dull, Paul S. *A Battle History of the Imperial Japanese Navy, 1941–1945.* Annapolis, MD: Naval Institute Press, 1978.

Fahey, James J. *Pacific War Diary, 1942–1945.* Boston: Houghton Mifflin, 1963.

Feldt, Eric A. *The Coast Watchers.* Melbourne: Oxford University Press, 1946.

The Four Stack APDs: The Famed Green Dragons. Paducah, KY: Turner Publishing Company, 1999.

Frank, Richard B. *Guadalcanal.* New York: Random House, 1990.

Hall, D. O. W. *Coastwatchers*. Wellington, New Zealand: Department of Internal Affairs, War History Branch, 1951.

Hammel, Eric M. *Munda Trail: The New Georgia Campaign*. New York: Orion Books, 1989.

Henderson, William, Jr., ed. *Escape from the Sea*. Los Altos, CA: Henderson & Associates, 2001.

Horan, James D. *Action Tonight, the Story of the Destroyer* O'Bannon *in the Pacific*. New York: G.P. Putnam's Sons, 1945.

Japanese Self Defense Force: War History Office. *Senshi Sosho (War History Series) Volume 83: Southeast Area Naval Operations, Part II*. Tokyo: Asagumo Shibunsha, 1975.

Lord, Walter. *Lonely Vigil: Coastwatchers of the Solomons*. New York: Viking Press, 1977.

Miller, John, Jr. *Cartwheel: The Reduction of Rabaul*. Washington, DC: Office of the Chief of Military History, Department of the Army, 1990.

Morison, Samuel Eliot. *History of United States Naval Operations in World War II Volume VI: Breaking the Bismarcks Barrier, 22 July 1942–1 May 1944*. Edison, NJ: Castle Book, 2001.

———. *The Two-Ocean War: A Short History of the United States Navy in the Second World War*. Boston, MA: Little, Brown, 1963.

Petty, Bruce. *At War in the Pacific: Personal Accounts of World War II Navy and Marine Corps Officers*. Jefferson, NC: McFarland & Company, 2006.

Rottman, Gordon L. *World War II Pacific Island Guide: A Geo-Military Study*. Westport, CT: Greenwood Press, 2002.

United States Navy. *The Bluejackets Manual*. Annapolis, MD: Naval Institute Press, 1946.

Watts, Anthony J., and Brian G. Gordon. *The Imperial Japanese Navy*. New York: Doubleday, 1971.

Whipple, Chandler. *Code Word Ferdinand: Adventures of the Coast Watchers*. New York: Putnam, 1971.

Action Reports and Official Documents

"Biographical Sketch of Rear Admiral Charles P. Cecil." Washington, DC: Naval Historical Center. August 1, 1946.

"Biographical Sketch of Vice-Admiral John L. Chew." Washington, DC: Naval Historical Center. July 10, 1970.

Bureau of Ships. "U.S.S. Helena (CL-50) Loss in Action." September 15, 1944. (Final War Damage Report.)

BIBLIOGRAPHY

Chambliss, William C. "How to Abandon Ship." United States Navy: Bureau of Personnel Information Bulletin. September 1943.

CO Destroyer Squadron Twelve to CinCPac. "Rescue of Approximately 165 Helena Survivors from Vella Lavella, Solomon Islands, 16-17 July, 1943." July 25, 1943.

CO Destroyer Squadron Twenty-One to CinCPac. "Rescue of Survivors of U.S.S. Helena from the Island of Vella Lavella (New Georgia Group); Report of." July 24, 1943.

CO Marine Detachment to Commandant, U.S. Marine Corps. "Report of Marine Detachment, U.S.S. Helena, subsequent to loss of ship in operations of war." July 27, 1943.

CO Task Force 67 to CinCPac. "Vila-Stanmore Bombardment." January 28, 1943.

CO Task Group 36.1 to CinCPac. "Action Report, Night Bombardment of Vila-Stanmore and Bairoko Harbor, Kula Gulf, 4-5 July 1943." July 30, 1943.

CO Task Unit 36.1 to CinCPac. "Action Report - Night Engagement off Kula Gulf during the Night of 5-6 July 1943." August 1, 1943.

CO Task Unit 36.1.4 (Commander Destroyer Squadron Twenty-One) to CinCPac. "Action Report - Shore Bombardment of Enemy Positions on Kolombangara Island and New Georgia Island (Kula Gulf) on the Night of July 4-5, 1943." July 12, 1943.

CO Task Unit 36.1.4 (Commander Destroyer Squadron Twenty-One) to CinCPac. "Surface Engagement with Enemy (Japanese) Forces off Kula Gulf, New Georgia Group, Solomon Islands on the Night of July 5-6, 1943; Action Report of." July 20, 1943.

CO USS *Grampus* to Commander Task Force Forty-Two. "U.S.S. *Gampus* (SS 207) - Report of Fourth War Patrol - August 30 to November 23, 1942." November 23, 1942.

CO USS *Helena* to All Officers. "Succession to Command." April 1, 1943.

CO USS *Helena* to Chief of the Bureau of Ships. "U.S.S. Helena (CL50) - War Damage Report." July 31, 1943. (Preliminary War Damage Report.)

CO USS *Helena* to CinCPac. "Action Report - Attack by Japanese Aircraft- January 24, 1943." January 28, 1943.

CO USS *Helena* to CinCPac. "U.S.S. Helena - Night Action against Japanese Surface Forces off Kula Gulf, New Georgia Group, Night of 5-6 July, 1943 - Report of." July 30, 1943.

CO USS *Helena* to CinCPac. "U.S.S. Helena - Shore Bombardment - Kolombangara Island and Bairoko Harbor, New Georgia Group, Night of 4-5, July 1943." July 30, 1943.

CO USS *Helena* to CinCPac. "Vila-Stanmore Area - Kolombangara Island - Bombardment of 1500 Zebra, 23 January, 1943." January 28, 1943.

CO USS *Nicholas* to CinCPac. "Action Report." July 7, 1943.

CO USS *Radford* to CinCPac. "Night Surface Engagement off Kula Gulf During Night of July 5-6, 1943; Action Report of." July 11, 1943.

Deck Logs: *Dent, Honolulu, Nicholas, Radford* and *St. Louis*. National Archives and Records Administration (Archives II), College Park, MD.

United States Navy, Office of Naval Intelligence. *Combat Narrative IX: Bombardments of Munda and Vila-Stanmore*. Washington, DC: Office of Naval Intelligence, United States Navy, 1944.

United States Navy, Office of Naval Intelligence. *Combat Narrative X: Operations in the New Georgia Area*. Washington, DC: Office of Naval Intelligence, United States Navy, 1944.

United States Navy, Office of Public Relations, *History of the U.S.S. Helena (CL-50)* Washington, DC: United States Navy, Office of Public Relations.

War Diaries: *Gridley, Helena, Waters*, and *Woodworth*. National Archives and Records Administration (Archives II), College Park, MD.

Articles

"161 Helena Survivors Quit Enemy-Held Isle: Naval Units Daring Exploit Effects Rescue." *New York Times*, July 19, 1943.

"Adm. John Chew, 89, Dies; Officer on WWII Cruiser." *Washington Post*, June 8, 1999.

Biesenbach, Betsy. "Celebrating Survival." *Roanoke Times & World News*, July 15, 1993.

Cant, Gilbert. "Rescue in the Pacific." *Saturday Evening Post*, January 29, 1944.

———. "They Live to Fight Again." *Sea Power*, April 1944.

Chew, Commander John L., and Charles Lee Lewis. "Some Shall Escape." *United States Naval Institute Proceedings*, August 1945.

"Cruiser Helena Set Firing Mark at End." *New York Times*, July 13, 1943.

Groverman, William Heald. "I Like Destroyers." *Popular Science Monthly*, July 1944.

"Kicks Sharks Off as He Waits Rescue." *New York Times*, August 8, 1943.

Lodge, J. Norman. "Rescue of 157 of Helena's Crew from Jap Isle." *Chicago Tribune*, July 20, 1943.

McLoughlin, Thomas J. "Heroic Rescue of Helena's Survivor's." *World War II*, July 2001.

Penfold, John B. "The Amazon of Kula Gulf." *Our Navy*, September 1943.

"Shipwrecked Sailors put on Show in the Sea." *Chicago Tribune*, August 8, 1943.

"Survivor Tells How Helena Sank." *New York Times*, October 23, 1943.

Twidwell, Kevin. "500 in town to Celebrate Helenas." *The Independent Record* (Helena, MT), August 25, 1989.

Undated newspaper articles courtesy of Bill Bunker, Howard Kavon, and Eugene Robinson.

Zurlinden, Sergeant Pete. "Chicago Marine Major Tells of Helena Sinking." *Chicago Tribune*, October 25, 1943.

Interviews, Oral Histories, and Unpublished Narratives

Cellozzi, Frank. "The Death of a Lady: The Aftermath of the Sinking of the Light Cruiser Helena CL 50." Unpublished narrative.

Cochran, Bin. Interviewed by the author and narrative sent to author, October 8, 2007.

Dudley, Remmel. Interviewed by the author, January 21 and December 18, 2008.

"Ensign Donald Charles Bechtel. Sinking of the U.S.S. Helena and Rescue from Vella Lavella." Washington, DC: United States Naval Historical Center, NRS 1971-16. November 2, 1943.

Gilbert, Gayle. Interviewed by the author and misc. documents sent to author, November 24, 2008 and June 10, 2009.

Hensler, Don. Interviewed by the author, September 18, 2007.

Howe, Robert M. "By the Grace of God." Unpublished narrative.

"Interview with Lieutenant John C. ("Jack") Fitch." By Ronald E. Marcello. Denton, TX: University of North Texas Oral History Collection. March 19, 1995.

Kavon, Paul. Untitled Narrative.

Layton, Jim. Interviewed by the author, February 25 and March 18, 2008 and June 8, 2009.

"Lieutenant W.L. McKeckney, USNW. U.S.S. Helena, Sinking of." Washington, DC: United States Naval Historical Center. NRS 1971-16. November 2, 1943.

Miller, Mason. Interviewed by the author, October 29, 2007.

Morison, Samuel E. "Conversation with Lt. Comdr. Warren Boles of Marblehead, Late Gunnery Officer of U.S.S. Helena, Now Gunnery Officer of new Vincennes. Fore River, 23 September 1943." Washington, DC: United States Naval Historical Center, NRS 1971-16. September 23, 1943.

"Reminiscences of Vice Admiral John L. (Jack) Chew, U.S. Navy Retired." Annapolis, MD: United States Naval Institute Oral History Collection. 1979.

Robinson, Eugene. Interviewed by the author and misc. documents sent to author, December 4, 2007 and January 3, March 26 and June 8, 2009.

Sears, Franklin EM2c, and Edwin J. Rick, SF 3/c. "The Sinking of the U.S.S. Helena in Kula Gulf." Washington, DC: United States Naval Historical Center, NRS 1971-16. August 31, 1943.

"Transcript of Recording by Captain C.P. Cecil, U.S.N., 7 August 1943, Intelligence Center." U.S. Navy World War II Interviews. College Park, MD: National Archives II. August 7, 1943.

Wendt, Walter. Interviewed by the author and misc. documents sent to author, November 5, 2007.

Weisenberger, Paul. Interviewed by the author, January 9, 2009.

Internet Sources

Discovery Survival Zone. "Sea Survival." Accessed December 9, 2009. http://dsc.discovery.com/convergence/survival/guide/environment/sea/sea.html.

Fitch, J. C. "Memorandum for the Commanding officer, U.S.S. Nicholas (DD 449)." Accessed November 24, 2008. http://destroyerhistory.org/fletcherclass/index.asp?r=44934&pid=44973.

Hemstock, Cliff. "The Rescue of the U.S.S. Helena Survivors at Kula Gulf." Accessed September 28, 2009. http://bellsouthpwp2.net/e/a/ea_herr/BoatTrip.htm.

Higgins PT305 Restoration Project. "Specification for the Higgins Industries 36-Foot LCVP." Accessed January 12, 2010. http://www.higginsboats.com/html/eureka.html.

Imperial Japanese Navy Page. Accessed on various dates. http://www.combinedfleet.com.

"Marietta: Deale Cochran, wartime experience defined his life." *Atlanta Journal-Constitution*, January 15, 2009. Accessed January 19, 2010. http://infoweb.newsbank.

"Miller, Mason Jr." *Roanoke (VA) Times*, December 12, 2008. Accessed October 10, 2009. http://infoweb.newsbank.

Moll, Joe. "Rescue at Kula Gulf." Accessed October 21, 2009. http://ussnicholas.org/fletcherclass.asp?r=44905&pid=44934.

Naval History and Heritage Command. "Dictionary of American Fighting Ships." Accessed on various dates. http://www.history.navy.mil/danfs.

BIBLIOGRAPHY

"Navy Department Communiqués and Pertinent Press Releases, December 10, 1941 to May 24, 1945." Accessed July 2, 2009. http://www.ibiblio.org/pha/comms/index.html.

Silvester, Archie Wharton Ellesmere. "Papers, 1908 - 1997." Auckland War Memorial Museum Library. MS 2006/53. Accessed on November 18, 2008. http://muse.aucklandmuseum.com/databases/Muscat/69648.detail.

USS *Helena* Web Page. Accessed on various dates. http://www.usshelena.org.

INDEX

Adam, Burt, 165
Ainsworth, Walden, 40, 45–50, 55–57, 63; during Kula Gulf battle, 66–68, 71, 73–74, 76, 78, 83, 103, 106–7, 127–29, 131, 179; during Vila-Stanmore Bombardment, 12–14, 17–18, 20, 23, 25–27
Akiyama, Teruo, 65–66, 68, 74, 77, 79
Amagiri, 65, 80, 103, 112–14
Anderson, John, 140, 144
Aore Island, 29
Arkansas, 16
Atkinson, Burton, 117
Atkinson, Grady, 173
Avenger (TBF), 28

Baird, William, 19, 116
Bairoko Harbor, New Georgia, 47
Barnet, Bill, 89
Bausewine, George, 163, 169–70, 179, 186
Bechtel, Donald, 167, 172, 178, 180

Beisang, Robert, 100
Benham, 120
Black Cats. *See* Catalina (PBY)
Blackett Strait, 42, 73, 103
Blahnik, Ted, 150
Boles, Warren, 59, 138, 150, 161, 163, 188
Boston, MA, 202–3
Bougainville Island, 49, 152
Brisbane, Australia, 147
Brooklyn Navy Yard, 5–6
Buerkle, Elmer, 92, 111
Bunker, Bill, 205
Buin, Bougainville, 54
Bush, George H. W., 105

Cape Esperance, Battle of, 2
Cape Esperance, Guadalcanal, 62
Carkin, Clayton, 109, 118–19, 123
Carpenter, Charles, 76
Catalina (PBY), 13–14, 17–20, 50

INDEX

Cecil, Charles, 3, 17–18, 20, 22, 26–28, 32, 35, 41, 48, 52, 61–63, 119; death of, 201; during Kula Gulf battle, 71–72, 74–77; on *Helena*'s sinking, 87–89; rescue from Kula Gulf, 120–21, 123, 125, 128, 134, 139

Cellozzi, Frank, 171, 174–75, 178, 188

Chevalier, 46, 50, 54–57, 62–64

Chew, John, 137–41, 143–44, 150–51, 197; death of, 201; during Vella Lavella rescue, 180, 183, 188–89, 193; on Vella Lavella, 156–57, 159, 163–66, 171–77

Chicago, IL, 8–9, 16, 24

Choiseul Island, 53, 68, 148

Chung, Sam, 159–61, 163–66, 171, 176–77, 184, 188

Ciunguin, Eli, 153, 186

Cleveland, OH, 23, 25, 32, 191, 198, 203

Cochran, Bin, 31, 59–61, 136–37, 198, 204; at Naval Academy, 15–16; at sea after *Helena*'s sinking, 140, 142, 149–50; at Sydney, 38; comments on Captain Cecil, 32; death of, 202; during Kula Gulf battle, 72–73, 76, 93–94; during Vella Lavella rescue, 187–89, 193–95; on Vella Lavella, 155–56, 160–61, 165–66, 168–69, 172, 176

Cook, Charles, 98–102

Coral Sea, 45

Corsair Fighter, 177

Craig, John, 147–48

Curran, James, 54

Dallas, TX, 6, 202

Dashing Wave, 196

Dauntless Dive Bomber, 28

DeHaven, 12, 20–22

DeJon, Edward, 97

Dent, 178, 184–86, 188, 192–93

Destroyer Squadron Twenty-One, 178

Dudley, Remmel, 40, 60–61, 195, 197–98, 205; death of, 204; during Kula Gulf battle, 92–93, 116; early years, 38–39; rescue from Kula Gulf, 116, 130; time at survivors' camp, 195–96

Dupay, William, 163, 179, 184

Edwards, Irvin, 129

Ellet, 179, 184

Enogai Inlet, New Georgia, 48, 56

Erskine Phillips, 63

Espiritu Santo, New Hebrides, 1, 3–4, 28–32, 40, 62, 196

Ewing, John, 167

Fiji Islands, 196

First Marine Division, 39

Firth, Robert, 152–53

Fitch, John, 109–10, 114, 118

Flanagan, Lawrence, 136

Flood, Charles, 89, 121

Florida Island, 41

Foster, Paul, 144

Frisbee, Molloy, 168

Fubuki, 2

Furutaka, 2

Gazis, Nicholas, 37

Gilbert, Gayle, 4–5, 29–30, 46–47, 51–52, 194, 196, 198; at sea after *Helena*'s sinking, 134–35, 140, 142–43, 145, 151; at Sydney, 37–38; during Kula Gulf battle, 91–92; during Vella Lavella rescue, 193; life after World War II, 202–3; on Vella

Lavella, 154, 162, 170–71, 173, 180–81
Gizo Island, 182
Gizo Strait, 182
Golden Gate Bridge, 196
Gonongga Island, 182
Grampus, 147–48
Great Depression, 6, 38–39
Great Lakes Naval Training Center, 5
Green Bay, WI, 5
Green, Ken, 143, 151
Gridley, 178, 184–85
Guadalcanal, 3, 11–14, 28, 41, 47, 49, 56, 62, 64–65, 67, 87, 127, 133–34, 139, 147, 152–53, 175, 178, 181; American invasion of, 2
Gwin, 124–26, 139

Halsey, William, 12, 38–39, 45, 47, 63, 65, 197
Hamakaze, 65
Hatsuyuki, 65, 80
Hayes, KS, 4
Helena, xv, 1, 15, 45–46, 56, 64, 83, 128–29, 133–34, 191, 201; air attack on, 26–27; armament of, 16–17, 21, 59–61, 72–73; at Mare Island, 5, 7, 10; at Sydney 35–36, 40; construction of, 2; during Kula Gulf battle, 71, 74–77; during Vila-Stanmore bombardment, 12–14, 19–20, 22, 41–42, 48–50, 52; early operations, 2, 6; hit by torpedoes, 78, 85–88; sinking of, 89–90, 105–6; survivors rescued in Kula Gulf, 107–10, 118–19, 124–26
Helena, MT, 205
Helena Reunion Association, 205
Hemstock, Cliff, 109, 118–19, 123–24
Henderson Field, Guadalcanal, 28

Henley, 35
Hensler, Don, 120, 122
Hiatt, Ken, 152
Higgins Boat, 185–86, 188–89
Hill, Andrew, 112, 114
Hitchon, Cobden, 100, 102, 114–15, 130
Hollingsworth, Sam, 140, 150
Holly Springs, MS, 15, 38
Honolulu, 41, 48–50, 55, 63–64, 68, 79, 104, 108, 127, 132
Hoover, Gilbert, 3
Houston, 203–4
Howe, Robert, 64, 129

Iringila, Vella Lavella, 152
Iwo Jima, 204

Java, Vella Lavella, 141, 170
Jenkins, 62–64, 66, 78, 82, 104, 178
Jintsu, 192
Johnson, James, 165
Jonesboro, AR, 38
Josselyn, Henry, 147–49, 152–53, 162, 175, 179, 188–89

Kanawha, 41
Kasaan Bay, 202
Kavon, Paul, 169–70, 180–81, 183, 186
Keenan, John, 147–48, 152
Kelly, Bernard, 93, 205; at sea after *Helena*'s sinking, 138, 144, 152; during Vella Lavella rescue, 184, 187–88; on Vella Lavella, 161, 163–64, 168–69, 177
Knuckles, Rollo, 185, 188
Koerner, Ozzie, 89
Koli Point, Guadalcanal, 47, 181
Kolombangara, Battle of, 180, 192

Kolombangara Island, 11–12, 65, 68, 80, 106–8, 194; American bombardment of, 13, 21, 25, 47, 50; Japanese airfield on, 12; location of, 11, 147; near *Helena* survivors, 115, 120–21, 133–134, 136, 138, 140, 141–43
Kolstad, Allen, 205
Korean War, 204
Kula Gulf, 13, 28, 53, 56, 62, 66–68, 72, 79, 82, 117, 124, 131–34, 141, 169, 178, 182, 191, 199; American naval operations in, 18, 22, 40–42, 47–49; *Helena* survivors in, 106–8, 120; Japanese naval operations in, 12, 40–41, 63; location of, 11
Kula Gulf, Battle of, xv, 69, 103, 117, 127–29
Kunizo, Kanaoka, 54

La Hue, David, 100
Lambu Lambu Cove, Vella Lavella, 141, 153, 159, 163, 177, 179–80, 183, 186
Larned, KS, 4
Lawler, Fred, 122
Layton, Jim, 16, 32, 194–96, 198, 201, 204; at Espiritu Santo, 30; at sea after *Helena*'s sinking, 135–36, 140, 142, 151–52; at Sydney, 38; during Kula Gulf battle, 95–96; during Vella Lavella rescue, 187–89; early years, 6–7; life after World War II, 202; on Vella Lavella, 154–55, 160, 166–67, 173–74
Leander, 194
Lew Wallace, 196
Liberator Bomber, 133, 139
Los Angeles, CA, 4

Mare Island Navy Yard, 2, 7, 16
Marietta, GA, 202
Maury, 178, 184
McInerney, Francis, 46, 49–50, 54–55, 57, 72, 74, 79, 103; during Kula Gulf rescue, 107–8, 112, 114, 117, 131; during Vella Lavella rescue, 178–79, 181–83, 185, 192–93
McKeckney, William, 64–65
McNaughton, WI, 199, 204
Memphis, TN, 15
Menakasapa Island, 122
Miami, 202
Mikazuki, 65
Miller, Helen, 9, 198
Miller, Mason, 7, 10, 21, 31–32, 51, 130–31, 196, 198; at midshipman school, 9; death of, 203; during Kula Gulf battle, 96–97; early years, 8; rescue from Kula Gulf, 110–11
Minegumo, 40
Mochizuki, 65, 103, 113, 117
Moffett, William, 133
Moll, Joe, 109
Mora, Jose, 144
Munda, New Georgia, 11, 14, 40, 45, 47, 65, 182
Murasame, 40

Nagatsuki, 49, 53, 65, 80–82, 117, 128, 133
Nashville, 3, 12, 18–22, 27
Nassau, 203
Naval Battle of Guadalcanal, 3, 40, 120
Neosho, 1
New Caledonia, 35, 38–39, 194–96
New Georgia Island, 13–14, 61, 67, 117, 120–22, 124, 132, 178; American invasion of, 45–47; location of, 11

INDEX

New York Navy Yard, 2
Ngawkosoli River, 184
Nicholas, 12–13, 18, 22, 46, 49, 53–54, 62–63; during Kula Gulf battle, 71–72, 74, 79; during Kula Gulf rescue, 103, 106–9, 112–14, 118–19, 121, 124, 127, 129, 131–32; during Vella Lavella rescue, 178, 185
Navy Blue and Gold (movie), 15
New Orleans, LA, 165
Niizuki, 49, 65, 68, 75, 77–78, 107, 112, 128–29
Noland, James, 134, 139
Nopper, Howard, 133
Northwestern University, 8

Oakland, CA, 25
Oakland Naval Hospital, 201
O'Bannon, 12–13, 18, 21–22, 27–28, 46, 50, 63, 178; during Kula Gulf battle, 71, 74, 79, 81, 104; rescuing *Strong* survivors, 55–57
Office of Naval Intelligence, 202
Oklahoma City, 202
O'Neil, Tex, 30
Operation Toenails, 45
Orita, Tsuneo, 117

P-38 Fighter, 28, 131, 186
Paraso Bay, Vella Lavella, 141, 153, 163, 179–80, 184
Pearl Harbor, Hawaii, 29, 196, 203
Pearl Harbor, Japanese attack on, 2, 4, 7, 24, 149
Philadelphia Navy Yard, 202
Phillips, Albert, 109–117
Point, Otis, 60, 93
Port Purvis. *See* Tulagi
Providence, 203

Quantico, VA, 39

Rabaul, New Britain, 11, 25
Radford, 12, 20–22, 27, 63–64, 66, 124, 127, 129–32; during Kula Gulf battle, 78–82; during Kula Gulf rescue, 103, 116–21; during Vella Lavella rescue, 178, 192
Rendova Island, 182
Rhinelander, WI, 5
Rice Anchorage, New Georgia, 47, 53, 120, 122–23
Richmond, VA, 9
Rick, Edwin, 62, 86
Ritter, Russ, 205
Roanoke College, 8
Roanoke, VA, 8, 203
Robinson, Eugene, 24–25, 30–31, 33, 42, 52–53, 191–92, 195–96, 198; at Sydney, 36–37; comments on Captain Cecil, 32; during Kula Gulf battle, 94–95; early years, 23; life after World War II, 203–4; rescue from Kula Gulf, 111, 131–32
Robinson, Mae, 25, 191, 192
Romoser, William, 63–64, 78, 80–83, 106, 112–13, 118, 129
Roxton, TX, 6
Russell Islands, 41, 62, 108, 127
Ryan, Thomas, 178–79, 181–82, 184, 186

San Antonio, TX, 30
San Cristobal Island, 62
San Diego, CA, 4–5, 7, 197–98, 202
San Francisco, CA, 9, 25, 110, 196–97, 203
Sandridge, James, 89
Santa Cruz, Battle of, 3
Saratoga, 28

Sasamboki Island, 18
Satsuki, 65, 80–81
Savo Island, 41, 62, 127, 193
Savo Island, Battle of, 2
Schank, Ken, 194
SC Radar, 2, 26–27
Segond Channel, Espiritu Santo, 1, 3, 29
Sereyko, Victor, 199
SG Radar, 2, 18, 21–22, 52, 67, 71, 76, 182, 184
Sharp, John, 60
Shortland Islands, 20, 66
Silvester, Archie, 148–49, 152–54, 162–64, 169, 174–74, 176; departure from Vella Lavella, 195; during Vella Lavella rescue operation, 179–80, 188–89
Simpson, John, 142
Slot, the, 12, 14, 40–41, 45, 47, 57, 65, 133, 143–44, 147, 179, 183, 192
Smith, Frank, 122
Smith, Rodman, 75
Solomon Islands, 1, 11, 128, 132, 147, 198
Spaulding, Lee, 140, 149, 187, 193
St. Louis, 41, 49–50, 81–82, 104, 108, 132
Strong, 46–47, 49; sinking of, 54–57, 66
Suzukaze, 65, 76–78, 103, 107–8
Sweeney, John, 179, 181, 184
Sweeney, Leroy, 76
Sydney, Australia, 35–37, 39–40, 43

Tanikaze, 65, 77–78, 103, 107–8
Task Force Thirty-Six, 45
Taylor, 178, 182, 184, 186
Tizzard, Thomas, 115

Tokyo Express, 49, 53, 63–64, 69, 71, 127, 180
Tulagi Island, 28, 41, 46–48, 57, 62–63, 124, 126–27, 131–32, 147, 181, 193–94
Turner, Richmond K., 45, 47, 124, 175, 178–79
Type 93 Torpedo (Japanese), 67

United States Naval Academy, 3, 15
University of Arkansas, 39

Vallejo, CA, 10
Vella Gulf, 82, 107, 141, 147, 149, 153, 182, 184
Vella Lavella Island, 141, 143, 162, 165, 170, 173, 175, 179–80, 182–84, 191–94, 197, 201; arrival of *Helena* survivors on 149–51, 153; coastwatcher operations on, 147–48, 152
Vila-Stanmore, Kolombangara, 13, 21, 41, 53–54, 65, 68, 81, 103, 117; Japanese air base at, 12, 40; American bombardment of, 18, 20, 28, 42, 47, 50, 52
Visuvisu Point, New Georgia, 49, 67, 121–22

Walker, Vic, 167, 188
Washington, DC, 202
Wasp, 2, 129
Waters, 178, 184–86, 189, 193
Waugh Rock, Kolombangara, 21, 80, 82
Weisenberger, Paul, 120, 122, 124–25
Wellings, Joseph, 57
Wendt, Walter, 6, 31–32, 42, 196, 199, 203; at Sydney, 36; during Kula Gulf battle, 97–98, 101–2; early years, 5;

life after World War II, 204; rescue from Kula Gulf, 114–15, 130
Wheaton, John, 138, 140, 167
Wildcat Fighter, 28
Woodworth, 124–25, 139

Yamashiro, Katsumori, 112, 114
Yunagi, 49, 53

Zero Fighter, 133, 140, 155

ABOUT THE AUTHOR

John J. Domagalski has had a lifelong interest in military history, with an emphasis on the Pacific side of World War II. In past years he has interviewed almost fifty veterans about their experiences during the Pacific War. Employed by a major retailer in the field of marketing, he resides in the Chicago area. His articles have appeared in *World War II History*, *Naval History*, and *World War II Quarterly* magazines and his first book, *Lost at Guadalcanal*, was published in 2010.